Convictions of Conscience

How Voices From the Margins Inform Public Actions, and Educational Leadership

A Volume in Issues in the Research, Theory, Policy, and Practice of Urban Education

Series Editor

Denise E. Armstrong
Brock University

Issues in the Research, Theory, Policy, and Practice of Urban Education

Denise E. Armstrong, Editor

Convictions of Conscience: How Voices From the Margins Inform Public Actions, and Educational Leadership (2019)
edited by Brenda J. McMahon and Lisa R. Merriweather

Teach & Thrive: Wisdom from an Urban Teacher's Career Narrative (2016)
by Kristina Valtierra and Denise E. Armstrong

Working (With/out) the System: Educational Leadership, Micropolitics and Social Justice (2016)
by James Ryan

Struggling for Inclusion: Educational Leadership in a Neo-Liberal World (2012)
by James Ryan

Student Engagement in Urban Schools: Beyond Neoliberal Discourses (2012)
edited by Brenda J. McMahon and John P. Portelli

Leadership from the Ground Up: Effective Schooling in Traditionally Low Performing Schools (2012)
by Michele A. Acker-Hocevar, Marta I. Cruz-Janzen, and Cynthia L. Wilson

Schools as Radical Sanctuaries: Decolonizing Urban Education through the Eyes of Youth of Color (2011)
by René Antrop-González

Including Families and Communities in Urban Education (2011)
by Catherine Hands and Lea Hubbard

Inclusion in Urban Educational Environments: Addressing Issues of Diversity, Equity, and Social Justice (2006)
by Denise E. Armstrong and Brenda J. McMahon

Convictions of Conscience

How Voices From the Margins Inform Public Actions, and Educational Leadership

edited by

Brenda J. McMahon

and

Lisa R. Merriweather
The University of North Carolina at Charlotte

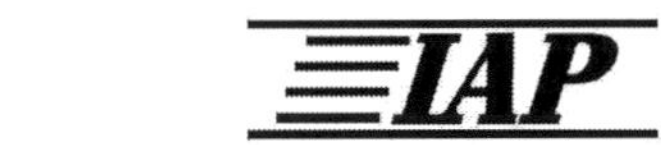

INFORMATION AGE PUBLISHING, INC.
Charlotte, NC • www.infoagepub.com

Library of Congress Cataloging-in-Publication Data

Names: McMahon, Brenda J., editor. | Merriweather, Lisa R., editor.
Title: Convictions of conscience : how voices from the margins inform public actions and educational leadership / edited by Brenda J. McMahon and Lisa R. Merriweather, the University of North Carolina at Charlotte.
Description: Charlotte, NC : IAP, Information Age Publishing, Inc., [2019] | Series: Issues in the research, theory, policy, and practice of urban education | Includes bibliographical references.
Identifiers: LCCN 2019029212 (print) | LCCN 2019029213 (ebook) | ISBN 978-1-64113-644-0 (paperback) | ISBN 978-1-64113-645-7 (hardcover) | ISBN 978-1-64113-646-4 (ebook)
Subjects: LCSH: Educational leadership--Social aspects. | Culturally relevant pedagogy. | Educational equalization.
Classification: LCC LB2806 .C585 2019 (print) | LCC LB2806 (ebook) | DDC 371.2--dc23
LC record available at https://lccn.loc.gov/2019029212
LC ebook record available at https://lccn.loc.gov/2019029213

Cover art by ke'ala lopez

Printed in the United States of America

DEDICATION

This book is dedicated to you, Brenda. You were more than a colleague, more than a professor, and more than a brilliantly conscious scholar. You were a good person as kind, supportive, and devoted as you were smart, witty, and fun. I will miss our conversation. We never had a shortage of life about which to make commentary and laugh. I will miss sharing good food with you at Caribbean Hut. I will miss our "road trips." The crystal blue waters of your beloved Barbados are still waiting on us. I will miss our listening to good music that spoke to the soul and reminded us that life was beautiful and to be lived to the fullest. You lived life without compromise. But most of all, I will miss you, that radiant smile, the purity of your spirit, and the heart of love for my family and me. Our spirits are forever intertwined. Thank you for always pushing me to see the "more" that my "next" promised. Thank you for being my sistah friend.

Love always, Lisa

CONTENTS

FOREWORD

Greg Wiggan

Brenda J. McMahon was a passionate author, scholar, professor, and a great colleague. She was an advocate for equity and justice, and as such, she was the embodiment of one who was willing to speak up against injustice even when it was unpopular to do so. When the reprisals came, as painful as they were, she would dutifully endure while never losing hope. These same qualities must guide the lives of educators and school leaders who seek to create positive change in schools and society.

As 21st century educators, historical (i.e., slavery, colonialism, and imperialism) and contemporary (i.e., neoliberalism and globalization) investigations and analyses must guide the work we do. To that extent, McMahon and Merriweather's *Convictions of Conscience: How Voices From the Margins Inform Public Actions and Educational Leadership* addresses the passions, hopes, and dreams of those who yearn to see the bitter consequences of educational inequalities, institutional racism, racial profiling, gender disparities, dehumanization, and other forms of oppression in schools rejected and eradicated. The phenomenon of the pipeline-to-prison and the underrepresentation of minorities in higher education and in selected programs, specifically, science, technology, engineering, and mathematics (STEM), are key concerns and education leaders must be challenged and equipped with strategies and resources to address these issues.

Convictions of Conscience: How Voices From the Margins Inform Public Actions, and Educational Leadership, pp. ix–xii

In the parlance of underrepresentation of minorities in STEM, there is somewhat of a paradox, as archeologically, historically, and scientifically evidenced, the earliest medical doctor on the human record was Imhotep (2600 BCE). Today, his manuscript is incorrectly called the Edwin Smith Papyrus as it was renamed in 1862 after the European antiquities collector who purchased it (see *Evolution of modern medicine* by William Osler [1913]). This renaming also speaks to dehumanization and the power of those with privilege to suppress the contributions of non-Whites. In fact, the evidence on Imhotep (later called Aesculapius by the Greeks) proves he was a Black African, to whom Hippocrates later expressed his indebtedness.

Suppression and oftentimes outright falsifications are common features of a canon, curriculum and school system that was intended to serve the dominant group. In this sense, how might the curriculum and lesson planning in schools change if it was more common knowledge that the Rhind Manuscript (housed in the British museum), which is often cited as the earliest mathematics work, was rightfully titled by the author's name, Ahmoses (Amhes/Ahmoses) [1500 BCE], who was a person of African descent, rather than Alexander Rhind, the man who purchased the papyrus in 1858. At a time when Blacks were generally thought to be non-educable property, a European was purchasing the oldest mathematical manuscript in the world, which was written by a Black African. The paradox threads even deeper because it is commonly believed that the University of Bologna [1088] of Italy and University of Oxford of England [1096], both founded as theological schools, were the first universities. However, Ipt Ast or University of Waset, also called the University of the Grand Lodge of Luxor in Egypt [2500 BCE], predates these institutions by more than a millennia. One wonders how this knowledge might become a staple of the curriculum, as part of human contribution, and not just a special topic for minority studies? One also wonders what would happen if the contributions, strategies and methods of Barbara Sizemore, a pioneering school leader and a champion of high achieving urban school districts, were more widely studied in higher education, modeled in school leadership, and practiced in public schools?

In the 21st century, the demonizing and criminalizing of Black and Brown bodies in schools and through the prison industrial complex speaks to the enduring legacies of racism while conjuring up the image of "disposable people," to which, the "Black Lives" and "Brown Lives" Matters movements have attempted to redress. In this sense, the relevance of Winston Churchill's little known book, *River War* (1899), still comes to mind as the young Churchill explained how Europeans conquered Sudan while killing millions of Africans and never being implicated or tried for the injustices. The suggestion is that crimes against humanity do not account for Black bodies, for in fact they are disposable. For at one time, the title of "chattel" suggested that they were not even human, and according to propagandist White supremacy theology, they had no souls. This is also the type of thinking and writing that demonizes Africans, Blacks, and Browns in general. Today, the notion of being disposable is translated in unfair school discipline, suspension and expulsion practices against Black and Brown students, and African American girls in particular. The cries of Trayvon Martin, Jonathan Ferrell, Tamir Rice, Eric Harris, Walter Scott, and countless others (and the echoes of Brenda J. McMahon) continue to urge us as educators that silence means consent. We must do more to advocate and create positive change.

In the context of the nation's record on achievement, the 2017 National Assessment of Education Progress data shows less than 46% proficiency nationally in fourth and eighth grade reading or mathematics by any school types (suburban, rural, urban, town) (National Assessment of Education Progress, 2018a, 2018b). This suggests that there are widespread systemic problems and the nation's schools are underperforming. These numbers are clearly not the school performance of a high-quality educational system. As an international scholar and former school leader, these were issues to which Brenda J. McMahon was privy. Preservice teachers and school leaders need a new kind of education, one in which equity, justice and multiculturalism are central tenants. Curriculum development and lesson planning must be addressed as curriculum violence is widespread in K–12 public schools and higher education institutions. Relatedly, the underrepresentation of minority faculty in higher education, at the higher ranks, and in positions of power speaks to the residual effects of institutions that were created as White-only space. Here again, paradoxically, the oldest universities in the U.S. were built by African American slaves, yet their descendants were not allowed to attend these institutions (e.g., Yale, Harvard, Princeton, University of Pennsylvania, University of North Carolina at Chapel Hill) (see *Ebony and Ivy* [2013] by Craig Wilder). This would gradually and painfully change over time. However, much more work is required. Similarly, in public schools, professional development and the training of a new generation of multicultural and culturally responsive teachers and education leaders are needed. In the current school context, how can we have multiculturalism with non-White cultures, bodies, and intellectual capital being omitted in the curriculum and in educational institutions? In this way, *Convictions of Conscience* explores modern forms of resistance to injustices in schools and society. It challenges school leaders, teachers, educational activists, parents, and community leaders to engage in positive change and inclusive practices in education and beyond.

REFERENCES

Churchill, W. (1899). *The river war.* London, England: Longman's, Green, and Co.

National Assessment of Education Progress. (2018a). "NAEP Reading: National-Achievement-Level Results." National Assessment of Educational Progress (NAEP) Nation's Report Card. Retrieved from https://www.nationsreportcard.gov/reading_2017/#nation/achievement?grade=8

National Assessment of Education Progress. (2018b). "NAEP Mathematics: National Achievement-Level Results." National Assessment of Educational Progress (NAEP) Nation's Report Card. Retrieved from https://www.nationsreportcard.gov/math_2017/#nation/achievement?grade=8

Osler, W. (1913). The evolution of modern medicine. In *Project Gutenberg*. Retrieved from http://www.gutenberg.org/files/1566/1566-h/1566-h.htm

Wilder, C. T. (2013). *Ebony and ivy: Race, slavery, and the troubled history of America's universities.* New York. NY: Bloomsbury Press.

SERIES EDITOR'S PREFACE

Denise E. Armstrong

Convictions of Conscience: How Voices from the Margins Inform Public Actions and Educational Leadership is the eighth volume in the series *Critical Perspectives on Research, Theory, Policy, and Practice in Urban Education*. Consistent with the goals of this book series, this coedited volume uses an equity and social justice lens to examine how education is currently conceived and enacted locally and globally. The chapters in this volume extend the critical focus of this series by highlighting the paradoxes and possibilities involved in working towards social justice in K–12, adult and higher education, and community settings. Using case studies, reflective vignettes, and personal narratives, each author provides evidence illustrating how leadership practice and education in Western democracies are increasingly dominated by state-imposed neoliberal ideologies that determine the topographical landscape of education and how power wielders envision and enact educational goals, purposes, and outcomes. Often combining conservative logic and technical-rational approaches that privilege narrow market-driven principles of competition, standardization, accountability, these hegemonies subvert democratic processes by pathologizing diversity, while at the same time containing and constraining multiple and intersecting forms of difference (e.g., race, gender, sex, socioeconomics, ability, etc.).

Given the present context and challenges, it is critical that educational leaders develop social, political, and historical consciousness and conscience and be courageous in working on behalf of traditionally marginalized

Convictions of Conscience: How Voices From the Margins Inform Public Actions, and Educational Leadership, pp. xiii–xv

individuals and communities. To this end, each chapter draws attention to the factors that facilitate and hinder inclusive educational leadership, while highlighting the importance of informed and intentional activism and advocacy. In particular, the authors call attention to the fact that socially just leadership is complex and contradictory work. This is because educational leaders, even those who express commitment to inclusive education espouse neoliberal ideologies, are deeply implicated in these hegemonic oppressive processes. They also experience ethical tensions as they work to resolve dilemmas associated with balancing managerialist values that favour imposed standards over local needs, standards over students, and technical-rational solutions over local and intuitive processes. Ethical action that is grounded in the moral goodness of character and conduct and guided by informed knowledge of, and challenge to oppressive and marginalizing hegemonic structures, ideologies, and discourses is critical in this process.

Each chapter in this volume provides examples of how leaders in K–12 and higher education communities can work together to disrupt narrow understandings of diversity and inclusion. The authors interrogate how multiple and intersectional identities interact with hegemonic power relations and how these macro and micro political dynamics impact educational opportunities and outcomes in urban and other marginalized spaces. Also emphasized is educational leaders' moral and legal responsibility to adopt transformative and decolonizing perspectives that challenge and counter oppressive managerialist, assimilative, and other oppressive trends while acting as advocates, activists, and allies.

Further this volume highlights successful innovative, asset-based, and wrap-around strategies and supports solutions that educators can use to recenter marginalized identities while recreating inclusive educational contexts that ensure equity and social justice for students, faculty, and communities. Researchers, practitioners, policy makers, and licensure and professional development providers will find this volume to helpful in understanding and resolving common tensions associated with social justice and ethical leadership as they explore the following questions that are raised by the different authors in this volume. These include, but are not limited to:

- What do critical theories offer the practice of educational leadership?
- How can professional licensure and development programs be supported in developing ethical, culturally competent, and responsive leaders?
- How can educators counter the noxious impacts of neoliberalism in K–12 and adult and higher educational institutions?

- How can educational leaders resolve ongoing conflicts and dilemmas between personal and professional ethics while challenging asymmetrical power relationship and dismantling oppressive hierarchical structures
- How can educators maximize their power and positionalities to support inclusive environments?
- How can they speak truth to power?
- How can educators build alliances and mobilize networks to sustain anti-oppressive and social justice work?
- How can educational leaders and communities be supported in their attempts to address systematic oppression in schools, districts, and the academy?

It is our hope that these questions, along with the dilemmas, case studies, vignettes, and innovative suggestions in this volume will motivate emerging and established scholars and practitioners of educational leadership to deeply reflect on their contexts and ideologies and act on their values.

INTRODUCTION

Decolonizing Educational Leadership for Social Justice

Brenda J. McMahon and Lisa R. Merriweather

Both inside and outside of the academy, incivility disguises itself as spirited discussion and "truth telling" in countless meetings that typically are pro forma, lacking substance and action. Such meetings inundate the workday of most faculty who understand the purpose as either meeting just to meet or sanctioning of a predetermined outcome, in spite of the invitation for discussion and debate. It was in a meeting of this nature that we birthed the idea for this edited volume, *Convictions of Conscience: How Voices from the Margins Inform Public Actions, and Educational Leadership*. This introduction is a prosopography of watercooler conversations about the colonizing of educational leadership and an exploration of new managerialism as hindrance to decolonizing the field.

Across countless academic departments and units, decisions are made that lack democratic merit, do not redress inequities, and are often aimed at replicating the status quo. Freire (2000) suggests that "social, political and economic contradictions" (p. 17) should be considered in order "to take action against oppressive elements of reality" (p. 17). For educational

Convictions of Conscience: How Voices From the Margins Inform Public Actions, and Educational Leadership, pp. xvii–xxix

leaders interested in transforming systems and decolonizing education geared toward socially just education and outcomes, democratic decision-making guided by an understanding of those contradictions is fundamental. Brown (2004) suggests that education has normative dimensions that are rooted socially, structurally, and ideologically in hegemony and often guide uncritically the process of decision-making.

Over the years we have engaged in numerous "watercooler" conversations with colleagues concerned that decisions devoid of wholistic social, political, as well as economic considerations had shifted priorities for some educational leadership departments from education to training, from rigor to convenience, and from concerns troubling humanity to the bottom "economic" line. Some have termed this shift new managerialism. Curricular decisions informed by new managerialism ideology were described as being fueled by antiquated notions of society and competition with for-profit institutions as opposed to observation and critique of contemporary society and its treatment of marginalized people and communities. Celoria (2016) posed the question of do "we want inclusive social justice school leaders who refuse to use colorblindness as a form of racism and marginalization, and who are well positioned to enact and support socially just strategies and practices?" (p. 201). New managerialism practices disembodied from society are less likely to result in the development of a school leader who is both activist and advocate, the type of leader emboldened to advance curricular and programmatic decisions, policies, and practices that center disenfranchised people.

Stories shared with us of doctoral students hungry for curriculum that "clapped back" at institutional and societal complacency toward hegemony, inequity, discrimination, racism, and inhumanity reflect an absence of decolonzing perspectives and behaviors in educational leadership preparation programs. This absence left future leaders clamoring for something more, something that did not reify the status quo ensuring that academic structures of domination remained intact and undisturbed. Celoria (2016) termed this a "thick" program (p. 210). Programs are

> thick when preparation programs provide a holistic, active, emancipatory, and inclusive curriculum and pedagogical approach that encourages depth involving both societal change and political action. In contrast, preparation programs are thin when the language is unclear and undefined, and does not lead to action and activism. (p. 210)

Brown (2004) concurs with the students' observation that professors and programs must attend to the complex contours of society and Celoria's (2016) idea of thickness. Brown wrote,

> a critical stance frames this discussion by outlining clearly the need for professors to retool their teaching and courses to address issues of power and privilege—to weave social justice into the fabric of educational leadership curriculum, pedagogy, programs, and policies. It recognizes and advocates for the social change role and responsibility of educational leaders. (p. 78)

Unfortunately the students' voices typically fell on deaf ears as departments, when given the chance, typically made a deliberate choice to remain stagnant, unchanged, and "thin" (Celoria, 2016, p. 210). This choice is a familiar one and one that does not surprise persons who seek to use the tool of criticality in program development.

Two faculty who sought to address issues of how to create space in the curriculum for students to engage deeply with discussions of equity in educational leadership while also attending to the challenges of students with limited time due to work and family shared this example. These faculty suggested coteaching paired courses. This entailed students signing up for two courses (one was required and the other was an elective) scheduled to follow each other on the same evening. The faculty planned to coconstruct the courses such that the topics were aligned with and built from each other. This format allowed students to earn six credits without having to travel to campus on separate days. The shared topic for the two courses was equity and social justice, with one course presenting theoretical considerations while the other looked at the theories as practical considerations. The faculty spent months advocating for this opportunity to allow for meaningful interactions and dialogue on how to engage equity as an educational leader while also dismantling barriers of access to students challenged with time restrictions. After months of mounting a vigorous argument as to the "why now" for these courses and "why us", they met one administrative roadblock after another. The courses eventually were taught with significant concessions. In spite of this, the courses were not only well-received but were the most heavily enrolled that semester. The arguments for "why now" though clear to the faculty and students continued to be met with disdain perhaps because of the inadequacy of the standards that inform educational leadership graduate programming (Celoria, 2016). Celoria (2016) lamented

> I was struck by what was included and what was excluded, as well as the language used and not used in the writing of these standards documents. Making me pause to ask whether or not the language used in these two sets of standards reflect racism in an era of colorblindness (Alexander, 2012; Ullucci & Battey, 2011)? … In considering these questions what hit me was the inadequacy of these standards—particularly when it comes to inclusiveness and social justice education leadership, due to the vagueness of the language used. (p. 200)

Other faculty discussed the consistency with which requests to bring conversations of equity and social justice into their programs by way of curricular changes were met with denial. Through hallway conversations at conferences and an informal survey of program websites, we learned that many programs of educational leadership do not require, much less offer a course on equity, diversity, inclusion, or social justice for future educational leaders. Some faculty described the resistance experienced when requesting to bring conversations of equity and social justice into their programs by way way of curricular changes. For instance a suggestion to require a course on equity and social justice for all doctoral students enrolled in the educational leadership degree was categorically denied. The reasons ranged from "we all teach diversity in our classes already" to "social justice means different things to different people" to "who among us has expertise to teach such a course" to "you are leftists bent on inculcating a particular ideology on the students." These faculty described *spirited discussions* that ended with bruised feelings, disheartenment with the system, and animosity. Faculty also described more ambitious goals that were met with similar reaction. For example, some faculty moved to include a concentration or cognate in social justice to better prepare their students for the diverse environs in which they would be working. To create the conditions for outcomes aimed at social justice, decolonizing of the mind, practices of the field and its preparation programs is needed. Brown (2004) said, "By exposing candidates to information and ideas that they may resist and by assisting them to stretch beyond their comfort zones, a critique and transformation of hegemonic structures and ideologies can occur" (p. 78).

Hegemonic structures resulted in horizontal adversaries (other faculty in the department) as well as vertical ones (department chairs and deans). Because courses, concentrations, new delivery methods were frequently challenged and rejected, faculty interested and passionate about awakening the consciousness of their learners often had to work subversively to create such learning opportunities. The double standard we heard expressed by our colleagues was strikingly commonplace as faculty were told no new concentrations could be approved even though new concentrations in "cash cow" disciplines, such as instructional systems technology often taught and assumed to be neutral in political positioning, had been approved. Faculty interested in teaching around issues of equity and social justice were told no new courses could be added even though new courses were actively being developed, taught, and supported by department chairs and other faculty. Faculty were met with a bevy of excuses to justify denials such as offering new courses would reduce enrollment in other courses. These interactions left faculty feeling marginalized in their departments amidst the denials and lack of support, and for some these interactions were interpreted as dismissal of their intellectual contributions to the program.

The experiences of our colleagues resonated with our own and created an urgency to act on our ethical responsibility. We needed to speak truth to power in the academy, to our colleagues, to our students by proffering a text that would convict the conscientious of the reader and inform public spaces and educational leadership programming.

The expression "speaking truth to power" appeared in 1955 in *Speak Truth to Power: A Quaker Search for an Alternative to Violence* (American Friends Service Committee, 1955). Many, who are White, were taught that either this originated from an unnamed (White) Quaker in the 18th century or that it arose spontaneously during a Quaker meeting in the 1950s. Like much of history from colonizers' perspectives, this is blatantly untrue. African American civil rights leader Bayard Rustin originated the phrase in 1942 and his contribution as a coauthor of the 1955 book was redacted. Brenda, as a member of the Quakers—an organization that prides itself in equity work, was appalled by how the Quakers participated in Malcolm X's *tokenism* while reinforcing endemic silencing. Tokenism is a type of feigned inclusiveness in which members of minoritized groups are provided in small measure and limited numbers with opportunities and favor. Tokenism is often experienced by those seeking to disrupt the status quo as a means of satisficing them. For instance, instead of being allowed to develop a full curriculum centered around equity and social justice, those in power would offer for a graduate certificate or a standalone course to be developed. Through our collective experiences and reflection on the experiences of our fellow sojourners, we understood more clearly than ever how tokenism, silencing, and marginalization worked in the academy. Replete throughout the experiences shared was the sense that the colleges' espoused commitments to diversity served instrumentally to assuage the universities' collective guilt while maintaining hegemonic structures that rolled back the project of social justice through their material practices.

Because tokenism, silencing, and marginalization are so rampant in the academy, each framed the context that shaped Brenda's work as a transformative educational leader with novice and aspiring public school administrators. Her work was paramount in a faculty of education where race is seen in "others" and a focus on the "achievement gap" is most often coded language for a deficit discourse. Brenda asserted her role to call into question the impacts of individual, organizational, and systemic privilege on student under and overachievement while remaining cognizant of the need to keep whiteness from occupying center stage in race discourses. For African American and Latinx graduate students the content in her classes was not new but the freedom to name it often was. For many White graduate students acknowledging a sense that what has been normed reinforced hegemonic structures was challenging. To their credit, many of these educational leadership students became excited by opportunities to question and challenge what they formerly took for granted while other White students retreated in anger, seeking solace, and finding support from faculty members who also felt threatened by discourses that called their privilege into question.

As a White Canadian female, Brenda felt righteous indignation that resulted in a moral obligation to generate and facilitate counter narratives to dominant discourses that shaped Western institutions, and attempted to use institutional power to silence racial discourses in the academy. An attempt to silence is what often gets experienced as advocates for social justice try to advance an institutionalized counter narrative of social justice, counter to the narrative that a stale curriculum developed in the previous century was adequate for addressing the needs of prospective school leaders who would encounter and impact a much more diverse constituency and inequitable society. Celoria (2016)

> strategically position(ed) the conversation of inclusion and inclusiveness within a broader context of social justice leadership that includes class, language, gender, race, ethnicity, gender identity, sexual orientation, and other historically and currently marginalized students, families and staff ... all isms [that] are endemic and engrained in the fiber of our society. (p. 214)

Celoria exhorts educational leaders to be

> prepared to address and abolish marginalization in schools and promote places of learning that are inclusive and diverse. Preparing educational leaders to serve as change advocates based on their awareness of explicit and implicit forms of oppression and marginalization within schools. (p. 214)

Brenda, like others in the silenced minority, understood the need to reimagine preparation of educational leaders. Throughout her career, Brenda responded to Brown's (2004) call to change how educational leaders were prepared and socialized with the knowledge, skill, and emotive capacity to address policies and practices in schools and to recognize the full humanity (e.g., race, gender identity, sexual preference, religion, class) of each stakeholder (students, parents, teachers, community members). Brown sees change occurring when programs attend to the confluence of context, theory and pedagogical strategies within the field of educational leadership. Brenda's desire laid a foundation for future educators to engage in the practice of decolonizing their practice of educational leadership and rejecting the false promises of new managerialism.

NEW MANAGERIALISM

As we unpacked those unsettling but all too common experiences, we bore witness to the insidious nature of new managerialism in programs of educational leadership, specifically, and higher education more generally. New managerialism is not just a new practice or managerial style but it represents a paradigm shift, a shift entrenched in neoliberal ideology. Neoliberal ideology eschews more human centered practices in favor of more business leaning ones. It attempts to delude its actors and audiences that the practices are just technical activities and not political ones (Deem, 1998; Lynch, 2014). Lynch (2014) suggests new managerialism

> is best understood as an ideological configuration of ideas and practices brought to bear on public service organization, management and delivery with a view to aligning organizational practices with those in the market system. It is about creating new management orthodoxy as to how public services are run. (p. 2)

But management has always been essentially about people, not tasks and as such it is inevitably a political project that is informed by the culture, economics, and society (Lynch, 2014). The neoliberal project of management seeks to maintain an amnesia-like state about its influences, and highlight just the economic market. This lunges it and its adherents into a false sense of neutrality of both purpose and process.

Kandiko (2010) writes "Neoliberalism assumes that the market is more efficient than the state, so goods and services once considered public [i.e., education] should become privatized, which also frees up capital for the market" (p. 156). Neoliberalism emphasizes product over process, output over input, production over development, efficiency over quality, and metrics over people (Lynch, 2014). Lynch (2014) posits the managerialism under this banner includes "a change of nomenclature from that of citizens, rights, welfare and solidarity to that of customers, service users and competition" (p. 1). Competition and marketplace demands within new managerialism therefore should hold the most sway on educational policies and practices. Correspondingly there is a strong belief that the market naturally corrects itself without any intervention informed by the lived experiences of those most affected by it. Neoliberalism promotes the value of individualism while devaluing a more communalistic worldview. It also places a premium on the freedom to make autonomous decisions, decisions free of consideration for others and societal good not measured by economic and status indicators (Kandiko, 2010).

New managerialism in higher education seeks to understand the market forces in order to cater to the idiosyncratic, often self-promoting needs and interests of the few and seeks to respond with programs and policies aligned with those forces and interest. An aim to be more inclusive in terms of who gets the opportunity to further develop and progress is a minor concern. As a result "academic stratification and academic consumerism, along with academic management, are leading to academic restructuring of higher education" (Kandiko, 2010, p. 158). This restructuring is based on a market perspective, which dictates not just the content of education, but also the perceived quality of education that in turn impacts how educational leadership is understood as best practiced. It equates accountability with standardization and requires that educational leaders focus on narrow understandings of evidence-based reporting, teaching and learning. This shift of priorities changes the character of education from being relational to being technical rational (Schön, 1983). As Lynch (2014) puts it

> major concerns expressed regarding new managerialism's prioritization of efficiency and effectiveness is that it occurs at the expense of more broadly-based moral and social values related to care, autonomy, tolerance, respect, trust and equality. This has the ultimate impact of defining human relationships in work organization in transactional terms. (p. 5)

In effect it becomes leadership without human context, leadership without people centered values, leadership without soul. Leadership fueled by such ideological practices are antithetical to leadership for social justice.

DECOLONIZING EDUCATIONAL LEADERSHIP

Convictions of Conscience is a call on educational leaders who are committed to success for all students to reject new managerial approaches at all levels of educational leadership (pre-K–12, higher education, and adult and community education) and is an invitation to expand their emphasis to concerns rooted in human context, particularly identity politics. This is an opportunity for educational leaders to challenge themselves to move beyond celebrating and embracing differences to ensuring equity and social justice through their practice for disenfranchised and oppressed people groups. Educational leaders must appreciate that creating a culture of inclusion requires intentionality and sustained commitment to working within and across groups for capacity building not just monitoring the market to better commodify education and those who it educates (Lynch, 2014).

A decolonizing philosophically grounded practice of educational leadership is required to move toward a more socially just praxis, a praxis informed by diverse people groups and their unique needs, a praxis that seeks equitable outcomes not dictated by market forces. How educational leaders understand difference as well as the very function and nature of difference highlight the need for a philosophically grounded practice not rooted in neoliberal ideology. Difference demands a rejection of the core tenets of a new managerialism practice. Abdi (2012) suggests a turn to decolonizing practices. These practices center the lived experiences of the marginalized. Abdi using the frame of colonialism says "The experiences of colonialism, in their psycho-cultural, educational, philosophico-epistemological and social development dimensions have been extensive, and with respect to the lives of the colonized, severely limiting in their onto-existential locations and outcomes" (p. 1). Abdi raises the consequential nature of colonialism, the relationship between the colonized and the colonizers, and the relationship of each to the hegemonically determined structures of power.

Abdi (2012) further states decolonizing practices "should also partially aim to problematize and interrogate the potentially misnamed postcolonial outcomes of colonial education and how that needs to be decolonized in contemporary spaces of learning, teaching and human well-being" (p. 1). Educational leaders whose practice is informed by decolonizing ideology therefore question the status quo and problematize the taken for granted to create more equitable outcomes for those who have been disenfranchised by systemic racism and personal prejudice. Fanon (2005) invokes violence as a critical method for decolonizing.

> In decolonization, there is therefore the need of a complete calling in question of the colonial situation.... The naked truth of decolonization evokes for us the searing bullets and bloodstained knives which emanate from it. For if the last shall be first, this will only come to pass after a murderous and decisive struggle between the two protagonists. That affirmed intention to place the last at the head of things, and to make them climb at a pace (too quickly, some say) the well-known steps which characterize an organized society, can only triumph if we use all means to turn the scale, including, of course, that of violence.... The native who decides to put the program into practice, and to become its moving force, is ready for violence at all times. From birth it is clear to him that this narrow world, strewn with prohibitions, can only be called in question by absolute violence. (p. 37)

Violence, in Fanon's estimation, however is not simply armed revolt and overthrow of oppressive regimes, but it more importantly refers to the disruption of static relations to the structures of power wrought by colonialism.

Colonial legacy and its contemporary practice have geographical, political, psychological, and ideological fault lines. These fault lines shape how individuals relate to each other in and across space and time, demarcating place and personhood. Disruption of those fault lines—education, residential, economic, social—are at the heart of the violence advocated by Fanon (2005). Each impacts how the colonized and the colonizer see themselves, often in relation to the other. That is, identity as the colonized cannot exist separate from an identity as the colonizer. Disruption requires a restructuring of those relationships and identities. Disruption is a process and product of which necessitates violence—a tearing down and tearing apart of the status quo and taken for granted identities and relationships. Fanon states this point more poignantly and eloquently.

> The violence which has ruled over the ordering of the colonial world, which has ceaselessly drummed the rhythm for the destruction of native social forms and broken up without reserve the systems of reference of the economy, the customs of dress and external life, that same violence will be claimed and taken over by the native at the moment when, deciding to embody history in his own person, he surges into the forbidden quarters. To wreck the colonial world is henceforward a mental picture of action. (p. 39)

Educational leaders committed to a decolonizing practice of leadership are committing to this project of violence, that is to say geographical, political, and ideological restructuring in classrooms, school buildings, institutions of learning and systems of education. Market trends, and capitalistic priorities cannot dictate such projects nor can the ill-informed assumption that colonialism has ended. Coloniality is still the root cause and intentional by-product of the enduring, persistent, and still present nature of the problem it created. Conversations of decoloniality are not occurring after the problem has ended but rather as a consequence of colonialism continuing and insidiously occupying the practice, policy, and politics of society. Recognition of the originating violence to the well-being—emotional, psychological, physical, economic—of children, families, and communities enduring colonization ignites a social justice practice of educational leadership and recalibrates the responsibilities and sensitivities of educational leaders, sensitivities that comprehend the gravity of subjugation.

> To subjugate people, willfully rob their resources, de-ontologize the main fabrics of their being, and eventually achieve the above mentioned naturalness of the project which convinces the oppressed to voluntarily partake in the de-centering of their world, an organized mental de-patterning must take place, and beyond what is done to the indigenous people, the implementers of the project must also be psycho-culturally deconstructed. (Abdi, 2012, p. 3)

Decolonizing educational leadership is not just actionable behavior but is also a mindset, both of which must be attentive to the cartographies and geographies of reason that frame learning and education. Lewis (2017) wrote:

> We therefore need to consider what it means not only to value what we think, but also value being valued by each other, when engaged in such thought. Shifting the geography of reason, then, also demands a shift in the orientation and possibilities of value. Valuing each other requires engaging each other. (para. 9)

An educational leader who assumes the project of decolonizing education through decolonizing leadership theories, policies and practices necessarily seeks to build through relationship the capacity of the disenfranchised to have and exercise agency that affirms their personhood and creates more equitable conditions of living and being. Educational leaders operating out of new managerialism and decolonizing both understand the power of education to shape the contours of living and being, but only those functioning from the framework of decolonizing strive for unilateral liberation and the suppression of "unfreedom" (Greene, 1988).

The chapter authors in *Convictions of Conscience: How Voices From the Margins Inform Public Actions, and Educational Leadership* seek to disrupt commonplace and unproblematized understandings of diversity and inclusion by emphasizing the integral role of equity and social justice as critical dimensions of human relationships. This collection considers how identity of place and person impacts power relations that in turn influence the quality of educational opportunities afforded based on location within society's hegemonic structure. We posit that hegemonically fueled understandings of identity (colonial products) govern both macro- and micropolitics and contribute to the ongoing stratification of our schools.

Authors were challenged to engage intersectional and integrated analysis of various educational conflicts and issues associated with educational leadership in urban spaces and explore innovative ideological solutions to the creation of inclusive educational environments related to various markers of identity such as race, gender, sex, socioeconomics, ability, and multiple or intersecting identities. Chapter authors intentionally interrogated the sociocultural dimensions that affect educational leaders.

In Chapter 1, Corpening and Frick situate activism as a dimension of educational leadership practice. They provide an historical look at the role of resistance and activism in the educational experiences of African Americans and develop the thesis that effective African American educational leadership is born within and from a culture of resistance. The next two chapters interrogate relationships as critical factors in educational leadership. In Chapter 2 authored by Camp and Foxx, counseling and educational leadership are integrally linked together through relational cultural theory. To be effective in either capacity, equitable relationship and non-hierarchical approaches are needed to ensure a praxis of inclusiveness. Niño, Garza, and Cordova in Chapter 3 insist that socially just minded educational leaders operate from a *pedagogy of critical reflection* that intones authenticity, reciprocity, and equity in mentoring relationships. Such relationships function to negate the dehumanization of education.

Butler and Triplett and Feldman and Rocco respectively in Chapters 4 and 5 interrogate discipline and policing in educational context as a means toward decolonizing education. Chapter 4 seeks to better understand the connection between identity politics and disciplinary outcomes in schools, while Chapter 5 deconstructs the impact culturally responsive law enforcement might have on the creation and sustaining of inclusive and socially just spaces for learning. In Chapter 6, Archibald, Cook, and Hopson consider the import of culturally responsive evaluations for increasing accountability and validity in community-based nonformal educational programs.

The remaining chapters look at programmatic efforts designed to create more equitable spaces of learning. In Chapter 7, Cruz and Benson tackle the mythology of gang affiliation and the subsequent demonization of Latino gang involved youth. In Chapter 8, Yang highlights photo-essay creation as a teaching method. Yang offers adult educators a window into the importance of affirming diverse immigrant identities and understanding how those identities influence relationships to learning. Cantu and Brooks similarly, in Chapter 9, focus on immigrant students in community college settings. They consider how English as a Second Language programming has been affected by neoliberal economic and political ideology. In the final chapter Holloway, Kerr, and Zacharakis extend the interrogation of neoliberalism's impact on K–12 educational leadership.

A unique feature of the compilation is that each chapter represents a collaboration between an established scholar and emerging scholar(s) (doctoral students, junior faculty, etc.). These collaborations provided opportunity for emerging scholars to receive mentorship in writing for publication and developing lines of socially just inquiry. We appreciate that mentorship is a key tool for cultivating desired attitudes and competencies in doctoral students and new scholars and reinvigorating or perhaps igniting the same in more seasoned scholars. The project of decolonizing educational leadership necessarily requires lighting, maintaining, and passing the torch forward to new generations of scholars.

Speaking truth to power is required in order to provide an institutional critique of action and inaction in the academia. It is required for those interested in the project of decolonizing. *Convictions of Conscience: How Voices From the Margins Inform Public Actions and Educational Leadership* speaks truth to power through addressing criticality in educational leadership. Educational leadership programs are often mimetic of the larger institutional and societal deficit and inequity framing models that govern what is taught by whom and to whom without question for whom the greatest benefits are accrued. It is our hope that this volume will contribute to the development of emerging scholars and practitioners of educational leadership and spur established scholars and practitioners to more deeply reflect on these ideas and execute decolonizing projects of educational leadership across the domains of pre-K–12, higher, and adult education.

REFERENCES

Abdi, A. (2012). Decolonizing philosophies of education: An introduction. In A. Abdi (Ed.), *Decolonizing philosophies of education* (pp. 1–14). Rotterdam, The Netherlands: Sense.

American Friends Service Committee. (1955). *Speak truth to power: A Quaker search for an alternative to violence*. Philadelphia, PA: Author.

Brown, K. (2004). Leadership for social justice and equity: Weaving a transformative framework and pedagogy. *Educational Administration Quarterly, 40*(1), 77–108.

Celoria, D. (2016). The preparation of inclusive social justice education leaders. *Educational Leadership and Administration: Teaching and Program Development, 27,* 199–219

Deem, R. (1998). 'New managerialism' and higher education: The management of performances and cultures in universities in the United Kingdom. *International Studies in Sociology of Education, 8*(1), 47–70.

Fanon, F. (2005). *Wretched of the earth.* New York, NY: Grove Press.

Freire, P. (2000). *Pedagogy of the oppressed.* New York, NY: Continuum.

Greene, M. (1988). *Dialect of freedom.* New York, NY: Teachers College Press.

Kandiko, C. (2010). Neoliberalism in higher education: A comparative approach. *International Journal of Arts and Sciences, 3*(14), 153–175.

Lewis, G. (2017, November 4). Decolonization matters [Blog Post]. Retrieved from https://www.rowmaninternational.com/blog/decolonization-matters/

Lynch, K. (2014). New managerialism: The impact on education. *Concept: The Journal of Contemporary Community Education Practice Theory, 5*(3), 1–11.

Schön, D. (1983). *The reflective practitioner. How professionals think in action.* New York, NY: Basic Books

CHAPTER 1

AFRICAN AMERICAN ACTIVISM AND THE STRUGGLE FOR EDUCATIONAL ACHIEVEMENT AND LEADERSHIP

A Historical Perspective

Brian K. Corpening and William C. Frick

ABSTRACT

The history of African American education is replete with struggle, courage and persistence. The struggle has often been in the form of activism with advocacy and agitation. Understanding how resistance and activism are developed and applied is important in the struggle for educational equality and opportunity. Utilizing historical examples that show how courage and persistence were hallmarks of community resistance and activism, this chapter discusses the development of educational resistance and activism within the African American community. This chapter also focuses on examples of African American educational leadership and how that leadership was developed and honed within the culture of community resistance and activism.

Convictions of Conscience: How Voices From the Margins Inform Public Actions, and Educational Leadership, pp. 1–19

> The whole history of the progress of human liberty shows that all concessions yet made to her august claims have been born of earnest struggle. The conflict has been exciting, agitating, all-absorbing, and for the time being, putting all other tumults to silence. It must do this or it does nothing. If there is no struggle there is no progress. Those who profess to favor freedom and yet deprecate agitation are men who want crops without plowing up the ground;
>
> This struggle may be a moral one, or it may be a physical one, and it may be both moral and physical, but it must be a struggle. Power concedes nothing without a demand. It never did and it never will. (Douglass, 1857, para. 7 & 8)

The above passage captures the spirit of the struggle for basic human rights for African Americans and other marginalized populations in this country. The power structure in the United States has never, in the course of its history, conceded basic rights to oppressed populations without some form of struggle and demand. This historical struggle for equality by marginalized populations has been in the form of acts of resistance to the ongoing denial of rights and opportunities. This resistance often emerged in the form of activism, and specifically, in acts of advocacy or agitation. Critical in any discussion of activism, advocacy and agitation in African American educational history and leadership is a firm understanding of their impact on the resistance to educational domination and deprivation.

Resistance is about change from an oppressive status quo to a freedom of opportunity and choice. As Alinsky (1971) noted: "Change means movement. Movement means friction. Only in the frictionless vacuum of a nonexistent abstract world can movement or change occur without the abrasive friction of conflict" (p. 20). The resistance offered by African Americans to educational denial and inequality has been about movement and conflict. Whether it was enslaved African Americans risking death to gain the power of literacy, or organized communities resisting established power structures preventing them access to a quality education, African Americans have always resisted in their effort to change an unfair system.

Activism has been the primary method of African American resistance to educational oppression. McKenzie (2016) defines activism as "action taken to solicit support for a candidate or policy that leads to social or political change" (loc. 65). Activism in the cause of educational opportunity and equality for African Americans is also at the core of the resistance to processes and structures that perpetuate the denial of educational equality and opportunities for African Americans. Throughout the long educational history of African Americans, engaging in acts of activism, through advocacy or agitation, has been a central feature of the struggle.

Frederick Douglass epitomized the struggle for educational opportunity and the resistance to oppression and denial of rights and opportunity. Douglass, a self-educated man, employed whatever means he could to acquire the power of literacy. He then used his newfound literacy to gain his freedom, escaping slavery to the North. Upon gaining his freedom, he used his literacy and education to become a powerful orator and abolitionist, using the force of his education in leading the struggle to end slavery and to transform the meaning and construction of his race. His call for resistance to slavery and oppression was based on the recognition that slavery and the oppression of African Americans would not end simply because it was morally right for the ruling class to end a system that was economically, socially, and politically beneficial for them. Douglass knew that the oppressors would never destroy such a system without demand from the oppressed, thus his advocacy for ongoing resistance and struggle. Douglass's words were also an acknowledgement that any progress and success experienced by an oppressed people would be the result of a concerted struggle.

The primary focus of this chapter is to understand the central role the history of resistance and struggle in the form of activism with advocacy and agitation has had in developing past, current, and future African American educational leadership. The history of this struggle for educational access and opportunity, seen through historical episodes and leaders, helps establish the frame in which African American educational leadership can be evaluated. Ultimately the only leadership that matters is that which effectively guides and supports the academic development of the children in the schools in which African American leadership exists. However, the role of history is important in the development of effective leadership. That is why opening this chapter with a quote from the important speech Douglass gave on the occasion of the 23rd anniversary of the ending of slavery in the British West Indies is appropriate to understand the cauldron in which African American leadership was developed.

This chapter introduces historical examples of effective resistance in the form of activism through advocacy or agitation in the cause of the education of African Americans. These instances are from the 19th, 20th and 21st centuries, and show how the resistance that emerged within African American communities impacted the educational opportunities and prospects of African Americans. In addition to the historical instances of educational resistance, the chapter will end with a discussion of two historical figures that represent effective African American educational leadership. The two individuals were community-oriented individuals who enjoyed long careers in urban schools educating African American children. They both openly advocated for educational opportunities within the African American community. They were also leaders in their communities who understood that community uplift was inextricably connected to educational uplift. Embracing the lessons and examples of history in creating the type of environments and structures that support the educational development of a historically marginalized population is invaluable when educating for the cause of freedom, which is the intent of the struggle for educational opportunity for African Americans. The past does inform the current and the future and provides important lessons for today's educational leaders.

A FOUNDATION FOR ACTIVISM AND RESISTANCE

Brown-Nagin (1999) discussed in her article on the educational activism of Septima Clark, a Civil Rights Movement educator, how Clark viewed the educational development of African American children as a form of resistance to the harmful effects of the inequalities and degradation of legalized segregation in the South. Clark believed that students could develop a "mental culture of resistance" (p. 90) to the effects of ongoing oppression through education. Clark understood that the ability to resist oppression was predicated on the mental acuity of those engaged in acts of resistance. Clark's later role in establishing "Citizenship Schools" which taught literacy, citizenship and activism to adults in the South was a manifestation of her philosophy on the role of literacy and education in the process of resisting oppression.

Septima Clark's efforts support the contention that engaging in acts of resistance to a system of domination and deprivation first involves the development of a critical consciousness within the dominated populations. Resistance to oppression and domination cannot effectively occur without some form of critique, which education facilitates. "Critique without resistance is empty and resistance without critique is blind" (Couzens Hoy, 2012, loc. 72). Critique in the form of a critical consciousness provides the lens that is required to understand the need for resistance and struggle while also ensuring that any form of resistance can succeed. Engaging in activism, in the form of advocacy or agitation is the mode of resistance that demands of power. It is resistance because those acts reject power structures that perpetuate an oppressive status quo. The form of resistance that can effectively employ activism, with advocacy, or agitation as a tool, is also able to both critique oppressive structures and motivate the oppressed to action. This form of resistance is critical in objectively critiquing the structures of oppression while summoning the awareness that Paulo Freire called "conscientização," or critical consciousness (Freire, 1970/2011, p. 35).

To develop the consciousness that is demanded to challenge and change oppressive structures requires the oppressed to embark on a process that will lead to a consciousness that will in turn inspire the activism, whether it is in the form of advocacy or agitation, required to challenge and change an oppressive status quo. Freire (1970/2011) accurately articulated this process: "To surmount the situation of oppression, people must first critically recognize its causes, so that through transforming action they can create a new situation, one which makes possible the pursuit of a fuller humanity" (p. 47).

The process of critical recognition of the causes of oppression does not occur in a vacuum. There must be a catalyst, an incident, an individual, something that starts this process of consciousness raising that leads to resistance in the form of activism, advocacy, or agitation. Septima Clark believed that the educator in communities suffering from the oppression of segregation must serve as the catalyst in developing the consciousness in students and community. These catalysts must galvanize marginalized and oppressed populations, encouraging (inciting, motivating) the movement from critical consciousness to actual action in the form of activism through advocacy or agitation. In the historical examples in this chapter it is the leaders, like Septima Clark, who emerged within the African American communities that led the challenge against the educational status quo that was depriving African Americans of the education that was necessary for their uplift and transformation.

Ward Randolph (2009) makes the argument that transformative leadership is required to advance the education of children in current and future educational environments. This transformative leadership, according to Ward Randolph, must account for the level of racism that African American educational leaders have always had to address in order to educate children in their schools. Present and future African American educational leaders must understand how "racism has structured the schooling experiences of African American youth, [and understand] they must also be willing to do something about it" (p. 33). Ward Randolph also lists four things African American transformative educational leaders must do in the communities they serve which are consistent with what transformative African American educators like Septima Clark have done in the past and what educational leaders who resist oppressive educational structures are required to do:

> 1. Understanding the historical, cultural, and present-day needs of the schools they serve. 2. School leaders must unlearn and examine their assumptions about African American beliefs about education. 3. School leaders must develop a vision for the school based on the cultural values and beliefs of the African American community in which the school resides. 4. School leaders must be willing to fight against political, social, and economic structures for the rights of African American youth to a quality education. (p. 33)

The four elements that African American school leaders must accomplish in their schools and communities captures the sense of critical consciousness described by Freire (1970/2011) that requires recognition of causes of oppression before transforming acts can occur to eradicate that oppression. The four elements also proscribe a necessity for resistance, in the form of ongoing activism through advocacy and, when necessary, agitation.

Dantley (2009) identifies African American educational leaders who approached their work from a critical perspective as "purposive leaders" (p. 45) because they engaged in critique and possibility. His description of purposive leaders is similar to how Ward Randolph (2009) described the role of transformative educational leadership. Dantley asserts that purpose-driven African American educational leaders are focused on removing structures of oppression against marginalized populations. Purposive leaders understand and embrace the necessity of engaging in activism, advocacy, or agitation when it is necessary to ensure that education, and specifically schools, become sites for transformation. Purposive leaders, who have the critical consciousness to recognize oppression and the ability to inspire, know that equity and justice are not gained without demand to power.

Both Ward Randolph (2009) and Dantley (2009), like Clark before them, understand that successful African American educational leaders can only succeed if they actively engage their communities in the necessity of developing consciousness and engaging in action while understanding the connection between the transformation of their schools to the transformation that occurs in the communities where the schools are located. The educational history of African Americans has countless examples of how the struggle for educational rights and opportunities was connected to the overall community resistance and struggle for basic rights and freedom.

Carter G. Woodson (1919) offers another example in his work *The Education of the Negro Prior to 1861*. Woodson argued that the education of African Americans prior to the Civil War fell into two distinct periods: 1619 to 1835, and 1835 to 1861. Woodson also argued that the supporters of the education of enslaved African Americans fell into three categories: slave-owners who wished to increase the efficiency of their slaves; sympathetic individuals who believed enslaved Africans should be educated; committed missionaries who believed that educated slaves would embrace Christianity. As early as the late 17th and early 18th centuries, slave-owners were providing basic literacy to enslaved Africans. While there were slave-owners who fell into Woodson's first category, and saw the economic benefit of having literate slaves, there were also slave-owners who believed that exposing slaves to Christianity through teaching them how to read the Bible was the means to keep them docile and obedient.

Woodson's (1919) second category—sympathetic individuals who believed it was the correct course of action that enslaved African Americans should be educated to the same extent as all Americans—are the individuals who exhibited the first real examples outside of the enslaved and free themselves of activism in the cause of African American education. The Presbyterians, and more notably the Quakers, actively promoted the education of African Americans, free and enslaved. In 1740, a Presbyterian, Hugh Bryan, opened a school for African Americans in Charleston. By 1755, the Presbyterians were operating schools for slaves in Virginia. At the beginning of the 19th century, Presbyterians in North Carolina were supporting John Chavis, a free African American Presbyterian minister, in his effort to open a school in Raleigh (Spraggins, 1970). Woodson's third category of supporters—committed missionaries who believed that educated slaves would embrace Christianity—were prominent in educating free and enslaved African Americans. In 1701, the Church of England formally got involved in the religious instruction of slaves through the creation of the Society for the Propagation of the Gospel in Foreign Parts. The teachers in the Society taught Scripture, reading and catechism (Franklin & Moss, 1994).

While groups like the Quakers, Presbyterians, and the Church of England were strong advocates for the education of free and enslaved African Americans, African Americans also started actively engaging in activism for their own rights to an education in the late 18h century. In 1787, Prince Hall, an African American War of Independence veteran and a Boston property owner, petitioned the City of Boston to support the education of African American children in the city in the same manner that White children were supported. In 1790, free African Americans opened a school in Charleston, South Carolina. Freemen opened schools in Washington, and Richard Allen and Absalom Jones open schools for African American children in Philadelphia (Spraggins, 1970).

UNDERSTANDING RESISTANCE AND ACTIVISM THROUGH HISTORICAL EXAMPLES

The conflict over control of the New York African Free Schools in the early 19th century is the first historical occurrence of African American educational resistance we would like to analyze. The struggle over control of the African Free Schools is an early example of African American community advocacy and agitation for control over how children were to be educated within schools and a clear indication of a "school leadership dimension long forgotten and ignored"—collective leadership as an ongoing "spiritual mission ... intentional about giving students experiences they would not otherwise have … and prepar[ing] students for life in and out of school" (Lambert et al., 2002, p. 25).

Founded in 1787 by the New York Manumission Society, an abolitionist organization, the New York African Free School was one of the first nondenominational charity schools in America. Eventually the schools founded by the Manumission Society would evolve into the public school system for African Americans (Mabee, 1979). In 1799, the trustees of the school hired an ex-slave, John Teasman, as principal. Teasman was a leader in the African American community and as a result of his hire the enrollment of the school increased dramatically. However, in 1809, the trustees of the school fired Teasman and replaced him with a White educator, Charles Andrews; in response to his termination, Teasman and his wife opened two new private schools that drew families from the African Free School (Harris, 2003).

The free African Americans in New York City started embracing the role and power of an education in their uplift at the beginning of the 19th century. To meet the demands of a growing African American population, the African Free School expanded, in 1820, to two schools. The African American community in New York was beginning to understand the power of education and was becoming more actively engaged in seeking a role in how the schools operated. The African American community, through the community's newspaper, *Freedom's Journal,* was very supportive of the schools with the newspaper stressing the importance of the schools for the future of African American children (Rury, 1983).

The African American community, after an important meeting in December 1827, started focusing on issues related to the operation of the school, such as the curriculum and the makeup of the teachers at the schools. In 1830, disagreement within the community emerged over the presence of White teachers, and the lack of African American teachers, at the schools. As a result of the dispute, the enrollment in the schools started dropping while at the same time private schools started by African American teachers made their appearance. The changes in the enrollment of the African Free Schools and the emergence of African American private schools between 1830 and 1832 signaled a shift in the attitudes of the African American community towards the education of African American children and its impact on the status of the community (Rury, 1983).

By the beginning of 1832, African American community resistance in the form of advocacy and agitation had forced the resignation of the educational leader at the school, Charles Andrews. In response to the resignation and the ongoing boycott of its schools by African Americans, the Manumission Society hired its first African American teacher as a replacement for Andrews. The Society hired more African American teachers for its schools and also a saw a significant increase in the enrollment after hiring the teachers. The success of the African American community in replacing Charles Andrews with an African American teacher was unprecedented and is an early example of community resistance to the educational status quo that the community found unacceptable. The activism, through advocacy and actual agitation, exhibited by the African American community worked. Power did concede to a demand.

The success experienced through the African American community's commitment to advocacy and agitation regarding how the African Free Schools were operating within the community was put to the test with the emergence of the Public Schools Society. The Public Schools Society was emerging as the primary entity in the education of the children of New York City. The Manumission Society saw its role in the education of African American children as anachronistic and transferred its African Free Schools to the Public School Society in 1834 (Rury, 1983). Even though the community did not enjoy the same influence with the schools when they were under the control of the Public Schools Society as it experienced when they were controlled by the Manumission Society, African Americans in New York where still able to affect the operation of the schools and thus, the education of their children.

This early historical example of educational resistance and activism within the African American community supports Douglass's contention regarding struggle, progress and demand. The case of the African Free Schools bears witness to the power of both advocacy and agitation on the behalf of educational opportunity. The case also highlights the role of courage and persistence within acts of activism. The courage and persistence of African Americans in early 19th century America to challenge the White power structure was impressive. Without the courage and persistence of community members to challenge how their children were being educated, the educational gains made by African American children attending the African Free Schools would not have occurred.

Courage and persistence have always been hallmarks of the African American struggle. When they are intertwined with resistance and activism, the ability to demand of power on behalf of any cause is enhanced. The legacy of the effort and success of African Americans in New York City, during the first half of the 19th century, would continue with the efforts of other African Americans in the cause of educational rights and equality.

The second historical occurrence of African American educational activism is from the 20th century. On May 17, 1954, Chief Justice Earl Warren delivered the unanimous opinion of the Court in the case of *Brown v. Board of Education of Topeka*. Warren opened his opinion by informing that *Brown* was one of five cases from Kansas, South Carolina, Virginia, Delaware, and the District of Columbia (*Brown v. Board of Education*, 1954). The case from South Carolina, *Briggs v. Elliot* (Burton, Burton, & Appleford, 2008) stemmed from the ongoing educational oppression of African American children in Clarendon County. What occurred in Clarendon County is the next example that we acknowledge of African American educational activism. While the outcome in Clarendon County may be outwardly different than New York City in the 1830s, nevertheless Clarendon is a strong example of the process of resistance to an oppressive educational system. Acts of activism, whether advocacy or agitation, may not always appear initially successful, but engaging in acts of resistance has symbolic and tangible value to any marginalized population and community.

Clarendon County was a sleepy county that seemed to be stuck in the slave-holding and Jim Crow eras of the past. At the middle of the 20th century, Clarendon was one of the poorest counties in South Carolina and, by extension, one of the poorest in America. The African American population comprised 70% of the county population; Whites owned 85% of the land. The segregated public school system served a student population that was nearly 70% African American; per pupil spending for White students was three hundred percent what it was for African American students (Burton, Burton, & Appleford, 2008). The old antebellum racial hierarchy was still in place in Clarendon in the middle of 20th century America. Most African Americans in the county worked as sharecroppers on the land of descendants of slave-owners. Other African Americans worked as domestics and in other service jobs. Most professional African Americans worked as teachers or preachers. The system that existed in Clarendon for African Americans "was nothing short of economic slavery, an unbreakable cycle of poverty and ignorance breeding more poverty and a bit less ignorance, generation upon generation" (Kluger, 2004, p. 7). The cycle of poverty and inequality that existed among African Americans in Clarendon County was on full display when it concerned education. In Clarendon County, at the time of the filing of *Briggs v. Elliot*, educational spending for White children was four times the amount that was spent on the 6,500 African American children in 60 dilapidated schools. African American children were educated in unequal facilities and were deprived of bus transportation to schools (De Laine Gona, 2011).

Reverend J. A. DeLaine, an African American, was also a teacher who lived in Clarendon County. He eventually took on the role of branch secretary for the NAACP and became instrumental in organizing African Americans in Clarendon to challenge the local school board responsible for the oppressive educational conditions African American children had to endure to attend schools in the county. Richard Kluger (2004) describes what happen to De Laine as a result of his advocacy and agitation in challenging the educational injustice occurring to African American children in Clarendon County:

> Before it was over, they fired him from the little schoolhouse at which he had taught devotedly for ten years. And they fired his wife and two of his sisters and a niece. And they threatened him with bodily harm. And they sued him on trumped-up charges and convicted him in a kangaroo court and left him with a judgment that denied him credit from any bank. And they burned his house to the ground while the fire department stood around watching the flames consume the night. And they stoned the church at which he pastored. And fired shotguns at him out of the dark. But he was not Job, and so he fired back and called the police, who did not come and kept not coming. Then he fled, driving north at eighty-five miles an hour over country roads, until he was across the state line. Soon after, they burned his church to the ground and charged him for having shot back that night, with felonious assault with a deadly weapon, and so he became an official fugitive. (p. 3)

Other African Americans in Clarendon County were also targeted as a result of their involvement in the legal case being led by De Laine. African Americans in Clarendon County exhibited real courage and persistence in fighting for an equal education for their children in a racially oppressive environment. Just as courage and persistence are hallmarks of activism, advocacy, and agitation, so is sacrifice. The African American people of Clarendon also sacrificed on behalf of educational equity. Individual sacrifice may never be at the level of the sacrifice of Reverend J. A. De Laine. However, some form of sacrifice may be required to successfully advocate or agitate for change. When individuals and communities are willing to sacrifice in some form for something as a powerful as a right to a quality education for children, the prospects of success increase. That is the lesson from Clarendon County.

Our last historical example involves advocating for the right of choice within communities that are often relegated to whatever is offered through the public schools. Advocacy in such an environment is as strong a form of resistance as the advocacy of the parents and community members in New York City in the 1830s. In 2002, the Supreme Court, in a 5 to 4 decision, determined that parents with children in Cleveland Metropolitan Public Schools had the right to use a publicly funded voucher program to move their children from failing public schools to private parochial schools. The case of *Zelman v. Simmons-Harris* (536 U.S. 639, 2002) was controversial because of the issue of using public funds to support what was in essence the private parochial school education of children in Cleveland. While the case involved the use of vouchers at parochial schools, and appeared to be in violation of the Constitution's Establishment Clause, the real issue behind *Zelman* concerned the ability of poor, urban, predominantly African American parents to have educational choices for their children. These parents did not want their children stuck in a failing school system with the foreclosed future opportunities that come with being miseducated in such systems. The parents' resistance to this educational fate for their children is another example of the need for resistance in the face of a failed status quo.

Saletta Harris was a 10-year-old girl at the time the Cleveland Choice Program of the Ohio Pilot Project Scholarship Program was being offered to parents with children attending Cleveland's public schools (Crisafulli, 2002–2003). As a result of the voucher part of the program, Saletta was attending Second New Hope Christian Academy, a private Christian school in Cleveland. Her parents had used the financial support available through the voucher program and moved their daughter out of a Cleveland public school where she had to repeat the first grade. At Second New Hope, Saletta was a successful student who was making excellent progress. In response to the systemic failure of the Cleveland Metropolitan School District, the Ohio General Assembly created the Cleveland Choice Program in 1996. The academic performance of the students in the district was so poor that a federal district judge declared a crisis and placed the entire district under the control of Ohio's Superintendent of Public Instruction. The Ohio General Assembly responded to the crisis with the creation of the Choice Program. The purpose of the program was twofold: provide financial support—in the form of a voucher—for low-income parents who wanted to give their children, in grades kindergarten through eighth grade, an alternative education to the public schools in Cleveland and provide resources for tutoring for those parents who wanted their children to remain in Cleveland's schools (Crisafulli, 2002).

Any private school located in Cleveland Metropolitan School District could participate in the voucher program. Participating private schools could either be parochial or secular as long as they followed state educational guidelines and did not discriminate. In the 1999–2000 school year, over 60% of the students in the program were from families that met poverty requirements. Of the students participating in program, 96% were attending religiously affiliated schools; there were not any public schools adjacent to Cleveland Metropolitan School District that participated in the program (*Zelman, Superintendent of Public Instruction of Ohio, et al. v. Simmons-Harris et al.*, 2002). Cleveland Metropolitan School District, at the time of the *Zelman* decision, failed to graduate two-thirds of its high school students. Of those students able to reach their senior year in the district, one of every four still failed to graduate. Those who did graduate were ill prepared to compete for jobs and career opportunities. In such a daunting and depressing environment any parent would want an educational alternative for their child. The parents of Saletta Harris, and countless other Cleveland parents who chose to participate in the Cleveland Choice Program, chose not to sacrifice their children to a failed educational system that would leave them with little or no prospects for the future. Activism also involves a willingness to challenge orthodoxies that often appears monolithic, unable to be moved or changed. Such challenges require courage, persistence, and sacrifice. A strong argument can be made that the parents who opted for the Cleveland Choice Program were not opponents of the public schools; they were proponents of a quality education for their children.

Regardless of the controversy over the Establishment Clause and the constitutionality of the voucher program, there were African American parents willing to challenge an educational system, that had educated them, and which they were oriented to believe would also educate their children. It is the most basic of parental responsibilities to struggle for the best for one's child. Challenging a system on behalf of one's children is what parents are supposed to do in their role as advocates. That is what the parents in Cleveland were doing when they looked beyond the public schools to educate their children. Their activism in the form of advocacy on behalf of their children was what Ward Randolph (2009) argued when she described what African American school leaders must do to transform the education of African American children. The lesson of the *Zelman* case and the parents of children in Cleveland public schools is that parents of African American children in ineffective public schools can also exhibit the type of transformative leadership in the education of their children that Ward Randolph (2009) and Dantley (2009) described as necessary for effective educational leadership

These historical snapshots provide a brief insight in how African Americans have challenged existing power structures to be able to secure for their children, and themselves, the right to participate in the American ideal of unfettered opportunity to success for all Americans regardless of race. The four examples also point to the understanding African Americans have had regarding the transformative power of education. African Americans have been willing to die for the right to an education and they also bear witness to the belief that education was their ticket to true freedom. African Americans willingly made demands of those in power and committed to an ongoing struggle for the basic right to an education.

AFRICAN AMERICAN EDUCATIONAL LEADERSHIP

Educational leadership for African American children and their communities should draw its guidance and inspiration from historical insights that provide the context for which leadership on behalf of children and community can be framed. The historical examples presented in this chapter provide insights on courage, persistence, resiliency, sacrifice, demand of power, spiritual intentionality, collective independence, and willingness to change. Throughout history there have been African American educational leaders who have successfully educated African American children. Those educators understood the environment in which they existed and despite countless hardships and obstacles were able to successfully educate African Americans.

The lessons that can be learned from these historical figures are what Adah Ward Randolph (2009) and Dantley (2009) argue educational leaders must provide in African American communities. You cannot effectively educate African American children, or children of any race or ethnicity, if you do not know their culture or history. You also cannot effectively address the educational needs of the community if you do not know the issues/needs impacting the community. Understanding the history and culture of African Americans affords a perspective regarding the strong role education has had in the community. Connecting a vision of the school with community cannot occur unless there is an awareness of history and culture.

Gooden (2012) asserts that African American educational leaders must embrace an "ethic of justice" to develop a leadership style that is inclusive rather than one that is unilateral and dominating. Gooden also calls for African American educational leaders to embrace an "ethic of care" in working with African American children who too often have been labeled and treated as problems (p. 80). Finally, Gooden asserts that African American leadership should "also know how to advocate, recognize, and address race-based inequities" (p. 82). Tillman (2004) provides insights to the critical school and community roles performed by African American principals in the pre-*Brown* era that supports Gooden's assertions regarding the role of educational leaders:

> They served as connections to and liaisons between the school and community. As principals, they encouraged parents to donate resources to the schools, helped to raise funds for schools, and served as professional role models for teachers and other staff members.... Understanding the importance of developing an educated Black community, these individuals held themselves accountable for the academic achievement of Black children and adults who attended all-Black public and private schools. (pp. 109–110)

This section discusses two successful African American educators: Maudelle Brown Bousfield and Marcus Foster and how they embodied the position of strong African American leadership in urban, predominantly African American communities in embracing the ethics described by Gooden (2012) and the pre-*Brown* roles described by Tillman (2004). Bousfield and Foster are both strong exemplars of courageous leaders who engaged in community resistance and activism on behalf of the education of the children they served. They are also examples of educational leaders who had their finger on the pulse of their communities and were not afraid to challenge community institutions that they felt were impeding the education of children in their care.

Maudelle Brown Bousfield had a long career in urban education in the first half of the 20th century. She was the first African American principal of both an elementary and high school in Chicago and for many years was the most visible and prominent African American educator in the city. Bousfield was an accomplished individual who was the first African American female to graduate from the University of Illinois in 1906. After moving to Chicago, she became principal of Keith Elementary School in 1927 and the principal of Douglas Elementary School in 1931 (Danns, 2009). At both schools, especially Douglas Elementary, Bousfield had White teachers under her supervision whose respect she had to earn, since many of them were resentful of having an African American principal. Dionne Danns (2009) recounts an incident where Bousfield confronted a White teacher about her neglect of her students in her classroom. The teacher was immediately transferred and other recalcitrant White teachers also transferred from the school. Bousfield stated that she had no other problems with teachers at Douglas after the transfers.

In 1939, Bousfield became principal of Phillips High School, another historic first in African American educational achievement in Chicago. Her appointment at Phillips was also unique in that she became the first African American to lead a multiracial school. Danns (2009) discusses how changing the negative perception of Phillips was one of the greatest challenges faced by Bousfield. Bousfield had to address the illicit activities —gambling, prostitution and drug dealing—occurring in the area around Phillips, while trying to change the perception of the school, among the students and the community. Bousfield was instrumental in cleaning up the community around the school, including a liquor store that was selling alcohol to minors. Bousfield's "strategy was to clean up the outsider's view of the school, and then instill pride in students and teachers so that academics could also be improved" (Danns, 2009, p. 9). She was so successful in turning around Phillips that students started using phony home addresses in order to be eligible to attend the school. Bousfield, who retired in 1950, was a school and community leader who embraced the four tenets offered by Ward Randolph and was the purposive leader described by Dantley (2009). Bousfield also embraced the ethics of care and justice described by Gooden (2012) in her educational leadership and she represented the pre-*Brown* educational leadership discussed by Tillman (2004).

Maudelle Brown Bousfield was a pioneering African American educator. She combined the skills of an educator and scholar with the courage of a community activist engaged in advocacy and agitation. She understood the connection between the education of children in a school with the issues in the community that impacted on the education of those children. By combining educational leadership and community activism Bousfield established a model of how educators can address systemic community issues while effectively educating children in those communities.

Another exemplar educational leader, Marcus Foster, was a teacher, principal and administrator in Philadelphia schools and who became the first African American superintendent of Oakland Unified School District in Oakland, California in 1970. In 1973, members of the Symbionese Liberation Army tragically assassinated Foster (Spencer, 2012). Born in Athens, Georgia, Foster was raised in Philadelphia. He received his undergraduate degree from Cheney State and his doctorate from the University of Pennsylvania. Foster started teaching in the School District of Philadelphia in 1957, eventually becoming a principal at three different schools and an associate superintendent in the district. It was Foster's work at Simon Gratz High School in North Philadelphia that was to bring him recognition and praise.

Foster became principal at Simon Gratz High School in 1966. At Gratz, Foster encountered a school that was in terrible physical condition, rife with gang violence and with students reading at a fourth grade level. Foster quickly connected with the students at the school and became widely known in the community around Gratz. He engaged parents and students to work with faculty in developing a more relevant curriculum. He pushed for higher academic expectations and achievement. Foster also led the community in a successful struggle with the school board and the city over the overcrowding and deplorable conditions at Gratz. Over 6,000 community members joined Foster in convincing the city and the school board to expand the facilities (Spencer, 2012). Foster was committed to involving the "total school community" in raising student achievement. "The total school community included parents who were upset by the school's failure to produce achievement and students who sought relevance and black history; but it also included teachers who were dismayed by their students' low motivation and skills" (Spencer, 2012, loc. 2898). By involving the total school community in the operation of the school, Foster successfully reduced dropout rates, raised academic achievement, college acceptance and scholarships.

Foster's success at Gratz led to a promotion as an associate superintendent in Philadelphia. In 1970, Foster left Philadelphia to become the superintendent in Oakland. In Oakland, Foster used the same community organizing skills he used at Gratz by mobilizing thousands of White and African American citizens in Oakland for a campaign to improve public education in the city. To accomplish that, Foster created a Master Plan Citizens Committee (MPCC) that consisted of citizens committees for each school in the district; he also created district-wide task forces and a central council, all as part of a greater effort to support community participation in the education of Oakland's students (Spencer, 2012). Foster was able to harness the community activism that was prevalent in the 60s and 70s. As an African American educator in a large urban community during those turbulent years, Foster understood the aspirations of the African American community to have a more prominent role in the education of their children. He supported those aspirations in Philadelphia and in Oakland by actively engaging the community as full partners in the education of children. It is tragically ironic that a fringe radical group that had targeted him because they mistakenly believed that he supported a nonprogressive agenda for Oakland's schools killed Foster. Foster completely epitomized an educational leader that pushed for high academic achievement, relevant curriculum and complete community involvement. In 1973, that was progressive. Marcus Foster represented purposive leadership that was transformative in the schools and communities he led and touched. He was not afraid to be an activist nor was he reluctant to successfully agitate on behalf of the needs of students and community as he did as Principal of Gratz High School in Philadelphia.

CONCLUSION

The African American struggle for educational opportunity and equity has been a centuries' long demand full of activism that has employed advocacy and agitation. This chapter offers the naming and recognition of a countervailing part of the dialectical dialogue between educational leadership concerned with equity, diversity, and social justice, and conversely, what can be understood as the privileged imperative of schooling (Blount, 2013). The struggle has not just been borne by parents and community members alone; it has also involved the contributions of educators. The resiliency, courage, sacrifice, persistence, and hope exhibited by countless individuals, Black and White, on the behalf of the fundamental right for all children to have access to a quality education should serve as a guide for how educational leadership should be framed to ensure that right. Educational leadership for African American children should involve an awareness of history and culture of the community, but it should also be steeped in activism with a focus on advocacy, and when necessary agitation. That is how educators like Maudelle Brown Bousfield and Marcus Foster led, and as a result was successful in raising the level of academic achievement in the schools they led.

History has made Douglass's admonition regarding power correct. The battles fought by African Americans in New York City in the early 19th century; South Carolina in the middle of the last century; and Cleveland earlier this century, as well as the demonstrated leadership of Bousfield and Foster, all highlight how progress can be made with resistance to inequities in the form of ongoing activism that is primarily focused on advocacy but is not reluctant to delve into agitation when necessary. If history provides any kind of lesson, in the future the struggle for educational equity and opportunity will still precede progress. Power will never concede without a demand.

REFERENCES

Alinsky, S. (1971). *Rules for radicals: A pragmatic primer for realistic radicals* [Kindle Edition]. Retrieved from Amazon.com.

Blount, J. M. (2013). Educational leadership through equity, diversity, and social justice an educational leadership for the privileged imperative: The historical dialectic. In L. C. Tillman & J. J. Scheurich (Eds.), *Handbook of research on educational leadership for equity and diversity* (pp. 7–20). New York, NY: Routledge.

Brown-Nagin, T. (1999). The transformation of a social movement into law? The SCLC and NAACP's campaigns for civil rights reconsidered in light of the educational activism of Septima Clark. *Women's History Review, 8*(1), 81–137.

Brown v. Board of Education, 347 U.S. 483 (1954).

Burton, O. V., Burton, B., & Appleford, S. (2008). Seeds in unlikely soil: The *Briggs v. Elliot* school segregation case. In W. B. Moore, Jr. & O. V. Burton (Eds.), *Toward the meeting of the waters: Currents in the Civil Rights Movement of South Carolina during the twentieth century* (pp. 176–200). Columbia, SC: University of South Carolina Press.

Couzens Hoy, D. (2004). *Critical resistance: From poststructuralism to post-critique.* [Kindle Edition]. Retrieved from Amazon.com.

Crisafulli, S. J. (2002–2003). *Zelman v. Simmons-Harris:* Is the Supreme Court's latest word on school voucher programs really the last word? *Fordham Law Review, 71*, 2227–2281.

Danns, D. (2009). Thriving in the midst of adversity: Educator Maudelle Brown Bousfield's struggles in Chicago 1920–1950. *The Journal of Negro Education, 78*(1), 3–16.

Dantley, M. (2009). African American educational leadership: Critical, purposive, and spiritual. In L. Foster & L. Tillman (Eds.), *African American perspectives on leadership in schools: Building a culture of empowerment* (pp. 39–55). New York, NY: Rowman & Littlefield Education.

De Laine Gona, O. (2011). *Dawn of desegregation: J. A. De Laine and Briggs v. Elliot.* [Kindle edition]. Retrieved from Amazon.com.

Douglass, F. (1857). If there is no struggle, there is no progress. *BlackPast.org*. Retrieved from http://www.blackpast.org/1857-frederick-douglass-if-there-no-struggle-there-no-progress

Franklin, J. H., & Moss, A. (1994). *From slavery to freedom: A history of African Americans* (7th ed.). New York, NY: McGraw-Hill.

Freire, P. (2011). *Pedagogy of the oppressed* (Myra Bergman Ramos, Trans.). New York, NY: Continuum. (Original work published 1970)

Gooden, M. A. (2012). What does racism have to do with leadership? Countering the idea of color-blind leadership: A reflection on race and the growing pressures of the urban principalship. *Educational Foundations, 26*(1–2), 67–84.

Harris, L. M. (2003). *In the shadow of slavery: African Americans in New York City, 1626–1863* [Kindle Edition]. Retrieved from Amazon.com.

Jordan, W. D. (1974). *The White man's burden: Historical origins of racism in the United States* [Kindle Edition]. Retrieved from Amazon.com.

Kluger, R. (2004). *Simple justice, The history of Brown v. Board of Education and Black America's struggle for equality.* New York, NY: First Vintage Books Edition.

Lambert, L., Walker, D., Zimmerman, D. P., Cooper, J. E., Lambert, M. D., Gardner, M. E., & Szabo, M. (2002). *The constructivist leader* (2nd ed.). New York, NY: Teachers College Press.

Mabee, C. (1979). *Black education in New York State: From colonial to modern times.* Syracuse, NY: Syracuse University Press.

McKenzie, T. (2016). *A comprehensive sociological glossary* [Kindle Edition]. Retrieved from Amazon.com.

Rury, J. L. (1983). The New York African Free School, 1827–1836: Conflict over community control of Black education. *Phylon, 44*(3), 187–197.

Spencer, J. P. (2012). *In the crossfire: Marcus Foster and the troubled history of American Schools* [Kindle Edition]. Retrieved from Amazon.com.

Spraggins, T. (1970). Historical highlights in the education of Black Americans. *National Education Association.* Washington, DC: Center for Human Relations.

Tillman, L. C. (2004). African American principals and the legacy of Brown. *Review of Research in Education, 28*(1), 101–146

Ward Randolph, A. L. (2009). The historical tradition of African American leadership in African American Schools: 1830–1955. In L. Foster & L. C. Tillman (Eds.), *African American perspectives on leadership in schools: Building a culture of empowerment* (pp. 17–38). Lanham, MD: Rowman & Littlefield Education.

Woodson, C. G. (1919). *The education of the Negro prior to 1861: A history of the education of the colored people of the United States from the beginning of slavery to the Civil War* [Kindle Edition]. Retrieved from Amazon.com.

Zelman, Superintendent of Public Instruction of Ohio, et al. v. Simmons-Harris et al., 536 U.S. 639. (2002).

CHAPTER 2

RELATIONAL-CULTURAL THEORY

Using Counseling Principles to Cultivate Inclusive Leaders

Ami Camp and Sejal Parikh Foxx

ABSTRACT

The theoretical underpinnings of relational cultural theory can be applied in the educational leadership context. These principles and skills can be used to cultivate leaders who foster equitable relationships and minimize a hierarchical approach to leadership. Furthermore, given inclusive leadership calls for developing a critical consciousness, this chapter discusses the basic tenets of relational cultural theory such as connections, mutual empathy, authenticity, and fostering growth. Case studies are used to demonstrate application in educational settings.

Educational systems experience perpetual change related to policy, curriculum, leadership, and personnel (Kershner & McQuillan, 2016). The aforementioned changes can engender negative, positive, temporary, or indefinite results that adversely affect the overall school climate (Kershner & McQuillan, 2016; Okçu, 2014). According to Okçu (2014), one of the most salient factors of effective schools is the leadership style of administrators. One example is transactional leadership where order and structure are valued but innovation and creative thinking are not. The status quo maintains

Convictions of Conscience: How Voices From the Margins Inform Public Actions, and Educational Leadership, pp. 21–33

educational systems of oppression that decrease access to quality teachers, instructional materials, and college and career readiness. Considering the perpetual, systemic changes experienced within school systems, it is challenging for administrators and faculty to not maintain the status quo; however, it is imperative that administrators model and foster the understanding and practice of multiculturalism by implementing culturally responsive leadership in their practice (Gooden, 2010).

One way in which educational leaders can promote inclusivity and sensitivity towards cultural differences is by encouraging staff to engage in professional development opportunities that addresses culturally and logistically appropriate practices and approaches (Santamaría, 2014). Additionally, leaders should work collaboratively with respective colleagues and local community stakeholders to develop inclusive communities and reciprocate accountability for positive student and community outcomes (Capper & Young, 2014). As such, growth and connected relationships are needed to accomplish inclusive practices. *Relational-cultural theory* (RCT) is a framework often employed by counselors that focuses on the growth that occurs when individuals are connected and relationships are fostered (Comstock et al., 2008) and can be vital in cultivating inclusive leaders.

RELATIONAL-CULTURAL THEORY

Relational-cultural theory (RCT) materialized from the belief that traditional models of psychotherapy did not address relational experiences of women and other marginalized individuals; grounded in feministic theory, this humanistic approach to counseling regards relational skills of the aforementioned populations as strengths (Comstock et al., 2008). Contrary to traditional theories such as psychoanalytic, existential, and cognitive behavioral that emphasize competition, autonomy, independence, and individual achievement, RCT promotes mutual empathy, mutual empowerment, and connections (Comstock et al., 2008; Tucker, Smith-Adcock, & Trepal, 2011). Additionally, psychological well-being is salient in RCT. Psychological well-being is characterized by an individual's desire for and movement toward connection with others rather than sole autonomy and independence (Headley & Sangganjanavanich, 2014). This movement, oftentimes, is experienced as an iterative process of relational movement wherein he or she transitions through connections, disconnections, and new, transformative connections with others, respectively. Well-being is further supported through the following basic tenets of RCT as described by Jordan (2001):

1. Individuals have an innate desire for connection and relationship and experience growth in their relationships throughout the lifespan.

2. Mature functioning is characterized by progression towards mutuality rather than separation.
3. One's psychological growth is characterized by his or her ability to maintain intricate relational development.
4. Mutual empathy and mutual empowerment are necessary in establishing growth-fostering relationships.
5. Authenticity is central to promoting growth-fostering relationships.
6. Intentional contribution to and involvement in cultivating growth-fostering relationships support ones' personal growth and maturation.
7. As an individual grows and matures throughout the lifespan, his or her relational competence increases.

Additional concepts that are central to RCT include condemned isolation, central relational paradox, and power-over dynamics. While connection promotes a mutually empathic and growth-fostering relationship, both of which are vital in a therapeutic alliance, there are several ways in which the connection can be ruptured, thus eliciting disconnection. According to Comstock et al. (2008), if unresolved, disconnection can precipitate condemned isolation, adversely causing an individual to experience distress, isolation, shame, frustration, and self-blame. For marginalized populations, in particular, condemned isolation further perpetuates and reinforces self-blame and negative relational perceptions. Behaviors such as blaming, minimizing, withdrawing, or attacking others are characteristic of disconnections that often emerge from feelings of shame and previous experiences of humiliation (Headley & Sangganjanavanich, 2014). If disconnections are traumatic or chronic they will likely influence individuals to remain isolated and withdrawn, thus refraining from establishing meaningful connections with others (Duffey & Trepal, 2016; Headley & Sangganjanavanich, 2014).

Although individuals intrinsically desire connection and belonging, they sometimes demonstrate a conflict in addressing relational situations that are presented and utilize distancing behaviors to manage their emotional safety, a process referred to as the central relational paradox (Comstock et al., 2008; Duffey & Trepal, 2016; Headley & Sangganjanavanich, 2014). Contrary to the innate desire to cultivate meaningful relationships and to have a sense of belonging, an individual with negative relational images may resist engaging in genuine, growth-fostering relationships because the negative images have impeded their ability to foster positive images. Relational images refer to internal connections developed by an individual's past experiences that affect current and future relationships with self and with others (Headley & Sangganjanavanich, 2014). Relational resilience is indicated as necessary to resolve relational conflict spurred by these relational images.

For example, a male student who has a relational conflict with his peers will avoid participating in activities (e.g., clubs, extracurricular events). In doing so, he allows less of himself to enter into relations with his peers, thus further isolating himself. To experience relational resilience, it is imperative that an individual be aware of his or her movement through connections and disconnections toward empowerment at intrapersonal, interpersonal, and societal levels. Additionally, relational competency, which is an intrinsic desire to attain mutual empathy, self-empathy, and empathy for others, is necessary in cultivating relational resilience (Headley & Sangganjanavanich, 2014).

Power-over is a dynamic that generates disconnection wherein either a dominant group or an individual of a dominant group utilizes his or her power to suppress another individual or group of individuals (Ruiz, 2012). Disconnection is engendered societally though misused power and institutional marginalization and oppression (Duffey & Trepal, 2016; Walker, 2005). In this contemporary culture and time, many individuals of underserved populations are becoming more fearful and less trusting of others due to perpetual forms of oppression, many of which are more overt. Birrell and Freyd (2006) stated,

> although oppression is often institutionalized at societal levels, it is necessarily enacted in the context of interpersonal relationships (p. 52), and the fragmentation caused by the violation of human bonds can only be healed by new and healing human bonds. (p. 57)

Oftentimes, feelings of isolation, humiliation, and shame, in addition to microaggressions, are central to the experiences of marginalized populations. RCT is an approach that supports the transformation of fear and disconnection into greater potential and ability to establish connections with others through growth-fostering relationships that engender resilience (Comstock et al., 2008). Awareness, or consciousness, of oppressive contexts and impacts on marginalized communities is vital in cultivating effective change.

RCT'S RELATIONSHIP TO CRITICAL CONSCIOUSNESS

Freire's (2000) notion of critical consciousness, *conscientizacao,* aligns with many tenets of RCT. Freire (1973) states, "*Conscientizaco* represents the development of the awakening of critical awareness. It will not appear as a natural byproduct of even major economic changes, but must grow out of a critical educational effort based on favorable historical conditions" (p. 15). According to Freire (2000), critical consciousness is the ability to perceive social, political, and economic oppression and to take action against the oppressive elements of society. This consciousness has the power to transform society as individuals take action to change their realities. Within the ideology of critical consciousness, marginalized people realize the importance of and learn to critically analyze their social conditions and engage in action to create change. *Conscientizacao* is achieved through critical dialogue. Critical dialogue occurs when individuals question social realities, change attitudes, and transform beliefs. For example Freire (1973) states "to every understanding, sooner or later an action corresponds. Onalce man perceives a challenge, understands it, and recognizes the possibilities of response he acts. The nature of that action corresponds to the nature of his understanding" (p. 44). Critical consciousness challenges the many forms of internalized oppression and disempowerment experienced by marginalized people. A comparable focus within RCT is the emphasis during the counseling process on improving the harmful impact of marginalization, social injustices, and other numerous forms of cultural oppression (Comstock et al., 2008).

Critical consciousness also values collaboration and rejects the notion of hierarchies that exist between student and teachers. Hierarchies that may be based on race, gender, sexual identity, religion, and so forth. Similarly, RCT values egalitarian relationships in which power is reconfigured between the client and counselor. In RCT individuals move toward connection and transform disconnections by realizing mutual empathy, developing resilience, broaching difficult conversations, and then being open and prepared to hear those responses. This is a multicultural perspective in which the onus is on the counselor to broach difficult subjects and to work toward understanding the racial identity of their clients as well as their own (Comstock et al., 2008).

An additional implication for critically conscious collaborative relationships is seen through Freire's (2000) concept of the banking system of education. Within this system, the relationship between teacher and student is transactional and consists of the teacher depositing knowledge into the students. Resulting in students having little to no contribution to the process of learning. Freire disavows the banking system and instead offers that education should liberate the student as a function of bi-directional relationships between student and teacher instead of unidirectional relationships. This supports the concepts of learning through collaboration and student agency in the learning process. Relatedly, this exercise of collaboration is evident in the practice of mutual empathy in counseling. The outcome of this practice is that counseling interventions are decided through a collaborative process between the client and counselor (Comstock et al,

2008). Many theoretical concepts of RCT relate to critical consciousness' philosophical principles discussed by Freire (2000) and have implications for educational leaders who desire to foster an educational environment that is systemically inclusive, empathetic, and promotes connections.

RELATIONAL CULTURAL THEORY FOR EDUCATIONAL LEADERS

Counselors have used RCT to support multiculturalism and social justice through promoting awareness and knowledge of the impact of oppression and social injustices on marginalized populations; however, there exists a paucity of literature addressing the integration of RCT within the field of educational leadership. This is surprising given previous research by Ryan (2010) found that principals recognize the political nature of schools, and attempt to use social acumen to establish effective working relationships with adults. However, the same study noted that the principals only spoke of other adults and omitted students, who were observed to have less power. As educational leaders are central in fostering an inclusive school environment, they must be aware of how the politicized nature of schools impacts the development of effective working relationships with all stakeholders and the capacity to engender trust. Trust must be established through addressing issues of class, ethnicity, race, as well as others in schools (Handford & Leithwood, 2013). Educational leaders who establish trust are able to counteract the "isms" that enter into classroom settings, form collaborative relationships, and move toward socially just schools (Rivera-McCutchen & Watson, 2014).

According to Walker (2002), relational development inevitably connects to an individual's racial, cultural, and social identities. Therefore educational leaders' awareness and knowledge of the ways in which marginalization and oppression at various levels impact students of underserved populations is vital in supporting their needs and fostering empowerment as well as building effective relationships. Educators increase the probability of creating inclusive school environments when they intentionally create connections and cultivate and sustain a culturally responsive environment.

Connection is important for the satisfaction and relational growth of individuals according to Tucker, Smith-Adcock, and Trepal (2011). In addition to relationships being central to ones' growth, balanced or shared power is central to establishing healthy relationships. Contrary to connection, disconnection is likely to occur and impede growth when power and privilege not only in relationships, but also in society, are imbalanced and remain unresolved. For many students, disconnection could manifest in either feelings of shame and isolation or maladaptive, distracting behaviors.

Fostering connection in the school environment should be a primary aim of educational leaders.

Cultivating and sustaining a culturally responsive environment is another important aspect. Effective learning experiences are predicated on the development of connections between students and their peers and faculty. The amalgamation of ones' beliefs and cultural knowledge can adversely affect how leaders lead and direct the implementation of instructional practices at all levels. For instance, one such practice is related to discipline. Research has demonstrated that African American students are 3.38 times more likely to receive a discipline referral to the office (Diem & Carpenter, 2013). Racial bias is considered a key influence on those referrals. Compounding the issue is that conversations related to ethnicity, race, and inequities in the classrooms are lacking in educational leadership preparation programs (Diem & Carpenter, 2013). This leads to what Nelson and Guerra (2014) refer to as deficit thinking, which is the propensity to view specific groups of students as deficient. Considering the impact of personal beliefs held by individuals on the decisions made regarding school policies, procedures, and practices, this type of thinking is detrimental and can impede efforts in creating a culturally responsive environment (Nelson & Guerra, 2014; García & Guerra, 2004). Educational leaders, then, should promote conversations that explore and challenge deficit based thinking in their efforts to engage in systemic change.

RCT is a culturally sensitive model from which educational leaders and school personnel can work with culturally, linguistically, and economically disadvantaged students and their respective families. Table 2.1 summarizes strategies that would be useful for educational leaders who desire to integrate RCT concepts into their practice. This theory can be used as a foundation to engage in open conversations about educators' belief systems, fostering relationships and connection with students, creating and sustaining a culturally responsive environment, and challenging deficit thinking. The tenets of RCT may also provide educational leaders with the tools and skills necessary to challenge the status quo. The following case studies illustrate how relational awareness, competencies, mutual empathy and empowerment can be applied in the school setting.

APPLICATION

Case Study 1

David is a 14-year old, Latino male beginning his freshman year in high school. The eldest of five children, David lives with his biological mother, biological father, twin sisters, and two younger brothers. As a result of his parent's recent job promotions, he and his family moved to a new home during the summer, resulting in David having to attend a new school that happens to be a rival to the school all of his closest friends will be attending. David is disappointed about separating from his friends, most of whom he grew up with, and concerned that he will not be able to make new friends at his new school.

Because of mistrust elicited by negative social and professional experiences with individuals of the majority dominant population, David's parents encouraged him to disclose as little information as possible to his peers and teachers, particularly those individuals of the majority, dominant population. During the first two months of school, David consistently made an effort to connect with a popular group of students. While receptive at first, this particular group of students began to distance themselves from David. Desperate for attention from the group and a sense of belonging and connection with his peers, David began to engage in externalizing behaviors that were disruptive and maladaptive both inside and outside of the classroom. Concerns about the once respectful and charming student echoed among each of his teachers and the administrators. His most recent

Table 2.1.
Strategies for Integrating Relational Cultural Theoretical Concepts

RCT Concept	Strategies for Educational Leaders
Mutual Empathy	1. Nurture dialogue 2. Transparency 3. Be vulnerable
Connectedness	1. Promote compassion 2. Foster a sense of community 3. Be culturally responsive
Egalitarian Relationships	1. Believe each person deserves to participate 2. Believe each person deserves to be heard
Authenticity	1. Promote engagement across hierarchies 2. Acknowledge cultural oppression, marginalization, and social injustices
Relational Awareness	1. Develop cultural competence 2. Be authentic and empathic
Promote Positive Relational Images	1. Recognize historical mistrust by oppressed groups 2. Confront stereotypes and biases

externalizing behaviors resulted in two subsequent in-school suspensions, prompting the ninth-grade administrator to initiate a one-on-one meeting with David to gain further insight into this change in behavior.

David's parents were aware of his most recent behavior, but were unable to attend a meeting at school during school hours as they would be at risk of demotion from their new positions should they miss scheduled hours. Although neither of David's parents had spoken with his teachers or the grade-level administrator, they were fearful David would be recommended to transfer to another school if his behavior remained unresolved.

David's administrator is a 45-year old, White male who had limited interactions with David prior to initiating the one-on-one meeting. Using RCT to conceptualize David's presenting challenges and provide support, the administrator recognizes David's underlying issue as his lack of connection and sense of belonging with peers and other individuals within the school. To foster mutual empathy, the administrator must be willing to have nonjudgmental dialogue with David about his most recent behavior, being transparent in his responses and comments regarding that which David discloses. It is through relational, nonjudgmental environments that an individual is challenged to self-examine their behaviors and themselves in relation to others (Tucker, Smith-Adcock, & Trepal, 2011). Having an opportunity to discuss recent maladaptive behaviors and self-reflect in a nonjudgmental environment may incite redirected thinking on behalf of David.

Through demonstrated compassion for and cultural sensitivity towards David, the administrator was able to connect with David in a way that he had not connected with him previously. The administrator's willingness to promote and model inclusivity while acknowledging marginalization and oppression of ethnic minorities fosters egalitarian relationships and reveals his authenticity and sincerity in providing support for David and his family, who had negative experiences with other individuals previously. Developing a personal understanding of transitions from disconnections to connections, mutuality, and empowerment, and developing a yearning for mutual empathy, self-empathy, and empathy for others are relational awareness and relational competencies, respectfully (Headley & Sangganjanavanich, 2014).

Obtaining this level of awareness and competency is a transformative experience, which extends beyond cultural awareness and knowledge to where deficit beliefs and practices can be acknowledged, challenged, and reshaped (Nelson & Guerra, 2008). To ensure that cultural competence among educational leaders and other school personnel are being cultivated, the administrator can work collaboratively with his team to arrange ongoing in-service professional development sessions that address ways in which cultural identity is embedded in many of the decisions related to instructional strategies, policies, and procedures (Delgado-Gaitan, 2006; Nelson & Guerra, 2014, 2008). Working to establish and maintain a culturally responsive climate among leadership, faculty, staff, and students would be conducive to a positive environment in which David can connect with peers and teachers, establish meaningful relationships, learn, and prepare to contribute to society.

Case Study 2

Dr. Sound is a current principal at a middle school. She was also an elementary school principal for five years and, just prior to the middle school principalship was a high school principal for three years. All were Title 1 schools. Despite several challenges presented within the school, namely high suspension and discipline referrals, low academic performance among students, and minimal parental involvement, Dr. Sound embraced the challenge and began the academic school year with confidence it would be one of the best years the students and faculty had experienced to date. During the summer, and before in-service professional development, Dr. Sound administered a brief school climate survey to all returning teachers, in which the identity of teachers remained anonymous. The results Dr. Sound received were astounding and disheartening as the majority of the responses reflected significant deficit thoughts among the faculty, unearthing an overall negative climate.

It was at that moment that Dr. Sound determined RCT would be appropriate to utilize in her efforts to revitalize the climate of the school, improve the perceptions of faculty and students about one another, and foster greater parental involvement. Dr. Sound, aware of how imperative it was for her to model concepts of relational-cultural theory such as mutual empathy, connectedness, authenticity, and relational awareness, was intentional in doing so to promote positive change in the perceptions and behaviors of faculty and students. She fostered mutual empathy through remaining authentic and attuned to faculty and students during their experiences of connections and disconnections. In the midst of these experiences, Dr. Sound maintained awareness of her personal worldview as well as the worldview of others (e.g., faculty, students, other school personnel) when addressing presenting concerns.

Her efforts to cultivate a more culturally responsive, inclusive academic setting were first initiated through collaborating with local community stakeholders to address cultural awareness during professional development training for teachers. The administrative team was also required to attend the workshop. The facilitators of the workshop reassured all of the faculty members in attendance that discussions addressed during the workshop would remain confidential. Additionally, their presence was acknowledged as a significant first step in pursuing change to the status quo.

Cultural competence promotes the cultivation of deep cultural knowledge, as well as presents the opportunity for surfacing, challenging, and reframing deficit thinking (Nelson & Guerra, 2014). Providing a forum where preexisting thoughts and beliefs regarding culturally and economically disadvantaged students and their respective families could be challenged and discussed was, to Dr. Sound, essential for the inception of school climate reform. Through nurturing dialogue and transparency among faculty regarding perceptions that may have previously reinforced institutional oppression, Dr. Sound is better able to foster mutual empathy and authenticity and model for her staff. Maintaining awareness of personal worldview and accepting the worldview of others is a framework for developing relational convergence of the similarities and differences between life experiences (Comstock et al., 2008). Aware of this, Dr. Sound emphasized to her staff that students and parents are more likely to work collaboratively and mutually agree on intervention strategies as needed, when their respective worldviews, beliefs, and values are addressed and considered.

To promote equality and egalitarian relationships within the school, particularly for students of historically marginalized and oppressed populations, Dr. Sound requires teachers to nominate a different student each month for their observed strengths and contributions to the learning environment. This recognition reassures all students of their belonging in the student body. Lastly, teachers are encouraged throughout the school year to engage in professional development and training opportunities that further promote relational awareness and images. With regard to the minimal resistance she received from some faculty, primarily veteran faculty members, Dr. Sound remained consistent in modeling appropriate, inclusive behavior for teachers as well as demonstrating mutual empathy towards faculty through welcoming open dialogue regarding concerns, challenges, and adjustments experienced.

Progressively, with the collaborative efforts of faculty and students, the overall climate of the school improved as evidenced by results from a school climate survey disseminated by Dr. Sound at the conclusion of the academic school year. The pre-post survey was administered at the beginning of the academic school year and, again, at the end of the academic school year. A greater sense of community among staff, students, and their respective families became more visible. The efforts of Dr. Sound, teachers, students, and parents to integrate and adapt to concepts of RCT within the school setting presented many challenges; however, persistence in changing the status quo and consistency in modeling behaviors such as mutual empathy, empowerment, relational awareness, and regard for cultural differences cultivated a school climate more conducive for positive growth-fostering relationships and student outcomes.

CONCLUSION

RCT is based on feminist principles of connection, relationships, and empowerment of traditionally marginalized groups. In many ways RCT challenges individuals, particularly those in leadership positions, to dismantle the status quo and to foster inclusivity through valuing egalitarian relationships, authenticity, and mutual empathy. Leaders within education have the ability to promote relational awareness and practice relational competencies to support the development of inclusive and equitable communities that will elicit immediate and long-lasting impacts (Capper & Young, 2014; Kershner & McQuillan, 2014). Relational cultural theory provides one way to assist educational leaders in cultivating educational systems wherein the status quo does not persist but instead inclusive environments flourish.

REFERENCES

Birrell, P. J., & Freyd, J. J. (2006). Betrayal and trauma: Relational models of harm and healing. *Journal of Trauma Practice, 5,* 49–63.

Capper, C. A., & Young, M. D. (2014). Ironies and limitations of educational leadership for social justice: A call to social justice educators. *Theory into Practice, 53*, 158–164.

Comstock, D. L., Hammer, T. R., Strentzsch, J., Cannon, K., Parsons, J., & Salazar, G. (2008). Relational-Cultural Theory: A framework for bridging relational, multicultural, and social justice competencies. *Journal of Counseling & Development, 86*, 279–287.

Delgado-Gaitan, C. (2006). *Building culturally responsive classrooms: A guide for K–6 teachers*. Thousand Oaks, CA: Corwin Press.

Diem, S., & B. W. Carpenter. 2013. Examining race-related silences interrogating the education of tomorrow's educational leaders. *Journal of Research on Leadership Education, 8*, 56–76.

Duffey, T., & Trepal, H. (2016). Introduction to the special section on relational-cultural theory. *Journal of Counseling & Development, 94,* 379–382. doi:10.1002/jcad.12095.

Freire, P. (1973). *Education for critical consciousness* (Vol. 1). New York, NY: Bloomsbury.

Freire, P. (2000). *Pedagogy of the oppressed*. New York, NY: Continuum.

García, S. B., & Guerra, P. L. (2004). Deconstructing deficit thinking: Working with educators to create more equitable learning environments. *Education and Urban Society, 36*, 150–168.

Gooden M. (2010). *Culturally relevant leadership: How principals can support student learning now*. Retrieved from http://www.mmabse.org/Culturally_Relevant_Leadership_Gooden_ 2010. pptx.pdf

Handford V., & Leithwood K. (2013). Why teachers trust school leaders. *Journal of Educational Administration, 51*, 194–212.

Headley, J. A., & Sangganjanavanich, V. F. (2014). A recipe for change: Promoting connection through relational-cultural theory. *Journal of Creativity in Mental Health, 9*, 245–261.

Jordan, J. V. (2008) Recent developments in relational-cultural theory. *Women & Therapy*, 31:2-4, 1–4, doi:10.1080/02703140802145540

Kershner, B., & McQuillan, P. (2016). Complex adaptive schools: Educational leadership and school change. *Complicity: An International Journal of Complexity and Education, 13*, 4–29.

Nelson, S. W., & Guerra, P. L. (2008). Four-stage process changes individuals and entire schools. *Journal of Staff Development, 29*, 55–56.

Nelson, S. W., & Guerra, P. L. (2014). Educator beliefs and cultural knowledge: Implications for school improvement efforts. *Educational Administration Quarterly, 50*, 67–95.

Okçu, V. (2014). Relation between secondary school administrators' transformational and transactional leadership style and skills to diversity management in the school. *Educational Sciences: Theory and Practice, 14*, 2162–2174.

Rivera-McCutchen, R. L., & Watson, T. N. (2014). Leadership for social justice. *Journal of Cases in Educational Leadership, 17*, 54–65.

Ruiz, E. (2012). Understanding Latina immigrants using relational cultural theory. *Women & Therapy, 35*, 68–79.

Ryan, J. (2010). Promoting social justice in schools: Principals' political strategies. *International Journal of Leadership in Education, 13*, 357–376.

Santamaría, L. J. (2014). Critical change for the greater good. *Educational Administration Quarterly, 50*, 347–391.

Tucker, C., Smith-Adcock, S., & Trepal, H. C. (2011). Relational-cultural theory for middle school counselors. *Professional School Counseling, 14*(5), 310–316.

Walker, M. (2002). *How therapy helps when the culture hurts* (Work in Progress No. 95). Wellesley, MA: Stone Center Colloquium Series.

Walker, M. (2005). Critical thinking: Challenging developmental myths, stigmas, and stereotypes. In D. Comstock (Ed.), *Diversity and development: Critical context that shape our lives and relationships* (pp. 47–66). Belmont, CA: Brooks/Cole.

CHAPTER 3

SOCIAL JUSTICE RELATIONSHIPS

Embracing a Process of Searching and Unfinishedness

Juan Manuel Niño, Encarnación Garza, Jr., and Amanda Jo Cordova

ABSTRACT

Considering the continued failure of school improvements efforts (Sarason, 2004) and "inadequate to appalling" quality of university leadership preparation programs (Levine, 2005), leadership for social justice has never been of greater importance. This chapter suggests social justice is more than becoming aware of and implementing cultural competencies. It asserts social justice leaders must engage in deep collective critical reflection known as the Pedagogy of Collective Critical Consciousness (Garza, 2015) to fashion relationships of authenticity, reciprocity, and equity with the aim of claiming space for a liberatory education. This chapter highlights mentorship, which is reconceptualized as comradeship (Freire, 2000) as a strategy for developing socially justice leadership. We share their own *testimonios* to demonstrate how mentorship can be reconceptualized to privilege humanizing relationships

Convictions of Conscience: How Voices From the Margins Inform Public Actions, and Educational Leadership, pp. 35–53

in educational leadership. We contend our praxis of comradeship enables us to collectively fight against the dehumanization of education and navigate towards a more socially just world.

INTRODUCTION

The *testimonios* of mentorship in this chapter originate from relationships fostered in the Urban School Leadership Collaborative (USLC), a graduate level cohort program of the Educational Leadership and Policy Studies at the University of Texas at San Antonio (UTSA). The codirectors of the USLC Program, Encarnación Garza, Jr. and Juan Manuel Niño, integrate Freire's (2000) conceptualization of liberation into the praxis of reciprocal learning relationships conceptualized as comradeship that they facilitate with USLC members. In the context of the USLC, members (including students and professors) come together to examine oppressive conditions of the school system and interrogate their roles as the oppressed and oppressor (Freire) to discover who they are as social justice leaders. As Freire asserts "This discovery cannot be purely intellectual, but must involve action; nor can it be limited to pure activism, but must include serious reflection, only then will it be praxis" (p. 65).

Freire (2000) describes comradeship as a "communion with the people" (p. 61) in which status is not imposed. In this communion, comrades walk side by side unraveling the depths of their colonized minds for a profound rebirth of the humanizing self, enabling them to confront dehumanizing educational systems. Together, they unearth and walk new paths together, reflecting upon and enacting their liberated selves. This lies in opposition to traditional mentorship, that situates a mentor as the holder of knowledge to direct the mentee on a clearly defined, and delineated path conforming to existing structures, as well as the hierarchies of these structures. Juan, Amanda, and Encarnacion's *testimonios* illuminate comradeship as a counter-story to traditional mentorship models. By sharing *testimonios* of comradeship, comradeship is situated as essential for social justice leadership.

LITERATURE REVIEW

Bordas (2012) contends that American leadership has been culled largely from a White male perspective, focusing on mainstream values and an ethnocentric orientation. Incidentally, Wheatley (2006) argues leadership is like a science, in which practices can be measured, synchronized, and predicted. Current trends privilege leadership preparation directed toward a skill sets approach, managerial responsibilities, and test scores for accountability (Waite, Boone, & McGhee, 2001). In contrast, leadership for social justice is grounded in the inclusivity of all ways of knowing to establish equitable educational systems. It is this collective effort, enveloped in authenticity that sets the foundation for comradeship centering on the integration of personal and academic growth.

Given the shifts in demographics, the diversity in languages, and the richness in cultures, leadership preparation needs to go beyond a skill set approach to develop champions for justice (Garza, 2004; Merchant & Garza, 2014; Prieto & Niño, 2016). With this mindset, the USLC prepares educators to center authentic mentoring relationships at the heart of educational leadership. We contend, comradeship, grounded in social justice, is critical in developing educational leaders who adopt a praxis of equity.

Garza (2004) suggests social justice is an attitude. It is an attitude formed by the values, beliefs, and lived experiences of those seeking to make equitable change for marginalized students trapped in a perpetuating cycle of exclusion. The union between comradeship and social justice calls upon school leaders to work together to claim equitable spaces of educational opportunity, by enacting authentic relationships embodying equity, reciprocity, and engaging in deep collective critical reflection known as the Pedagogy of Collective Critical Consciousness (Garza, 2015). In this manner, relationships, evolve together as well as challenge each other to integrate their personal and professional lives toward humanizing the educational experience.

Rethinking Mentorship

Hinsdale (2015) challenges us to rethink our pedagogical relationships with students, especially those across differences of race, class, gender, sexuality, and ability" (p. 16) as a mechanism to counter higher education's history of exclusion, colonialism, and the minimization of other ways of knowing. In her decade review of mentor programs, Haring (1997) concurs the status afforded mentors as "one with benefits to offer and ways" (p. 7) to be emulated reinforces a mindset in which the mentee is perceived as needing help, due to intellectual deficits. The traditional role of a mentor as an omniscient guide, perpetuates a devaluing of the knowledge and lived experiences of students.

Swoboda and Millar (1986) also call upon educators to deconstruct their perception of mentoring as a grooming relationship, in which a protégé is hand-picked and often a mirror-image of the mentor, to instead incorporate a networking-mentoring stance in which both participants are mutually benefiting. In the latter mentoring dynamic, a greater number of individuals can be mentored, and those who are often denied a grooming mentoring relationship, such as women and minorities, are empowered to discover new spaces of professional growth in multiple mentoring relationships (Higgins & Kram, 2001; Swoboda & Milar, 1986). Healy and Welchert (1990) propose a more comprehensive definition of mentoring. They emphasize a "dynamic, reciprocal relationship in a work environment between an advanced career incumbent (mentor) and a beginner (protégé) aimed at promoting the career development of both" (p. 16) through the identity transformation by both mentor and protégé. This foundation of reciprocity in mentoring relationships negates the basis of hierarchical relationships, often demanded of traditional teaching/supervisory arrangements.

Reciprocity. The trend toward reciprocity as a foundation in mentoring relationships can be further illuminated by an understanding of the specific ways in which mentor and mentee experience these phenomena. These dynamics include two-way dialoguing with feedback and reflections, and establishing safe, risk-taking environments to welcome newly learnt teaching practices (Hudson, 2013). This is also put forth as being partners in "creative dialogue and cooperation" (Franke & Dahlgren, 1996, p. 632) in which mentor and mentee reflect openly about how they experience teaching affirmed in their own unique understanding, effectively establishing their ability to become cocreators of knowledge.

In doctoral programs, this reciprocal learning is gleaned from "mentoring practices that challenge and reshape status quo understandings" (Hall & Burns, 2009, p. 49) to allow diverse epistemologies to emerge, cultivating all ways of knowing. Hall and Burns (2009) suggest that practice of reflection and dialogue be emphasized as a crucial component in minimizing the marginalization of one's unique identity. In fact, explicit ongoing discussion and critique of the white centered identity in academia, and the tensions non-White scholars experience negotiating their own identity in this arena are necessary to acknowledge the intersections of lived experiences, of both mentor and mentee, as fundamental to more authentic participation in higher education (Hall & Burns, 2009).

Reciprocity then, extends beyond mutually beneficial relationships to encourage the integration of critical consciousness of our thoughts and behaviors across our multi-faceted existence in both our personal and professional lives. In this manner, all participants of mentoring can become more culturally responsive (Gay, 2004) to counter the marginalization of scholars of color in the academy, and to interrogate implicit bias formed throughout our socialization into educational systems. Woods (2001) adeptly makes this argument in his discussion of the difficulties Black women face in mentoring relationships at the graduate level in which they feel their "ideas and opinions are devalued" (p. 111). Similarly, in

Dillard's (1994) work with preservice teachers, he describes a student of Mexican descent who asked: "If I come to your university will I be more than a number. I guess what I mean is, can I be a Mexicana and a teacher?" to exemplify the "duality of race manifested in critical consciousness" (p. 9). These researchers direct our attention to the idea that reciprocity and critical consciousness are interwoven into the fabric of mentorship if the premise of the relationship rests in broadening our understanding of self within the complexities and tensions of individual and collective ways of knowing.

Equity. Research studies suggest the role of mentorship as perceived by mentors is evolving to encompass a more mutually beneficial relationship (Jacobi, 1991). For example, in their study of 11 paired mentor-mentee relationships Hudson (2013) asserts the very dynamics of reciprocity diminishes an imbalance of power found in more traditional apprentice type mentorships. Kwan and Lopez-Real (1990), researchers at the University of Hong Kong, analyzed 259 questionnaires answered by teacher mentors. They indicated, although still important, mentors' emphasis of a more skills based role nurtured through providing feedback, shifted more toward a relational role characterized as counselor, equal partner, and critical friend (Hudson, 2013; Kwan & Lopez-Real, 1990). Research of higher education faculty members found faculty members believe successful mentoring relationships engender "reciprocity, mutual respect, clear expectations, personal connection, and shared values" (Straus, Johnson, Marquez, & Feldman, 2013, p. 7). Echoing these findings Awaya, McEwan, Heyler, Linsky, Lum, and Wakukawa (2000) describe mentorship as a journey that "involves the building of an equal relationship characterized by trust, the sharing of expertise, moral support, and knowing when to help and when to sit back" (p. 45).

Comradeship. Comrade originates from the Spanish word *camarada* to mean a room-mate; from the Latin word *camera* or a room. Comrade refers to someone who shared the same room or tent who was often a fellow soldier (Cresswell, 2009). In examining the original context of the word comrade, we can better understand why Freire (2000) chose this particular word to convey the totality of liberatory relationships. A comrade, or a person who shares a room with you, has intimate knowledge of an individual, not often known in the confines of the work environment. In this manner, Freire is negating the superficiality of relationships in which individuals compartmentalize their professional and personal lives.

When you share a room with someone, it strips away the pretense of enacting specific roles, and engages us in the intimate interaction of knowing one another. As educators, we share the rooms of academia, but as a comrade, we share and reflect upon the rooms of our lives. We become vulnerable to one another connecting our past, our struggles, our flaws, our fears, and our hopes as a mechanism of cocreating our knowledge of the world. This also means, we are comrades as soldiers are in our fight to emancipate our knowledge and reshape an educational system inclusive of this knowledge. As comrades we come together, in our knowledge of one another, ascertained through authentic relationships to claim spaces of equity for all. Comrades continually seek to deepen their relationships through reflection of their thinking and feeling, in a joint effort to dismantle the confines of status, hierarchy, and patriarchy rampant in our educational systems.

Pedagogy of Collective Critical Consciousness. Encarnación's teaching, mentoring, and leadership philosophy is firmly grounded in the notion of social justice advocacy and operationalized through the Pedagogy of Collective Critical Consciousness in which teaching is mentoring and mentoring is teaching. It is also shaped by his lived experiences as a migrant student, pedagogical training, and his experiences as a teacher, counselor, principal and superintendent working with students in diverse settings.

Encarnación's most significant contribution to pedagogical innovation has resulted from the work he has done as instructor and coordinator of the Urban School Leaders Collaborative (USLC) and cocoordinator of the UTSA Winter Garden doctoral program. Such experiences and reflections have influenced him to coin and identify this notion as the Pedagogy of Collective Critical Consciousness. This framework evolved from a combination of instructional activities, instructional methods and personal and professional growth engagement that he developed since the inception of these alternative leadership programs at the doctoral and master's levels.

Coupled with constructivist learning theory, the Pedagogy of Collective Critical Consciousness engages students intensely in collective learning activities including shared critical reflection, and writing autoethnography. Students and professors learn together and from each other and they are coconstructors of knowledge. Both are teachers and learners. The central premise of this framework is to engage students in a continuous cycle of collective learning experiences.

As professor, Encarnación has come to understand retrospectively that he has been engaged in writing his own story and facilitating the process for students to write their own for many years. Students know the transparent Encarnación. They know his vulnerabilities and he knows theirs. As a young middle school teacher, Encarnación's students in his Spanish class wrote their own one-act play based on their life histories. They *collectively* performed before their peers and teachers and gained their respect and admiration.

As a school counselor, Encarnación worked with a group of migrant children and asked them to write their stories. They produced scripts that combined their experiences into five mini-dramas and shared their stories at the state and national migrant conferences. Through critical reflection, they realized the assets of their migrant lifestyle. They no longer felt stigmatized by the migrant label, they were proud of it. During this process, Encarnación learned about himself as well. At the end, Encarnación felt his students' stories were his stories too. Currently as a professor, Encarnación engages his students in writing their autoethnographies that focus on their personal, professional and transformational journeys. Students not only write their individual autoethnographies, but they also analyze their life stories collectively. As Encarnación shares,

> Many years later, as a scholar and professor (after thirty-two years as a K–12 practitioner), it has become obvious to me that I have been facilitating the process of collective critical consciousness with and for my students at all levels. Whether this was through the writing and acting of personalized "one-act" plays or the dramatization of personal stories of migrant students, this kind of work is aligned and congruent to autoethnography as a method for personal and professional transformation.

TESTIMONIOS

Using *testimonios* (Anzaldúa, 2002; Moraga & Anzaldúa, 1981) as a methodological approach, helps create salient depictions of experiences, identities, and new ways of knowing that center of culture and identity. A *testimonio* is viewed as a written journey (authentic narrative) of one's life with a focus on the effect of injustice (Reyes & Rodriguez, 2012). *Testimonio* as a genre evolved around the 1960s, as a genre to define the documentation of Latin American or Caribbean reality from a direct source, as told by the individuals involved (Nance, 2006; Reyes & Curry Rodríguez, 2012). The experience of the speaker, in this case, each author, is representative of a larger class, a larger experience. Thus, *testimonios* embody both individual and group memory, and may represent a collective or common struggle, though without claim to universal representation (Brabeck, 2001). Each author uses their *testimonio* to offer a language of hope and insights for others to promote equity, consciousness, and agency with the hope of influencing the lives of others as they develop as leaders for social justice.

In the following section we narrate how each author has personally influenced the mentorship process. In each *testimonio* we highlight our own lived realities to create and give voice to our knowledge. We concur with Anzaldúa (1990) who states, "by bringing in our own approaches and methodologies, we transform that theorizing space" (p. xxv). Centering on Anzaldúa's (2002) mindset, we share our experiences in the hopes of influencing and conceptualizing the reciprocity of mentorship.

Juan Manuel Niño

I have been fortunate to experience great mentorship opportunities throughout my life. At home I had nurturing experiences from my parents, family, and friends. As a professional, I experienced mentorship from educators who I value more as friends than colleagues. During my doctoral studies I solidified a true appreciation for my professors who genuinely took concern about my professional and personal advancement. It was during the doctoral program that I valued the sincerity of great mentors and came to acknowledge how people help others develop into caring individuals. My experiences in the program helped me better understand the academy but at the same time introduced me to an authentic approach of caring for students, where professors and students learn from each other. These experiences also helped me understand that relationships formed in school can and should go beyond the walls of the classroom setting.

As a student. I was introduced to Dr. Garza at my first academic conference. My professors knew him personally and I believed I could learn from his experience. Incidentally, I also met his wife, who was also in the academy. Meeting him during my first year as a doctoral student was inspiring. His background was very similar to mine and out of that similarity grew hope and aspiration towards the professoriate.

Through the years I became more familiar with who he was as I started reading his research. In a traditional scholar's mindset, research interests and personal interests never intersect; however, the more I read, the more I realized the marriage Dr. Garza formed between his research and the person he is. For this and many other reasons, I invited him to be part of my dissertation committee. Luckily, he agreed. Having Dr. Garza on my committee was very instrumental for my study. As a former superintendent, he brought a specific perspective to my study and to the committee. He was able to help me secure a participant for my study, provided feedback on my writings, and was always willing to meet and discuss findings.

As a colleague. The life of an academician can be overwhelming. Much of the work centered on this profession focuses on research for publications. In contrast, there is not much done in this profession to welcome new faculty into the academy. I have been fortunate to work with a colleague who naturally understands the demands of the job and at the same time mentor new faculty. As a new faculty member at the University of Texas at San Antonio, I was assigned to Dr. Garza for mentorship. Naturally, other colleagues in the department understood the fit as there was already a relationship prior to my arrival at the institution. The mentorship has been nurtured and solidified based on an authentic and reciprocal caring relationship.

Since my first semester, Dr. Garza and I have shared our classroom for instruction as coteachers. This opportunity to learn from each other has helped me better understand who I am as a scholar, researcher, and a person. Although, team teaching is not a common practice in higher education, we do this with the approach of developing people to better understand who they are as leaders. We do not teach with a mindset of training people to be good leaders because we wouldn't know what metric to follow. However, we use a pedagogy to embrace the caring aspects of what leadership can be for more equitable practices. In our times of instruction, reflection becomes a critical component of our pedagogy. It is through this approach that we, and the students, are able to internalize and make meaning of what research and practice look like for each individual person in the room. It is through these moments that we learn from each other and share our differences and we celebrate them.

The mentorship from Dr. Garza extends beyond the classroom and to research opportunities. Many of the research projects and publications I have been part of stem from an invitation from Dr. Garza. With his mentorship, he has introduced me to his international network of colleagues with whom I collaborate. Additionally, he has also mentored me with administrative responsibilities in assisting him in coordinating the Urban School Leaders Collaborative, an award winning leadership preparation program and the Winter Garden Doctoral Program. Under this assignment, we are responsible for recruiting, selecting, and advising students in a master's program. In all mentoring opportunities I have experienced, none have been prescriptive. Each moment provides flexibility where I can claim my own space and define my practice according to who I am. Mentorship is not about teaching the ropes of the trade but encompasses authentically helping others be successful in their own right. For me, my mentorship opportunities have given me space to grow and develop professionally and personally.

As a friend. Many junior faculty can attest that the road to tenure can be hard and lonely. For scholars of color, the process can be even more challenging. The advice often heard from colleagues is to publish and focus on research. I have experienced the tenure process quite differently. While I have focused on my publications, having a mentor who is honest, trustworthy and caring has been instrumental to my success. The relationship Dr. Garza and I formed a few years ago has matured to a lifelong friendship. As such, Dr. Garza has been there to help me out when significant relationships come into question, when I experienced family difficulties and more importantly, when I need someone to listen to me. He has unselfishly spent numerous hours helping me process my personal issues, as well as embraced me on research projects. I strongly attest that our mentorship is based on this reciprocal relationship centered on caring for each other.

In our conversations, classes, meetings, and every opportunity we get to talk, we engage each other in a mutualistic endeavor of helping each other. In such experience, help is not defined as what one wants to hear or do. Rather, our encounters are described as growing moments where we actively listen to each other and model the care in our words and actions. Our relationship is rooted in the power of understanding the self as humans.

Self as mentor. As I reflect on my past three years in academia, I acknowledge I have been privileged to engage in authentic relationships with faculty, staff, and students. My mentor and colleagues have been critical in cultivating me as a faculty member who embraces students. As such, I have taken the responsibility to follow the practice that I experienced. In this approach, I welcome students to self-reflect, and engage them in an authentic caring relationship where we learn from each other.

I now have the opportunity to continue this cycle of mentorship with current students. I had the opportunity to meet Amanda as a graduate student. During class, she was always reflective and welcomed different ways of knowing. Her receptiveness and willingness to challenge herself and others encouraged her to apply into the doctoral program. As a graduate and doctoral student, Amanda has been open and caring in her learning development as a student, scholar and woman. It has been this sincere approach that has influenced my mentorship relationship with her as unique. During the years, Amanda and I work, reflect and think together to help each other develop as scholars and friends. Much like my mentorship with Dr. Garza, Amanda and I do not limit our moments to just sharing the academic realms. We learn from each in research, class, and from personal moments. She has showed me how to embrace my role as a junior faculty member and owning my stance as a professor. Additionally, I have welcomed her to my academic and personal realms; all with the hopes of providing support for her aspirations. My mentorship with Amanda helps me better understand my responsibility as a scholar. As such, I embrace my mentorship model with all students I encounter.

The USLC program has been a perfect setting for nurturing mentorship opportunities. Here, students and professors contribute to the space of learning. There are no hierarchies in play, rather an honest and caring trust to help each other better understand and respect experiences. In this physical space we all embrace the mentorship role, where the mentor-mentee roles become fluid. In this coteaching space, we learn that titles, genders, and ages become multiple factors that influence who we are as individuals. However, these differences are not perceived as deficits, rather they are accepted as necessary to create a safe learning environment.

Amanda Jo Cordova

The first time I led a presentation at an international conference I was a ball of nerves. Everything I worked on over the last year to complete my first research project all came down to a 15-minute presentation to professors completely unknown to me. When it was all over, and the haze of moment passed, I immediately looked in the audience to see the expression on my mentor's face. With one glance at him I knew all the questions buzzing in my mind would be answered. Did the presentation go well? Were the ideas presented in a scholarly manner? Could I contend as a researcher among an array of international professors? My emotions were surging as I quickly caught his gaze to see a tear in his eye. I looked away quickly, not wanting the floodgates of my own emotions to overwhelm me in the sea of academics in our midst. We've never talked about that moment. We didn't have to. With that one unshed tear I knew he understood the transcendence of that moment in time, in which I realized my own power to claim my space in the Academy. I felt the rush of our collective pride wash over me, as one of the highpoints of our mentoring relationship undergirded in reciprocity, equality, and a collective critical consciousness.

As a graduate student. My relationship with my mentors, Dr. Garza and Dr. Niño began in graduate school. The ways in which they modeled reciprocal relationships was truly different when compared to my other mentoring experiences. They modeled reciprocal relationships centered on facilitating learning by dismantling the traditional teacher-student relationships and replacing them with learner-learner relationships. By our initial class meeting, Dr. Garza knew all the cohort members by name, taking time to make sure he pronounced each name correctly, and seeking clarification when needed. With each interaction he exuded the importance of knowing the details of who we are as individuals. He thoroughly read our personal statements required for admission as another way to get to know us before the first day of coursework. He then reciprocated by sharing some of his personal history, speaking passionately about his convictions of social justice, and inviting us to read his autoethnography; all with the purpose of knowing him on a deeper level. With each interaction from the first e-mail correspondence to the day of graduation, our professors deliberately embodied Freire's (2000) concept of dialogue that demands equality among participants where mutual trust and respect exists through the ethics of care (Noddings, 2005).

With this mentoring relationship firmly in place we continued toward collective critical consciousness molded through conscientization, the development of critical awareness, practiced with ongoing reflection and action (Freire, 2000). As a cohort we engaged in this process by writing an autoethnnography over a two-year period, with the first section focusing on our personal history. Complementing this strategy, we engaged in weekly reflection where each member (including professors) responded to a prompt, listened to all others, and then followed-up with questions or comments. Committing to this reflection reminded us each week to connect as people, to be open and vulnerable, to acknowledge other ways of knowing, and to validate personal experiences. It served as a mirror to reflect our humanity in our daily struggles and deconstruct the compartmentalization of our complex identities. Furthermore, participating in reflection at the beginning of class centered our collective experience in our personal and professional lives strengthening our resolve to act upon our awakened consciousness.

Within this new reality of learning, we were all students, we were all professors, we all challenged thinking together. No one was the expert and no one's knowledge was less than another. We could all become vulnerable to the critique of our epistemology, the influence of socialization on our identity, our role in perpetuating an inequitable system, and our struggle to confront both internal and external barriers to social justice leadership. Following reflection, we continued our classroom formation in a semicircle with professors sitting among students to begin the presentations of the week, facilitated by students. A learner-learner stance was maintained and dialogue ensued to deepen our understanding of coursework. The norms of engaging with the coursework encouraged openness, confrontation of peers, articulating intuitive ways of knowing, and expressing unfiltered emotions. Our learning was not sanitized by diluting our expression to polite professionalism, often characterized by an agreeable tone and raising one's hand for permission to speak. The rawness of our dialogue and the trust we built with one another became the spine of our self-awareness and praxis, emphasizing our flexibility to reach for intellectual depth and breadth, over conforming to students as depositories of knowledge (Freire, 2000). Dr. Garza coined this concept as the Pedagogy of Collective Critical Consciousness. This pedagogy fosters a continuous process of engaging in individual and collective critical consciousness to center relationships in social justice leadership. Through the pedagogy of collective critical consciousness all new learning becomes connected to our individual identity, we then critically reflect upon in writing and class discussion. When mentorship is approached from this stance, it is not reduced to grooming a select few to emulate a skilled professional. Instead, mentorship becomes a mechanism of transformation whereby both parties are critically conscious of how they choose to navigate the reality of their personal and professional lives.

As a doctoral student. With the completion of the USLC program, my mentors encouraged me to become more open to different routes of social justice activism in the field of education. I applied to the doctoral program, not truly believing I could be accepted, because I still harbored negative self-perceptions of intellectualism imposed on me throughout my early schooling years. To my astonishment I was not only accepted into the program but was also selected as a doctoral fellow, providing a path toward aspirations as a researcher and professor, committed to the Pedagogy of Collective Critical Consciousness. A central tenet of this pedagogy rests in the multiple levels of reciprocity in the mentoring relationship. For example, I am beginning the doctoral program with a reflective mindset and already established reciprocal relationships with my professors of the USLC Program. This established relationship permeates our personal and professional lives in which we have a collective experience of internalizing ideals of social justice. In addition, we have organic relationships allowing us to challenge one another, supporting or ongoing process of identity development. Lastly, we have fostered an unbreakable bond centered on helping one another to develop equally as individuals and scholars grounded in social justice.

It is difficult to choose what to write about to convey the deepening of my mentoring relationships during my first year of doctoral studies. On the one hand, leaving teaching to become a full-time student and doctoral fellow working alongside my mentors, allowed my creativity as a thinker, researcher, and writer to flourish. On the other hand, as a social justice leader, I could not ignore the history and continued reality of elitism and exclusivity threaded through the norms of higher education. In my work as a teacher I was considered the leader of my classroom and as such, cultivated actions bound in inclusivity, reciprocity, and authenticity, modeling a learner-learner stance internalized from my mentors. Now, in the doctoral program, I became the student again, and struggled to find a way to navigate the tensions between critical consciousness, social justice, and more traditional student-teacher relationships.

At first, I regressed and deferred to my subordinate position as a student. I ignored the tensions inside of me and narrowed my focus toward immersing myself in reading, reflecting, and improving my scholarly abilities. It wasn't until the middle of my first course with Dr. Niño that I was able to openly grapple with my reality of being a woman in higher education where male-privilege and patriarchal pedagogy are the norm. In this ethics course I was exposed to feminist writings that spoke to the depths of my multifaceted experiences as a woman. Reading Anzaldua's (1999) "How to Tame A Wild Tongue" and delving into the concept of "the other," my eyes were no longer simply reading print, my being grasped the soul of them (Freire, 2000). At times, it felt like the readings were an unstoppable glacier rolling through my body, tearing down my imposed, internalized image of womanhood, unearthing my perfectly preserved way of knowing, that had been patiently waiting to emerge. In the midst of this reawakening of my feminist conscious, my mentors were not only concerned about broadening my thinking through the study of multiple epistemologies, they attentively listened to how this transformation of thinking began to mold me personally, academically, and professionally. In turn, they too opened themselves to understanding my unique experience as a Latina aspiring to become a member of the Academy that differed from their own.

They did not "mentor" their "protégé" through the male privileged world of academia, teaching me how to assimilate to the dominant culture of the professorate. I had no pressure to conform, nor was my feminism stifled. Instead, they shared their own stories of entering the professorate as Latinos, the challenges they faced, and the internal struggles they forged emphasizing the importance of maintaining their whole identity every step of the way. Our lived experience, explored collectively, provided the space I needed to firmly grasp hold of the freedom I have to transform my own reality as a Latina scholar who values *educación* over schooling. This dialogue with my mentors is the essence of how they practice *educación*. *Educación* is guided by the belief that

> Education either functions as an instrument which is used to facilitate integration of the younger generation into the logic of the present system and bring about conformity or it becomes the practice of freedom, the means by which men and women deal critically and creatively with reality and discover how to participate in the transformation of their world. (Shaull, 1990, p. 34)

As our fourth year of mentoring relationships ends, I have come to appreciate how rare an experience it is to have mentors who can truly engage in reciprocal relationships unafraid of the nature of duality, and unafraid to commit themselves to dismantling an oppressive educational system present in our everyday lives. A few days ago, for his birthday, I offered Dr. Niño a small token and on the gift tag I wrote "To: My professor, my mentor, my friend." Although this may sound insignificant, it goes to the heart of reciprocal relationships in that they are dynamic, fluid, and informed by both professional and personal experiences where all knowledge is valued. In this manner our cultural wealth is shared collectively to broaden our way of thinking, cultivating an ability to garner strength to confront both internal and external conflicts faced as social justice educators. In closing, the true measurement of successful mentorship is mutual transformation fashioned in the reciprocal nature of collective critical consciousness.

DISCUSSION: ENCARNACIÓN GARZA, JR.

Do we do the work as mentors because it is human nature to help others? Do we do it because we feel valued? Or do we do it because it is our moral duty? Maybe it is all of the above and more. One would hope that it is human instinct to help and support others. As a mentor, I have often wondered if I have done it for purely unselfish reasons because I draw equally, if not more from an authentic reciprocal relationship with my mentee. And, as a leader for social justice, it is my moral responsibility to create a hopeful and just world.

A truly meaningful mentor/mentee connection is possible only if the relationship is authentic and reciprocal. I argue that the greatest challenge of this relationship is the perceived positionality of the mentor and mentee respectively. As a mentor, I have to be critically conscious of my position as an equal partner to avoid assuming the role as the expert imparting knowledge upon "my" mentee who accepts it willingly. The initial mentor/mentee interaction tends to be embodied in an oppressor/oppressed relationship. To develop an equal and equitable mentor/mentee relationship, it takes significant effort that is deliberate, genuine, and authentic. We have to maintain a constant state of deep critical reflection and consciousness to stay true to the reciprocal relationship. A reciprocal relationship can only be accomplished when we break down these inequitable role perceptions. As a mentor, I must see myself as a learner and a teacher and my mentee must see herself/himself as learner and teacher too. We are both coconstructors of knowledge; we are both mentors and mentees.

Mentoring and teaching are simultaneous activities. As a professor, I am always a teacher, a mentor, and a mentee. These roles do not manifest themselves in isolation. As a student, practitioner and scholar, I have learned from both good and bad models and I am especially cognizant of the importance of the affective domain. Teachers have phenomenal influence and power, positive or negative, on the children they serve. I learned some hard lessons from my own painful experiences of cruelty and humiliation at the hands of teachers. I was fortunate I had parents who supported me through my struggles in school and who "repaired" me when I came home emotionally and physically damaged at the end of the school day. When I became a teacher, I pledged to myself that I would create an environment of care and empathy for all students in my classroom. I do not feel any differently about students at the graduate level. I invite all of my graduate students to come into my "claimed" space; a space where they feel safe to engage in deep self-discovery and critical reflection about serving students as advocates for social justice. I must share that not too long ago, I was proud to say that it was my obligation to "create" space for the students I served. I have come to realize that this is an arrogant, if not oppressive approach to liberation. If we think we have the power to create space, we also have the power to take it away. Through deep critical reflection, I have learned my responsibility is to facilitate a process to help students "claim" their own space because the space belongs to all of us.

Reflection. I have learned that the Pedagogy of Collective Critical Consciousness has served as the foundation that has helped Juan, Amanda, and me achieve an authentic reciprocal relationship. Juan posits, "that our mentorship is based on this reciprocal relationship based on caring for each other." Amanda attests that "the true measurement of a successful mentorship is mutual transformation fashioned in the reciprocal nature of collective critical consciousness.

I have known Dr. Niño (Juan) for a number of years; I was the chair of the search committee when he was hired. Juan indicated that he "was assigned to Dr. Garza for mentorship." Interestingly, I was never told I was his mentor but Juan immediately showed high interest in the work I was doing and I welcomed his participation. In retrospect, this is when the mentor/mentee relationship started. The Pedagogy of Collective Critical Consciousness facilitates a process where according to Juan "I can claim my own space and define my practice according to who I am. For me, my mentorship opportunities have given me space to grow and develop professionally and personally."

I met Ms. Córdova (Amanda) when she was accepted (Spring 2013) to the USLC cohort 6. Both Juan and I were her instructors during this two-year program. Upon graduation from the USLC, Amanda applied and got accepted to our doctoral program and she has our student and has worked closely with us as a research fellow. I have had the honor to witness Amanda's inspiring transformational journey "as a female, Latina, scholar who values *educación* over schooling." Amanda eloquently captures the essence of our collective experiences as mentors and mentees. "I have come to appreciate how rare an experience it is to have mentors who can truly engage in reciprocal relationships unafraid of the nature of duality, and unafraid to commit themselves to the dismantling an oppressive educational system in their everyday lives." As we collaborate in writing this chapter, we model the central premise of our mentoring framework. We work collectively within our own "claimed" spaces as we learn from each other, grow within our own realities and maintain our unique identities. That speaks to the core of an authentic and reciprocal relationship.

CONCLUSION

We have collectively shared our *testimonios* as a way to highlight how students and teachers can mentor each other for leadership development. Our stories are not shared to provide a replicable model, but rather a pedagogy that centers on people and the way we learn from each other. Instead, we propose that school systems can be understood as living systems where people can learn, reflect, and grow. The USLC program is grounded on the notion of respect and authentic relationships with a social justice advocacy curriculum. In this program, professors foster a genuine relationship with students. Additionally, professors are caring individuals who are able to transcend the space of the transmission of knowledge to the collective construction of multiple realities. In all, we become vulnerable as an approach to invite students to claim grounding of their own power, knowledge, and resiliency. This pedagogy offers hope and opportunity for all students to learn who they are and what they stand for. It also calls for leaders to question practices and to advance equitable opportunities for all. It is our hope that leadership preparation programs embrace a clear sense of the true and evolving purpose of an education where no perfect model exists. As such, leadership preparation is a relationship, where mentorship becomes part of the pedagogy.

Since the inception of No Child Left Behind in 2001, schools around the country have begun to operate more than ever from a technical rational viewpoint. The pressure of accountability has stressed the importance of workplace coordination, predictability, and accountability for the success of the school's goals (Ingersoll, 2003). While rationalizing schools might maximize efficiency, it does so at the expense of human growth and development of people. Leadership is not about following the status quo and implementing a packaged practice. According to Weber (1947), the efficiency of a bureaucracy may propel an organization's ends; however, "the rigidity, inflexibility, and inhumanness created by rationalization locks humans in an iron cage" (p. 31).

With Pedagogy of Collective Critical Consciousness in the USLC program, everyone is vital in the development of social justice leaders where authentic care extends beyond professional roles, centers on human values and invites everyone to claim their space. We share our *testimonios* so that others may see the blurring of teacher-student roles. We invite colleagues to embrace a notion of comradeship, where care, wholeness, and liberation are central aspects for leadership development and social justice.

REFERENCES

Anzaldúa, G. (1990). *Making face, making soul.* San Francisco, CA: Aunt Lute Foundation Books.

Anzaldúa, G. (2002). Now let us shift...the path of conocimiento ... inner work, public acts. In G. E. Anzaldúa & A. Keating (Eds.), *This bridge we call home: Radical visions for transformation* (pp. 540–578). New York, NY: Routledge.

Awaya, A., McEwan, H., Heyler, D., Linsky, S., Lum, D., & Wakukawa, P. (2003). Mentoring as a journey. *Teaching and Teacher Education 19*, 45–56.

Bordas, J. (2012). *Salsa, soul, and spirit: Leadership for the multicultural age* (2nd ed.). San Francisco, CA: Berrett-Koehler.

Brabeck, K. (2001, June). *Testimonio: Bridging feminist ethics with activist research to create new spaces of collectivity.* Paper presented at the meeting of Bridging the Gap: Feminisms and Participatory Action Research Conference, Boston College.

Cresswell, J. (2009). *Oxford dictionary of word origins*. Oxford, England: Oxford University Press.

Dillard, C. (1994). Beyond supply and demand: Critical pedagogy, ethnicity, and empowerment in recruiting teachers of color. *Journal of Teacher Education, 45*(1), 9–17.

Franke, A., & Dahlgren, L. (1996). Conceptions of mentoring: An empirical study of conceptions of mentoring during the school-based teacher education. *Teaching & Teacher Education, 12*(6), 627–641.

Freire, P. (2000). Pedagogy of the oppressed (30th anniversary ed.). New York, NY: Continuum.

Garza, E. (2004). Social justice is an attitude: Response to: " 'Yes, but ...': Education leaders discuss social justice." *Journal of School Leadership, 14*, 578–584.

Garza, E. (2015). *The pedagogy of collective critical consciousness: The praxis of preparing leaders for social justice.* Paper presented at UCEA Conference, 2015. Denver, CO.

Gay, G. (2004). Navigating marginality en route to the professoriate: Graduate students of color learning and living in academia. *International Journal of Qualitative Studies in Education, 17*(2), 265–288.

Hall, L., & Burns, L. (2009). Identity development and mentoring in doctoral education. *Harvard Education Review, 79*, 49–70.

Haring, M. J. (1997). Networking mentoring as a preferred model for guiding programs for underrepresented students. In H. T. Frierson (Ed.), *Diversity in higher education* (pp. 63–76). Greenwich, CT: JAI.

Healy, C., & Welchert, A. (1990). Mentoring relations: A definition to advance research and practice. *Educational Researcher, 19*(9) 17–21.

Higgins, M., & Kram, K. (2001). Reconceptualizing mentoring at work: A developmental network perspective. *The Academy of Management Review, 26*(2), 264–288.

Hinsdale, M. (2015). *Mutality, mystery, and mentorship in higher education*. Boston, MA: Sense.

Hudson, P. (2013). Developing and sustaining successful mentoring relationships. *Journal of Relationships Research, 4*, 1–10

Ingersoll, R. M. (2003). *Who controls teachers' work?: Power and accountability in America's schools.* Cambridge, MA: Harvard University Press.

Jacobi, M. (1991). Mentoring and undergraduate academic success: A literature review. *Review of Educational Research, 61*, 505–532.

Kwan, T., & Lopez-Real, F. (2005, November). Mentors' perceptions of their roles in mentoring student teachers. *Asia-Pacific Journal of Teacher Education, 33*(3), 275–287.

Levine, A. (2005). *Educating school leaders.* Washington, DC: The Education Schools Project.

Merchant, B., & Garza, E, Jr. (2015). The urban school leaders collaborative: Twelve years of promoting leadership for social justice. *Journal of Research on Leadership Education, 10*(1), 39–62.

Moraga, C., & Anzaldúa, G. (1981). *This bridge called my back: Writings by radical women of color.* New York, NY: Kitchen Table Women of Press.

Nance, K. A. (2006). *Can literature promote justice? Trauma narrative and social action in Latin American testimonio.* Nashville, TN: Vanderbilt University Press.

Noddings, N. (2005). *The challenge to care in schools.* New York, NY: Teachers College Press.

Prieto, L., & Niño, J. M. (2016). *Testimonios* of Latin@ professors: Teaching for social justice leadership. *National Forum of Educational Administration and Supervision Journal, 29*(1), 54–63.

Reyes, K. B., & Curry Rodríguez, J. E. (2012). Testimonio: Origins, terms, and resources. *Equity & Excellence in Education, 45*(3), 525–538.

Reyes, K., & Rodríguez, J. (2012). *Testimonio*: Origins, terms, and resources. *Excellence and Equity in Education. 45*(3), 525–538.

Sarason, S. B. (2004). *And what do you mean by learning?* Portsmouth, NH: Heinemann

Straus, S., Johnson, M., Marquez, S., & Feldman, M. (2013). Characteristics of successful and failed mentoring relationships: A qualitative study across two academic health centers. *Academic Medicine, 8*(1), 82–89.

Swoboda, M. J., & Milar, S. B., (1986). Networking-Mentoring: A career strategy of women in academic administration. *Journal of NAWDAC, 49*, 8–13.

Waite, D., Boone, M., & McGhee, M. (2001). A critical sociocultural view of accountability. *Journal of School Leadership, 11*(3), 182–203.

Weber, M. (1947). *The theory of economic and social organizations.* New York, NY: Oxford University Press.

Wheatley, M. J. (2006). *Leadership and the new science: Discovering order in a chaotic world* (3rd ed.). San Francisco, CA: Berrett-Koehler.

Woods, R. L. (2001) Invisible women: the experiences of Black female doctoral students at the University of Michigan. In R. O. Mabokela & A. L. Green (Eds.), *Sisters of the academy: Emergent Black women scholars in higher education* (pp. 104–115), Sterling, VA: Stylus.

CHAPTER 4

THE INFLUENCE OF ADMINISTRATIVE LEADERSHIP ON RACIAL DISPARITIES IN SCHOOL DISCIPLINE

A Closer Look at White Male Principals

Bettie Ray Butler and Nicholas P. Triplett

ABSTRACT

A long history of research has firmly established that African American students in urban schools are disciplined more often and more harshly than their White peers. In identifying the determinants of disciplinary disproportionality, studies have demonstrated that the perspectives of school administration are one of the strongest predictors of racial disparities in school discipline. While this finding has been well-substantiated by empirical research; few studies have offered an explanatory framework for thinking about principal perspectives and inequitable school discipline. Even fewer have examined suburban school contexts, which contain disproportionately high numbers of White principals. The purpose of this chapter is to draw theoretical connections between principals' disciplinary philosophies and

Convictions of Conscience: How Voices From the Margins Inform Public Actions, and Educational Leadership, pp. 55–74

the occurrence of punitive, racially disproportionate discipline outcomes. A theory building methodology, side-by-side theory integration which combines racial/group threat theory and the benign neglect hypothesis is used to interpret the impact of White, male principals' perspectives about discipline on the frequency and severity of school punishment experienced by Black male students in suburban schools. It is anticipated that this chapter will increase understanding of what is needed to reduce school suspensions within this specific schooling context. Recommendations for practice, policy, and research are offered to guide educational stakeholders to this expected end.

INTRODUCTION

Decades of research have demonstrated that African American students are overselected for exclusionary discipline (i.e., out-of-school suspensions) across a wide variety of school contexts (Children's Defense Fund, 1975; Fabelo et al., 2011; Wallace, Goodkind, Wallace, & Bachman, 2008). This research also acknowledges the continued significance of race when attempting to understand the unique and varied schooling experiences of children of color (Skiba et al., 2011). Yet, there remains a paucity of information on the contributing factors of racial disparities in school suspension. Student factors, such as socioeconomic status or variation in misbehavior rates, have consistently proven insufficient to explain racial disparities (Fabelo et al., 2011; Krezmien, Leone, & Achilles, 2006; Rocque & Paternoster, 2011). Recent evidence suggests that school level characteristics, including principals' perspectives on school discipline, are potentially important predictors of racialized disciplinary outcomes (Skiba et al., 2014). Despite the importance of these empirical findings; conceptually, it remains unclear why this type of inequitable treatment has been perpetuated (Finn & Servoss, 2014), particularly when considering substantial evidence that the overuse and misuse of exclusionary discipline harms students academically, socially, and emotionally (Losen & Martinez, 2013; Wallace et al., 2008). Therefore, the aim of this chapter is to draw upon theoretical insights that help to make sense of the relationship between White, male principals' disciplinary philosophies (i.e., their perspectives about school discipline) and the occurrence of punitive, racially disproportionate disciplinary outcomes for students of color, namely African Americans, in suburban schools.

To begin, this chapter provides a brief overview of the literature on racial disparities in school discipline. Next, two separate, yet interrelated, conceptual frameworks are introduced to help explain the influence of principal leadership on exclusionary discipline practices. Upon outlining these theoretical assumptions, this article concludes with implications for reducing suspension and producing more equitable discipline outcomes within suburban schooling contexts.

RACIAL DISPARITIES IN SCHOOL DISCIPLINE

In an analysis of national data, utilizing over 2800+ school districts, the Children's Defense Fund (CDF) determined that Black students were between 2 to 3 times more likely to be suspended in comparison to their White counterparts (CDF, 1975). Since the publication of this seminal report, numerous studies have remained remarkably consistent in their finding that Black students are overwhelmingly overrepresented in out-of-school suspensions (Krezmien et al., 2006; Raffaele Mendez & Knoff, 2003; Wallace et al., 2008). Studies reveal consistently higher rates of suspension for African American students after accounting for individual student factors such as socioeconomic status and rates of misbehavior (Kewel Ramani, Gilbertson, Fox, & Provasnik, 2007; Rocque, 2010; Welch & Payne, 2010). For instance, Fabelo et al. (2011) conducted a longitudinal, multivariate study of *all* seventh grade students in Texas (approximately 5 million students) over the span of six years. The researchers controlled for 83 different variables; such as student behavior, school discipline policies, socioeconomic class, language proficiency, attendance, teacher experience/qualifications, and school resources/per-pupil expenditures. These controls allowed them to isolate the effect of race on disciplinary consequences. The study found that African American students were 31% more likely to receive disciplinary sanctions compared to otherwise identical White and Hispanic students. Similarly, Skiba and his colleagues, studying 364 elementary and middle schools during the 2005–2006 school year, found that Black students were 2.19 (elementary) to 3.78 (middle) times more likely to be referred to the office as their White peers for the same or similar problem behaviors (Skiba et al., 2011).

The results from both studies are disconcerting, to say the least. That these inconsistencies in school punishment persist today, nearly four decades after the CDF report is both puzzling and disturbing. Not only have racial disparities in discipline remained virtually unchanged but it is plausible that they have even worsened over time. To reduce disproportionality one must first understand why it exists; and because there remains great uncertainty around who gets suspended and why, it seems that schools are no closer than they were 40 years ago to remedying inequities in discipline. And still, researchers are more determined than ever before, to understand the source of racial disproportion in school suspension rates as discussed in the following section.

Who Gets Suspended and Why?

As the research on school discipline grows in popularity the topic, itself, has become more pervasive and highly controversial. *Who* gets suspended and *why* are deeply varied concerns that have consistently remained at the forefront of the discipline scholarship. While these questions appear simple in nature, scholars have discovered that there is no single predictor that fully explains why certain students are suspended more than others. Studies maintain that the causes of disproportionality in school discipline are determined by a host of variables (Morrison & Skiba, 2001; Raffaele Mendez, Knoff, & Ferron, 2002; Skiba et al., 2013). Over the years, researchers have noted differential behavior (Shaw & Braden, 1990; Skiba, Michael, Nardo, & Peterson, 2002), differential treatment (Nicholson-Crotty, Birchmeier, & Valentine, 2009), implicit bias/microaggressions (Carter, Skiba, Arredondo, & Pollock, 2017), and student-teacher cultural mismatch (Irvine, 1990) as commonly cited contributing factors to disciplinary disproportionality. Despite these well-articulated arguments, it has taken decades and increasingly sophisticated statistical methodologies to determine which of these factors have the greatest explanatory power with regard to understanding the predictors of disparities in discipline.

Gregory and Weinstein (2008) used multilevel modeling to examine the relationship between student and teacher characteristics and the circumstances that resulted in discipline referrals. They found that African Americans were overrepresented in referrals for defiance and that these students seemingly behaved more defiantly and less cooperatively with teachers perceived as being untrustworthy (Gregory & Weinstein, 2008). Furthermore, in a study of middle schools, Skiba, Peterson, and Williams (1997) found a significant association between the seriousness of infractions and the severity of punishment given by administrators, suggesting that variation in administrator perspectives on school discipline can produce differential discipline outcomes in office referrals given that principals are primarily tasked with determining the punishment for rule violations. These findings, taken together, are important in the sense that they make it readily apparent who is most susceptible to receiving exclusionary sanctions. Equally important, they begin to reveal the influence of principals' perspectives on discipline outcomes.

According to Morrison, Morrison, and Minjarez (1999) principals' typically adhere to one of two discipline philosophies: a *get tough* approach or a *supportive/preventative* orientation. Principals that adopt the get tough approach are more likely to endorse the use of suspensions; whereas, principals that view discipline from a preventative lens will most often have fewer suspensions in comparison (Skiba & Edl, 2004). Proponents of the get tough approach often argue that their punitive practices increase school safety and improve the learning environment (Casella, 2003; Skiba, Eckes, & Brown, 2009). However, studies have shown that supporting harsher discipline practices create a negative, unwelcoming school environment fraught with mistrust and resistance (American Psychological Association Zero Tolerance Task Force, 2008; Noguera, 1995).

In looking at how principal leadership impacts school discipline, Skiba and his colleagues (2014) used a multilevel examination to determine what variables predicted the strongest probability of receiving a suspension at the administrative level. They examined a host of variables including infraction type, student-level characteristics (race, class) and school-level variables (percent African American, principal perspectives). Prior to conducting their study, they hypothesized that racial disproportionality in discipline was a function of an intermixing of factors found at all three levels. Not only were their assumptions correct, what they found would ultimately change the way in which school discipline would be studied from that point forward. For instance, although decades of previous research found student race to be an indispensable explanatory predictor of suspension (Wu, Pink, Crain, & Moles, 1982; Skiba et al., 2002), Skiba et al. (2014) showed that the effect of student race could be reduced to statistical insignificance when school level characteristics, including principals' perspective on school discipline, were accounted for separately. The study's ability to parse out the variables that predicted suspension across nested groups of students, teachers and schools/principals demonstrated the powerful impact of principals when it revealed that the strongest predictor of disciplinary disproportionality was not race, but rather principals' perspectives on discipline.

Principal Characteristics

Examining principal characteristics by gender, race, and geography is also telling. Skiba and Edl (2004) found that female principals generally held a more preventative perspective, while male principals largely assumed a very strict punitive stance when making disciplinary decisions. While women make up a clear majority of the teaching force, their representation in educational administration remains disproportionate, particularly in the role of principal (Jean-Marie, 2013). According to the National Center for Education Statistics (2016), women accounted for nearly 77% of teachers, but only 52% of the proportion of principals. Males, on the other hand, constituted nearly half (48%) of all principals (Bitterman, Goldring, & Gray, 2013) and were only a small subset of the teaching population. Furthermore, at the secondary school level, 77% of principals are male (Jean-Marie, 2013). Insofar as race is concerned, principals are majority

White, and over 81% of White principals oversee schools in suburban districts. These statistics paint a picture of the widespread representation of White, male principals in secondary schools. All things considered, given that the rates of suspension are higher at the secondary school level for Black students, and that disparities between Black and White suspension rates are just as pervasive in higher resourced suburban districts as they are in urban schools (Skiba, Shure, Williams, 2012), it is plausible that the pervasive presence of White male principals holding more punitive views of school discipline may be connected to the overrepresentation of African American students in the application of harsh discipline found in suburban, predominantly White schools.

These collected findings warrant a closer look at the salience of school building-level administrative leadership, specifically the role of the White male principal, and its effect on discipline outcomes for African American students. A perspective that, until now, has remained underexplored in theory.

BUILDING A THEORY OF RACIALIZED EXCLUSIONARY DISCIPLINE

Within the discipline literature, study after study, has shown that Black students are suspended more frequently than any other group. This research has made a compelling argument for further exploring the antecedents of exclusionary discipline, including the role of the White male principal. While large, rigorous studies have increased our understanding of who gets suspended and why (Fabelo et al., 2011; Skiba et al., 2014), empirical results have not been accompanied by equally robust conceptual and theoretical arguments intended to explain the reasons that inequitable discipline outcomes persist. Consequently, an epistemological shift in discipline processes - how one comes to understand and interpret what is known about disparities in discipline from empirical studies—has been slow if not altogether, absent.

To try to explain school discipline disproportionality through the use of a singular theory is problematic at best, and misleading at worst. Due to the complexity of the phenomenon, what is needed is a multidimensional theory of processes and outcomes that informs the relationship between principal leadership and school discipline. Therefore, the primary goal of this study is to use an integrated approach to provide an in-depth conceptual framework for understanding the influence of principals' disciplinary philosophy on racial inequities in school suspension. This approach takes what is known about White male principals' perspective on school discipline and combines *racial/group threat theory* with the *benign neglect hypothesis* to explain why Black students have high suspension rates. Given this emphasis on threat, the present study focuses primarily on the unique experiences of African American males, acknowledging the pervasive and long-standing racial stereotypes that negatively position young Black men as more threatening, and at times, inherently dangerous (Cogburn, Chavos, & Griffin, 2011; Majors & Billson, 1992; Monroe, 2006).

A brief description of each theory is provided below, followed by a discussion of the process in which these theories have been integrated to explain the potential impact that White male principals' perceptions about discipline have on the disproportionate suspension of Black males in suburban schools.

Racial/Group Threat Theory

Racial/group threat theory posits that as the proportion of a marginalized group (i.e., non-Whites) increases, they are perceived to present an economic, cultural, and/or criminal threat to dominant (i.e., White) social groups (Blalock, 1967; Finn & Servoss, 2014; Rocque & Paternoster, 2011). Majority groups respond to this perceived threat by imposing punitive social controls, such as heightened surveillance (policing) and increased security, in order to maintain social dominance. While racial/group threat theory was developed within the fields of legal studies and criminal justice (Hughes, 2012), the growing overlap between school discipline, juvenile justice and criminal justice systems (Advancement Project, 2005; Casella, 2003; Hirschfield & Celinska, 2011) has led to recent studies that explore racial/group threat in education (Rocque & Paternoster, 2011; Welch & Payne, 2010).

Broadly speaking, in the context of school discipline, racial/group threat theory helps explain how cultural differences (in communication, social behavior, hairstyles, dress, posture, etc.) can contribute to exclusionary discipline outcomes when Black students are perceived to present a threat to dominant cultural hegemony (Butler, Robinson, & Walton, 2014; Majors & Billson, 1992). More specifically, in this chapter, racial/group threat theory helps explain why White male principals in suburban schools that have growing African American populations may over-select Black male students for more punitive discipline when they perceive (a) a criminal threat based on pervasive, but unsubstantiated racial stereotypes, or (b) a threat to the dominant culture in historically White contexts. Though not directly suggested by racial/group threat, such perceptions of criminal or cultural threat, as is theorized here, strongly imply indifference and/or unresponsiveness to cultural differences between White and non-White social groups.

Rocque and Paternoster (2011), along with Noguera (1995), help to support the perceived threat claim introduced in this chapter to explain school discipline. They suggested that racial threat is rooted in a climate of fear and intimidation and has very little to do with the issue of preserving school safety (Noguera, 1995; Rocque & Paternoster, 2011). In other words, the threat of losing power may be internalized by White males in leadership when Black male students are perceived as rejecting or resisting traditional school culture. Furthermore, White principals in suburban schools, specifically, may feel social pressure to maintain the cultural and academic norms historically associated with Whiteness (Watts & Erevelles, 2004; Vavrus & Cole, 2002). As such, Black students are then viewed as a threat to school governance and are, in effect, removed under the guise of creating safe, orderly schools (Casella, 2003; Skiba et al., 2009). Because of the negative stereotyped image of the Black male as dangerous, their removal is seldom disputed, when in actuality—the reasons that contribute to their displacement are much deeper and more intricate than could ever be fully understood by a simple school safety argument.

Benign Neglect Hypothesis

The benign neglect hypothesis (Liska & Chamlin, 1984) emerged from the study of racial threat as legal scholars found that not only the size of minority populations, but also the degree of segregation, that is, the chance of interaction available between groups, affected White's perception of minority threat and the severity of attendant social control measures. Benign neglect suggests that White authorities increase punitive social control measures as minoritized populations increase, but at a certain threshold, when Whites no longer perceive a threat from non-Whites, punitive social control measures decline. Original formulations of benign neglect focused on criminal threat, suggesting that when Whites perceive that non-White criminality victimizes other non-Whites as opposed to them, they feel less threatened and relax social controls (Liska & Chamlin, 1984). An example of this could be longer police response times for crimes reported in Black neighborhoods in contrast to shorter police response times for crimes reported in Black neighborhoods.

While there is no evidence that principals perceive the same kind of criminal threat from African American students, it is suggested that benign neglect can be extended to perceived *cultural* threats in school (Rocque & Paternoster, 2011). The inclusion of this extension moves us toward a new way of thinking about the impact of perceived threat on school discipline outcomes. Specifically, in this chapter an emphasis is placed on how benign neglect assumes that White, male principals in relatively homogenous

White school populations, such as those prevalent in suburban schools, will diminish perceptions of racial/cultural threat in an effort to appear to be fair, but that the punitiveness of discipline meted out by these principals will remain as a form of social control. For the purposes of this chapter, the type of perceived threat predicted by benign neglect is called "benign cultural threat," which references the less acute perceptions of threat in homogenous racial contexts.

Support for the benign neglect hypothesis in school discipline was found in a study by Raffaele Mendez and colleagues (2002). They examined out of school suspension rates in a large, ethnically diverse school district across elementary, middle, and high school levels, differentiating between high- and low-suspending schools. Raffaele Mendez et al. assessed the impact of student homogeneity, which was measured by using a dichotomous variable to classify schools as *homogenous*—if one racial group made up at least 50% of the student population—or as *heterogeneous*, if no one racial group made up at least 50% of the student population. Their findings indicated that schools serving more racially heterogeneous groups of students had a higher rate of suspension. Although the authors attributed this finding to issues of racial tension between students, the potential impact of principal leadership on student suspensions, as posited here in this chapter, should not be dismissed. Therefore, a closer look at how combining racial/group threat theory with the benign neglect hypothesis becomes necessary.

Integrated Approach

An integrated theory building methodology is used to develop a conceptual framework that draws upon racial/group threat theory and the benign neglect hypothesis to articulate how White, male principals' disciplinary philosophies impact racial disparities in exclusionary discipline for Black males in suburban schools. Theory integration occurs when the strengths of two or more theories are combined to advance a new way of thinking about a given phenomenon (Hoffmann, 2011). Utilizing side-by-side integration, a multidimensional process-outcomes model is used to demonstrate how principals' perceptions of threat (input) translate into punitive disciplinary decisions (outcome). With this integrated approach, only the organizational/internal (i.e., school) inputs and outcomes are considered, as nonorganizational/external (e.g., law enforcement, community, etc.) factors are beyond the scope of this study. Specific indicators of organizational inputs include, principals' perceptions *of threat to control and culture in heterogeneous environments* (increasingly diverse suburban schools) and principals' perceptions *of threat to control and culture in homogenous environments* (predominantly White suburban schools); whereas the indicators for organizational outcomes include *frequency of suspension* (a proxy of disciplinary disproportionality) and *severity of sanction* (a proxy of disciplinary punitiveness). By developing an integrated conceptual framework, using the identified inputs and outcomes, the ability to theoretically explain disparities in school discipline as a function of principal leadership in suburban schools is given more credence.

A Specialized Integrated Process-Outcomes Model of Discipline Disproportionality

Figure 4.1 is an illustration of a specialized integrated process-outcomes model of discipline disproportionality. The model presented here is not designed to capture the interplay of variables that perpetuate disparities in discipline in multiple schooling contexts, but instead its intention is to explain how a very specific type of principal leadership (White, males' perspectives about school discipline) could potentially lend itself to targeted disciplinary action, which adversely impacts Black males in suburban schools. Given this a specialized, rather than general, model is put forth.

There are a few assumptions that must be met in order to achieve optimum model fit: (a) the schooling context must be situated in a suburban setting; (b) the principal leader must be a White, male who takes a punitive stance toward discipline; (c) the student composition of the school must either experience increases in Black enrollment to the extent that the White enrollment begins to decline (indicating increasing school heterogeneity) or the school must have stable predominantly White enrollment (indicating school homogeneity); and (d) the school leaders that subscribe to a get tough approach will perceive the loss of control as an imminent threat to authority regardless of the school make up. Only when these conditions are satisfied, can the specialized integrated process-outcomes model of discipline disproportionality fulfill its intended purpose.

The model consists of four distinct stages. Each stage is framed using a side by side comparison of two distinct environment compositions (schools with student heterogeneity and schools with student homogeneity) to show how *inputs* (threat) are processed and *outcomes* (disciplinary decisions) are produced. This model begins with identifying the environment composition. A school is considered either heterogeneous (racially diverse) or homogenous (monocultural). Therefore, Stage 1 makes the assumption that White male principals in suburban settings will be positioned in school environments with either increasing Black student enrollment (see Figure 4.1, Stage 1a) or in school environments with stable, predominantly White student enrollment (see Figure 4.1, Stage 1b).

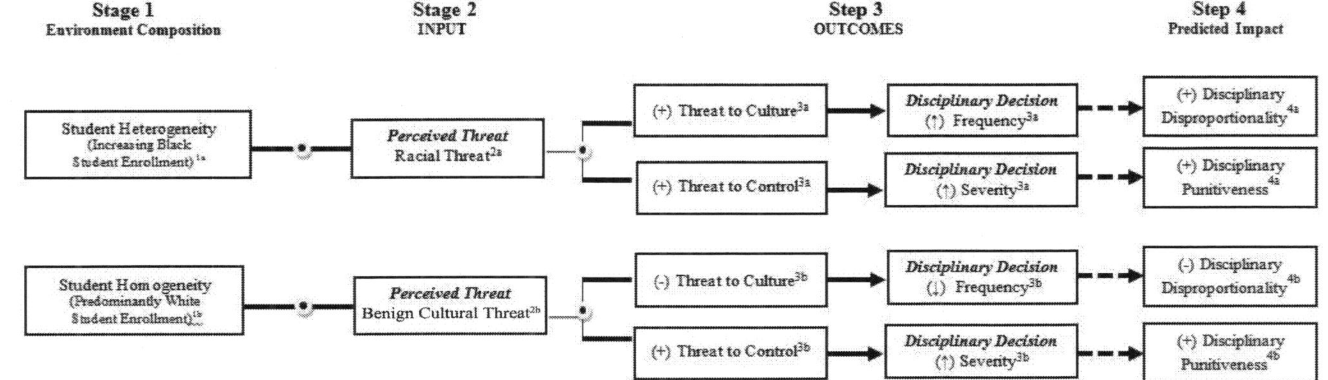

Figure 4.1. Specialized integrated process-outcomes model of discipline disproportionality. This model uses side by side integration to illustrate the effects of White male principal leadership on school discipline patterns in suburban schools.

Next, the model suggests that the environmental composition of the school will dictate the input (threat). As such, Stage 2 assumes that when White male principals in suburban settings are positioned in school environments with increasing Black student enrollment, there will exist a perceived racial threat to culture and control (see Figure 4.1, Stage 2a). Stage 2 also assumes that when a White male principal is in a suburban setting with a stable, predominantly White student enrollment, there will exist a perceived benign threat to culture only (threat to control remains constant; see overview of assumptions above) (see Figure 4.1, Stage 2b).

To process the effects of the input, the model then connects the perceived threat to an identified outcome (disciplinary decision). Stage 3 assumes that when White male principals in suburban settings are positioned in schools with increasing Black student enrollment; a perceived threat to culture (+) will result in more frequent (↑) disciplinary responses, and a perceived threat to control (+) will result in more punitive (↑) disciplinary responses (see Figure 4.1, Stage 3a). When White male principals in suburban settings are positioned in schools with a stable, predominately White student enrollment; Stage 3 suggests that there is no perceived threat to culture (–) and therefore fewer (↓) disciplinary responses, but there remains a (constant) perceived threat to control (+) which results in more punitive (↑) disciplinary responses (see Figure 4.1, Stage 3b).

The final stage of this integrated model attempts to link the perceived outcomes to predicted outcomes based largely in the literature and existing research. Stage 4 of the integrated model assumes that when White male principals in suburban settings are positioned in schools with increasing Black student enrollment; a perceived threat to culture (+) will result in more frequent (↑) disciplinary responses, and in turn, predict disciplinary disproportionality, and a perceived threat to control (+) will result in more punitive (↑) disciplinary responses, and subsequently, predicts disciplinary punitiveness (see Figure 4.1, Stage 4a). Stage 4 also makes the assumption that when White male principals in suburban settings are positioned in schools with stable, predominantly White student enrollment, there is a diminished perceived threat to culture (-) and therefore fewer (↓) disciplinary responses, which in turn, indicates (predicts) an absence of disciplinary disproportionality, but there remains a (constant) perceived threat to control (+) which results in more punitive (↑) disciplinary responses, and consequently, predicts disciplinary punitiveness (see Figure 4.1, Stage 4b).

CONCLUSION

Research has been remarkably unanimous in finding racial disproportionality, and in documenting the irreparable harm to children caused by exclusionary discipline practices. After four decades, it would seem that virtually all reasonable, educational explanations have been tested and found inadequate to explain inequitable outcomes. Therefore, we seek to add our voice to a growing body of scholarship that positions school discipline primarily as an issue of social justice, legal rights and civil rights (Losen, 2013; Losen & Skiba, 2010; Raffaele Mendez, 2003; Skiba et al., 2009; Skiba et al., 2011). In the face of a mountain of evidence, continuing to engage in discourse that focuses solely on student traits (behavior, culture, race) and school safety/order serves to reify the perspectives and ideologies that deny non-White students the full benefit of education. Put bluntly, it is well past time to accept that race and discipline are inextricably linked, and to recognize that the get-tough, zero-tolerance discipline policies have failed to adequately protect school children from unjust and discriminatory practices.

The theoretical model presented in this chapter suggests that White male principals in predominantly White, suburban school contexts may practice forms of school discipline that make non-Whites (particularly African American males) uniquely vulnerable to overly-punitive exclusionary discipline based on intergroup threat (Welch & Payne, 2010), negative stereotypes (Neal, McCray, Webb-Johnson, & Bridgest, 2003), and a lack of cultural responsiveness (Gregory & Mosely, 2010). While additional research is needed to test its utility, several implications and general recommendations flow from the ways the proposed model positions school authorities in the production of racially disproportional discipline outcomes. Below, we present a concurrent, two-part approach to help shift school discipline toward more equitable outcomes. First, we argue that students of color must, to the greatest extent possible, be protected now from unjust and discriminatory practices. Second, we discuss how educational institutions and stakeholders, particularly school administrators, might pursue consciousness-raising efforts to reduce the effect of racism, bias and discrimination on the discipline practices of principals, administrators, and school authorities.

Protecting Students Now

A conceptual shift toward a social and legal justice orientation amongst educational stakeholders and away from deficit discipline practices represents a critical step in protecting students' legal and civil rights. Law and social justice place great emphasis on *equitable outcomes*. Historically, school officials have been granted a large amount of discretion in handling disciplinary problems at their schools, and courts tend to defer to the judgements of school officials (Skiba et al., 2009). A social/legal justice lens that emphasizes equitable outcomes inverts this, deferring instead to the protection of students rather than the intent or discretion of school authorities. Further, it implies the need for some form of discipline accountability that involves the close monitoring of discipline disparities, and a process for intervention that can hold school authorities accountable for discipline policies and practices that are racially motivated (Triplett et al., 2016).

How educational stakeholders think about discipline, race and equity is not just a matter of perspectives and ideology. Indeed, in recent years, legal and regulatory actions have challenged racialized school discipline based on the appearance of unjustified and discriminatory practices (New York Civil Liberties Union, 2010; U.S. Department of Justice, 2012). Almost all cases related to school discipline rely on an analysis of the extent to which outcomes are equitable (disparate impact), rather than proving malicious intent (disparate treatment), which is very difficult to prove (U.S. Department of Justice & Department of Education, 2014). Therefore, an equitable outcomes-oriented conceptual shift serves to preserve the ability to intervene legally in cases of unjust discipline, which is an important protection for schoolchildren of color in today's disciplinary climate. Furthermore, promoting equitable outcome-focused frameworks may be able to reduce the extent to which negative stereotypes, perceptions of threat, and racialized school contexts leak into administrators' practice of school discipline.

Consciousness Raising

Given that conceptions of race and the practice of racism is deeply rooted in social institutions, schools, and everyday life to the point that it has attained a measure of permanency (Bell, 1973; Ladson-Billings & Tate, 1995), promoting social justice, equitable outcomes-focused intervention and some form of discipline accountability avoids the need to immediately convince educational stakeholders that race and racism affect discipline policy and practice. While this justifies our focus on protecting students now, it does not imply that consciousness raising is not an important part of reducing inequities in discipline. We use the term consciousness raising to refer to efforts intended to raise awareness about issues of race, bias, and discrimination in school discipline, and how the perspectives of individual actors can influence their decisions about school discipline. We recognize that changing perspectives is intensive and difficult work. However, research is clear that prejudice and bias (including racial attitudes) affect school discipline (Fenning & Rose, 2007; Okonofua & Eberhardt, 2015; Payne & Welch, 2010). Research shows that the influence of prejudice and bias can be attenuated under the right circumstances (Gawronski & Sritharan, 2010). Indeed, merely focusing attention on decisions can reduce the effect of prejudices and biases that influence judgement (Schooler & Engstler-Schooler, 1990; Wilson & Schooler, 1991). However, the most effective methods for creating lasting change require "intention, attention, and time" (Wald, 2014, p. 2014), and include strategies like perspective taking, counter-stereotypical examples and increasing positive contact with the subject(s) of one's biases (e.g., those of a different culture, race, gender, or nationality) (Devine, Forscher, Austin, & Cox, 2012).

Given the demands of being a principal, a promising site for consciousness raising with school principals is in preservice training programs and university departments of educational leadership. A growing body of literature on school leadership for social justice suggests that justice-oriented preservice programs can help future principals "to perceive social, political, and economic contradictions, and to take action against the oppressive elements of reality" (Brown, 2004, p. 77). In-service principals would likely benefit from similar programs in the form of professional development. Law and legal studies provide exemplars of such actions in this area. Legal scholars have long been concerned about prejudice and bias in criminal justice, and growing evidence has suggested that in the courtroom, "attitudes or stereotypes ... affect our understanding, decision-making, and behavior, without our even realizing it" (Kang et al., 2012, p. 1126). In response to this, the U.S. Department of Justice (2016) recently announced that it would mandate implicit bias training for all law enforcement agents and prosecutors. The Department noted that the trainees "will learn how to recognize and address their own implicit bias, which are the unconscious or subtle associations that individuals make between groups of people and stereotypes about those groups" (p. 1). While additional study is needed to determine the efficacy of a specialized integrated process-outcomes model of discipline disproportionality, we suggest that these are the kinds of interventions that can promote discipline equity at the school-building administrator level.

REFERENCES

Advancement Project. (2005). *Education on lockdown: The schoolhouse to jailhouse track.* Washington, DC: Author.

American Psychological Association Zero Tolerance Task Force. (2008). Are zero tolerance policies effective in the schools? An evidentiary review and recommendations. *American Psychologist, 63*(9), 852–862.

Bell, D. A. (1973) *Race, racism and American law.* New York, NY: Little, Brown and Company.

Bitterman, A., Goldring, R., & Gray, L. (2013). *Characteristics of public and private elementary and secondary school principals in the United States: Results from the 2011–12 Schools and Staffing Survey* (NCES 2013-313). U.S. Department of Education. Washington, DC: National Center for Education Statistics. Retrieved June 1, 2017, from http://nces.ed.gov/pubsearch

Blalock, H. M. (1967). *Toward a theory of minority-group relations*. New York, NY: John Wiley and Sons.

Brown, K. M. (2004). Leadership for social justice and equity: Weaving a transformative framework and pedagogy. *Educational Administration Quarterly, 40*(1), 77–108.

Butler, B. R., Robinson, D., & Walton, C. (2014). A perfect storm: How pose, perception, and threat converge to perpetuate discriminatory discipline practices for black male students. In J. Moore & C. Lewis (Eds.), *African American male students in pre-K–12 schools: Informing research, policy, and practice* (pp. 151–175). Bingley, England: Emerald Group Publishing.

Carter, P., Skiba, R. J., Arredondo, M. I., & Pollock, M. (2017). You can't fix what you don't look at: Acknowledging race in addressing racial discipline disparities. *Urban Education, 52*(2), 207–235.

Casella, R. (2003). Punishing dangerousness through preventive detention: Illustrating the institutional link between school and prison. In J. Wald & D. J. Losen (Eds.), *New directions for youth development: Deconstructing the school-to-prison pipeline* (pp. 55–70). San Francisco, CA: Jossey-Bass.

Children's Defense Fund. (1975). *School suspensions: Are they helping children?* Cambridge, MA: Washington Research Project.

Cogburn, C., Chavous, T., & Griffin, T. (2011). School-Based racial and gender discrimination among African American adolescents: Exploring gender variation in frequency and implications for adjustment. *Racial and Social Problems, 3*(1), 25–37.

Devine, P. G., Forscher, P. S., Austin, A. J., & Cox, W. T. (2012). Long-term reduction in implicit race bias: A prejudice habit-breaking intervention. *Journal of experimental social psychology, 48*(6), 1267–1278.

Fabelo, T., Thompson, M. D., Plotkin, M. D., Carmichael, D., Marchbanks, M. P., & Booth, E. A. (2011). *Breaking schools' rules: A statewide study of how school discipline relates to students' success and juvenile justice involvement.* New York, NY: Council of State Governments Justice Center.

Fenning, P., & Rose, J. (2007). Overrepresentation of African American students in exclusionary discipline: The role of school policy. *Urban Education, 42*(6), 536–559.

Finn, J. D., & Servoss, T. J. (2014). Misbehavior, suspensions, and security measures in high school: Racial/ethnic and gender differences. In D. J. Losen (Ed.), *Closing the school discipline gap: Research for policymakers* (pp. 44–58). New York, NY: Teachers College Press.

Gawronski, B., & Sritharan, R. (2010). Formation, change, and contextualization of mental associations: Determinants and principles of variations in implicit measures. In B. Gawronski & B. K. Payne (Eds.), *Handbook of implicit social cognition* (pp. 216–240). New York, NY: Guilford.

Gregory, A., & Mosely, P. M. (2010). The discipline gap: Teachers' views on the over-representation of African American students in the discipline system. *Equity & Excellence in Education, 37*(1), 18–30.

Gregory, A., & Weinstein, R.S. (2008). The discipline gap and African Americans: Defiance or cooperation in the high school classroom. *Journal of School Psychology, 46,* 455–475.

Hirschfield, P. J., & Celinska, K. (2011). Beyond fear: Sociological perspectives on the criminalization of school discipline. *Sociology Compass, 5*(1), 1–12.

Hoffmann, J. P. (2011). *Delinquency theories: Appraisals and applications*. New York, NY: Routledge.

Hughes, C. C. (2012). The impact of school discipline research on racial threat theory. In R. Rosenfield, K. Quinet, & C. Garcia (Eds.), *Contemporary issues on criminological research* (pp. 69–74). Belmont, CA: Wadsworth.

Irvine, J. J. (1990). *Black students and school failure: Policies, practices, and prescriptions*. Westport, CT: Praeger.

Jean-Marie, G. (2013). The subtlety of age, gender, and race barriers: A case study of early career African American female principals. *Journal of School Leadership, 23*(3), 615–639.

Kang, J., Bennet, M., Carbado, D., Casey, P., Dasgupta, N., Faigman, D., ... Mnookin, J. (2012). Implicit bias in the courtroom. *UCLA Law Review, 59*, 1124–1186.

Kewel Ramani, A., Gilbertson, L., Fox, M., & Provasnik, S. (2007). *Status and trends in the education of racial and ethnic minorities* (NCES 2007-039). National Center for Educational Statistics, Institute of Education Sciences, U.S. Department of Education. Washington, DC.

Krezmien, M. P., Leone, P. E., & Achilles, G. M. (2006). Suspension, race, and disability: Analysis of statewide practices and reporting. *Journal of Emotional and Behavioral Disorders, 14*, 217–226.

Ladson-Billings, G., & Tate, W.F. (1995). Towards a critical race theory in education. *Teachers College Record, 97*, 47–68.

Liska, A. E., & Chamlin, M. B. (1984) Social structure and crime control among macrosocial units. *American Journal of Sociology, 90*, 383–395.

Losen, D. J. (2013). Discipline policies, successful schools, racial justice and the law. *Family Court Review, 51*(3), 388–400.

Losen, D. J., & Martinez, T. E. (2013). *Out of school & off track: The overuse of suspensions in American middle and high schools*. Los Angeles, CA: The Center of Civil Rights Remedies.

Losen, D. J., & Skiba, R.J. (2010, September). *Suspended education: Urban middle schools in crisis*. Los Angeles, CA: The Civil Rights Project at UCLA.

Majors, P., & Billson, J.M. (1992). *Cool pose: The dilemmas of black manhood in America*. New York, NY: Touchstone.

Monroe, C. (2006). Misbehavior or misinterpretation? Closing the discipline gap through cultural synchronization. *Kappa Delta Pi Record, 42*(4), 161–165.

Morrison, G. M., Morrison, R. L., & Minjarez, M. E. (1999). *Student pathways through school discipline options: System and individual interactions*. Paper presented at the 23rd Annual Conference on Severe Behavior Disorders of Children and Youth, Scottsdale, AZ.

Morrison, G. M., & Skiba, R. J. (2001). Predicting violence from school misbehavior: Promises and perils. *Psychology in the Schools, 38*, 173–184.

National Center for Education Statistics. (2016). *Stats in brief: Trends in public and private school principal demographics and qualifications: 1987–88 to 2011–12*. Washington, DC: U.S. Department of Education.

Neal, L. I., McCray, A. D., Webb-Johnson, G., & Bridgest, S. T. (2003). The effects of African American movement styles on teachers' perceptions and reactions. *Journal of Special Education, 37*(1), 49–57.

New York Civil Liberties Union. (2010). *B.H. et al v. City of New York (Challenging the NYPD's school safety policies and practices).* Retrieved July 9, 2014, from http://www.nyclu.org/case/bh-et-al-v-city-of-new-york-challenging-nypds-school-safety-policies-and-practices

Nicholson-Crotty, S., Birchmeier, Z., & Valentine, D. (2009). Exploring the impact of school discipline on racial disproportion in the juvenile justice system. *Social Science Quarterly, 90*(4), 1003–1018.

Noguera, P. (1995). Preventing and producing violence: A critical analysis of responses to school violence. *Harvard Educational Review, 65*(2), 189–213.

Okonofua, J. A., & Eberhardt, J. L. (2015). Two strikes: Race and the disciplining of young students. *Psychological Science, 26*(5), 617–624.

Payne, A. A., & Welch, K. (2010). Modeling the effects of racial threat on punitive and restorative school discipline practices. *Criminology, 48*(4), 1019–1062.

Raffaele-Mendez, L. M., Knoff, H. M., & Ferron, J M. (2002). School demographic variables and out-of-school suspension rates: A quantitative and qualitative analysis of a large ethnically diverse school district." *Psychology in the Schools, 39*, 259–277.

Raffaele Mendez, L. M. (2003). Predictors of suspension and negative school outcomes: A longitudinal investigation. *New Directions for Youth Development, 99*, 17–33.

Raffaele Mendez, L. M., & Knoff, H. M. (2003). Who gets suspended from school and why: A demographic analysis of schools and disciplinary infractions in a large school district. *Education and Treatment of Children, 26*(1), 30–51.

Rocque, M. (2010). Office discipline and student behavior: Does race matter? *American Journal of Education, 116*(4), 557–581.

Rocque, M., & Paternoster, R. (2011). Understanding the antecedents of the "school-to-jail" link: The relationship between race and school discipline. *Journal of Criminal Law and Criminology, 101*(2), 633–666.

Schooler, J. W., & Engstler-Schooler, T. Y. (1990). Verbal overshadowing of visual memories: Some things are better left unsaid. *Cognitive Psychology, 22*(1), 36–71.

Shaw, S. R., & Braden, J. P. (1990). Race and gender bias in the administration of corporal punishment. *School Psychology Review, 19*(3), 378–383.

Skiba, R. J., Chung, C. G., Trachok, M., Baker, T., Sheya, A., & Hughes, R. (2014). Where should we intervene? Contributions of behavior, student, and school characteristics to out-of-school suspension. In D. Losen (Ed.), *Closing the school discipline gap: Equitable remedies for excessive exclusion* (pp. 132–146). New York, NY: Teachers College Press.

Skiba, R. J., Eckes, S. E., & Brown, K. (2009) African American disproportionality in school discipline: The divide between best evidence and legal remedy. *New York Law School Law Review, 45*, 1071, 1088.

Skiba, R. J., & Edl, H. M. (2004). *The disciplinary practices survey: How do Indiana's principals feel about discipline*? (Supplementary Analysis 2-C). Bloomington, IN: Center for Evaluation & Education Policy.

Skiba, R. J., Horner, R. H., Chung, C., Rausch, M. K., May, S., & Tobin, T. (2011). Race is not neutral: A national investigation of African American and Latino disproportionality in school discipline. *School Psychology Review, 40*(1), 85–107.

Skiba, R. J., Michael, R. S., Nardo, A. C., & Peterson, R. L. (2002). The color of discipline: Sources of racial and gender disproportionality in school punishment. *The Urban Review, 34(*4), 317–342.

Skiba, R. J., Peterson, R. L., & Williams, T. (1997). Office referrals and suspension: Disciplinary intervention in middle schools. *Education and Treatment of Children, 20*(3), 295–315.

Skiba, R. J., Shure, L., & Williams, N. (2012). Racial and ethnic disproportionality in suspension and explusion. In A. L. Noltemeyer & C. S. McLoughlin (Ed.), *Disproportionality in education and special education: A guide to creating more equitable learning environments* (pp. 89–118). Springfield, IL: Charles C Thomas Publisher, LTD.

Triplett, N. P., Bryant, A. C., Brown, K. E., Steele, A. S. L., Ardrey, T., Allen, A., & Lewis, C.W. (2016). Discipline disproportionality, student achievement and the Every Student Succeeds Act (ESSA). *Educational Law and Policy Review, 3*(1), 209–240.

U.S. Department of Justice. (2012, August 10). *Justice department releases investigative findings showing constitutional rights of children in Mississippi being violated*. Retrieved July 9, 2014, from http://www.justice.gov/opa/pr/2012/August/12-crt-993.html

U.S. Department of Justice & U.S. Department of Education. (2014, January). *Notice of language assistance: Dear colleague letter on the nondiscriminatory administration of school discipline*. Washington, DC: Office of Civil Rights, U.S. Department of Education

U.S. Department of Justice. (2016, June 27). *Department of Justice announces new department-wide implicit bias training for personnel*. Washington, DC: Department of Justice, Office of Public Affairs. Retrieved from: https://www.justice.gov/opa/pr/department-justice-announces-new-department-wide-implicit-bias-training-personnel

Vavrus, F., & Cole, K. (2002). "I didn't do nothin": The discursive construction of school suspension. *The Urban Review, 34*(2), 87–111.

Wald, J. W. (2014). Can "de-biasing" strategies help to reduce racial disparities in school discipline. *Summary of the literature. The Equity Project at Indiana University, Supplementary Paper II*, 1–8.

Wallace, J. M. Jr., Goodkind, S., Wallace, C. M., & Bachman, J. G. (2008). Racial, ethnic, and gender differences in school discipline among U. S. high school students: 1991–2005. *Negro Educational Review, 59*(1–2), 47–62.

Watts, I. E., & Erevelles, N. (2004) These deadly times: Reconceptualizing school violence by using critical race theory and disability studies. *American Educational Research Journal, 41*(2), 271–299.

Welch, K., & Payne, A. A. (2010). Racial threat and punitive school discipline. *Social Problems, 57*(1), 25–48.

Wilson, T. D., & Schooler, J. W. (1991). Thinking too much: Introspection can reduce the quality of preferences and decisions. *Journal of Personality and Social Psychology, 60*(2), 181–192.

Wu, S., Pink, W., Crain, R., & Moles, O. (1982). Student suspension: A critical reappraisal. *The Urban Review, 14*(4), 245–303.

CHAPTER 5

DILEMMAS AND CONTRADICTIONS

Police on Campus and the Learning Environment

Eric M. Feldman and Tonette S. Rocco

ABSTRACT

This chapter examines the history and growth of school-based policing in the U.S. while identifying and analyzing the dilemmas and contradictions that are found within the coverage of this topic. As educators work to create and sustain spaces of inclusive and socially just spaces for learning, it is hard to ignore the role of law enforcement within both K–12 schools and institutions of higher education. Arrests of minors in public schools, recorded and posted on social media, are raising public consciousness of the school-to-prison pipeline and the racially disproportionate fashion in which students are referred to law enforcement officials. The increased law enforcement presence on both K–12 and college campuses has outpaced enrollment growth in colleges and universities, while eclipsing funding for counselors in some public school districts. A constant public perception of increasing crime and terror on school campuses used to justify these actions may be juxtaposed against

Convictions of Conscience: How Voices From the Margins Inform Public Actions, and Educational Leadership, pp. 75–96

a national movement, rooted in identity politics, demanding more culturally responsive law enforcement.

INTRODUCTION

In July 2015, University of Cincinnati police officer Ray Tensing pulled over nonstudent Samuel Dubose for an equipment violation, half of a mile outside of campus grounds. Two minutes into the stop, Dubose restarted his car and shifted it into gear around the same time that Tensing reached into the car through the open window. Tensing, who would later say that he feared for his life, fired a single, fatal shot into Dubose's head (Murphy, 2016). In October of the same year, Richland County Sheriff's Deputy Ben Fields, a school resource officer assigned to Spring Valley High School was recorded on video lifting a student, who had refused to give up her cell phone, out of her desk, slamming her onto the floor, dragging her across the room, and handcuffing her (Fausset, Perez-Pena, & Blinder, 2015). Each of these incidents sparked national conversation about the role of police in educational settings, both at colleges and universities and in K–12 schools, and whether armed officers should be present in schools at all. The 2018 school shooting in Parkland, Florida, meanwhile, has swung the pendulum toward more police in schools, as evidenced by Miami-Dade, Florida schools almost immediately requesting authorization to hire 100 new school police officers and an increase of $30 million to their security budget (Hanks, 2018).

The purpose of this chapter is to briefly present the history of campus-based policing and, then, to identify specific dilemmas and contradictions concerning campus-based police forces based on recent articles in the popular press and academic outlets. The need to prepare schools for mass shootings is scrutinized against the detrimental effects on learning caused by the regular sight of rifles and armored vehicles. In order to be practically useful to educational leaders, the chapter concludes with options and recommendations for policy and pedagogy. Examples of rules designed to decrease school-based arrests, as well as dialogue programs between police officers and students, which can be proposed and implemented in readers' home districts and institutions, are presented.

DEVELOPING POLICE PRESENCE IN SCHOOLS: A HISTORY

Yale University (n.d.) established the first university police department in 1894. At the time, relations between the university and the city it inhabits, New Haven, were strained. Residents were infuriated over rumors that

Yale students were exhuming local graves; meanwhile, New Haven police officers never stepped foot onto campus, seen as a place of refuge from the law for "Yale boys." Two New Haven police officers volunteered to be permanently assigned to the campus grounds, inaugurating the American tradition of policing educational campuses, which has seen tremendous growth and its fair share of political controversy in the subsequent 122 years (Yale University, n.d.).

The unrest and social activism of the 1960s and 70s caused many colleges to open their own police departments, or spurred the growth of some existing modest college public safety departments (Lee, 2016; Thomsen, 2015). Subsequently, college police forces went through a period of professionalization and accreditation in the 1980s (Lee, 2016). Legislation passed in the 1990s, the Campus Safety Act and the Clery Act, mandated that institutions provide adequate safety measures for students and produce accurate reporting regarding crime on campus and further expanded the role of college police agencies (Jacobsen, 2015). Between 2004 and 2012, the growth of college police departments outpaced the increase in college enrollment; the number of full-time law enforcement personnel on campuses increased 16%, while student enrollment increased only 11% (Lee, 2016; Reaves, 2015). By the 2011–12 school year, 68% of American colleges and universities utilized 14,576 sworn law enforcement officers, those with the same weapons and arrest powers of city police (Reaves, 2015).

The policing of public K–12 schools by armed, sworn officers began in 1953 in Flint, Michigan (Merkwae, 2015). Similar programs in Tucson, Arizona and Miami, Florida were implemented in the 1960s (Kennedy, 2001), the same era in which the term "school resource officer," or SRO, was coined (Weiler & Cray, 2011). The expansion of SRO programs into a commonplace staple of American public schooling occurred in the 1990s as a result of federally funded programs, such as the $750 million COPS in Schools grant program, created in response to a general increase in violent crime among teenagers and school shootings (Kennedy, 2001; Merkwae, 2015; Myrstol, 2010). In 1998 alone, 2.7 million crimes were committed on school grounds, and 1994 saw the most "homicide, aggravated assault, robbery, and rape by young people" (Mallett, 2016, p. 17; Peak, 2015).

Even prior to the infamous 1999 Columbine shooting, legislation signed into law by President Bill Clinton after the 1998 Westside Middle School shooting in Arkansas provided additional funding for school security and increased the use and role of SROs (Mallett, 2016; Peak, 2015). By 2013, around 20,000 school resource officers were patrolling about 30% of public schools (Childress, 2016). The presence of police in schools is seen by many as a punitive and reactive measure, yet we live with increased support for police in schools. Proactive approaches such as community building, decreasing student alienation, increasing mental health support, school counseling, and smaller class sizes are regularly dismissed as too costly.

DILEMMAS

Police-in-schools create dilemmas around when police should intervene, when teachers or administrators should invite them to act, and when it is in a student's best interest (or not) to include police. A dilemma is a scenario where multiple options exist, and each option has a negative outcome for at least one of the actors who face uncertainty about the proper course of action. The scenario creates "a situation in which compelling moral considerations favor each of the courses of action" (Mason, 1996, p. 3) or where "a moral agent was obliged to perform an action of a specified kind and not to perform it" (Donagan, 1996, p. 13).

Dilemma 1: Police in the Classroom: Is There a Time and Place?

When a student acts out in a school where an SRO is present, teachers have the option to call the officer to remove the student, as opposed to handling the situation themselves, or invoking other available resources such as school administrators, guidance counselors, and special educators. Any option that involves removing the student from the classroom interferes with student learning. Teachers relinquish control of the classroom when they ask someone else to remove the student. If the teacher handles the situation, it may quickly resolve, and even be a teachable moment for the disruptive student and the class. It is also possible, though, that a delay of instruction and an escalation of the situation, including violence, may occur.

If the officer removes the student, the result may be legal proceedings, and a juvenile record. By utilizing the police in classroom discipline, teachers exacerbate the school-to-prison pipeline, a term representing "the widely accepted process of disciplining a student, removing that student from the classroom as punishment, wondering at that student's decreasing academic interest and skills, and watching that student flounder and eventually enter the judicial system" (Pane & Rocco, 2014, p. 3). Some parents are frustrated when teachers "don't try to deal with anything; they just call the police" (Spencer & Hooper, 2016, para. 15). One Texas judge suggested that some teachers outsource discipline to the police to redirect the ire of parents to the police department (McGreal, 2012). This overuse of the police further complicates the contradictory nature of the school-based officer's law enforcement and educational roles (McKenna & Pollock, 2014).

The school-to-prison pipeline cycle includes in class discipline, office referral, suspension, expulsion, school failure, dropping out, juvenile incarceration, and adult prison (Pane & Rocco, 2014). Schools place a student indirectly into the pipeline upon suspension from class or school because suspension from school means that the student is not in school and therefore not learning or learning instead that school is not a safe or welcoming space. The arrest of a student directly enters them into the criminal justice system and the prison pipeline. The types of behavior that land students into this pipeline are often part of adolescent ways of thinking and behaving. Disrupting class or playing pranks are offenses that do need to be addressed and corrected, but that do not usually pose a real threat to school safety in a way that would rise to the level of criminal activity (Childress, 2016; Theriot, 2009). Subjective charges such as disorderly conduct can be applied to a wide range of behaviors and are regularly used to arrest schoolchildren (Theriot, 2009).

Dilemma 2: Preparing for the Worst: How Much Is Too Much?

Decisions regarding the deployment of police officers on school grounds are influenced by the dilemma of the worst-case scenario—a fatal mass shooting. This applies to both K–12 school districts and colleges and universities. Support for increased school security and officers in schools has been fueled by high profile, fatal school shootings beginning in the 1990s, in spite of the fact that overall school crime was on the decrease, and incidents were usually nonviolent (Theriot, 2009). The dilemma becomes should school districts and universities work with law enforcement to prepare for mass shooting incidents, or focus on the types of crimes that are more likely to occur on school grounds?

Preparation for mass shootings often entails what some call "militarization" of the police, referring to the acquisition of surplus tactical equipment, such as assault rifles, grenade launchers repurposed to fire tear gas, and mine-resistant armored transportation vehicles, from the U.S. military through the Department of Defense 1033 program (Bauman, 2014). The necessity of this tactical preparedness is contested. The Los Angeles Schools Police Department (LASPD) returned all of its military equipment after months of protests by students and community members (Rivas, 2016). While the LASPD police chief cited the threat of mass shootings as the justification for acquiring such equipment, community members saw the purpose of the equipment as being intended for use toward the minority student body, and did not like the idea of local schools having the look and feel of a warzone (Rivas, 2016).

Though the imagery of hulking, armored equipment near schools almost certainly evokes a negative, fear response, such equipment should be evaluated in terms of how and when it should be used. For example, the Mine Resistant Ambush Protected vehicle, which is a controversial symbol of militarization, does not have any built-in weaponry. In fact, some schools have replaced their MRAP's seats with stretchers and have designated them solely as emergency medical evacuation equipment (Chokshi, 2014). The same vehicle re-framed in the public discourse as a rescue vehicle capable of ferrying children to safety during an emergency, rather than a tool of war, could very well change the perception of parents and the public as to their belonging in and near schools.

The answer to questions as to whether or not school authorities should have access to surplus military hardware may not be the same in every community. One municipality may have developed guidelines stipulating the vehicles cannot be deployed at protests where students are present, while others may intend to use them in exactly that sort of scenario. If police departments are willing to be transparent as to their policies on when and how they will deploy controversial tools, and members of the concerned public are willing to seek such information and debate it rationally, the conversation about equipment such as MRAPs can transcend generalized fearmongering.

Law enforcement leaders argue that much-maligned equipment such as rifles are needed if a school shooting takes place (Sneed, 2015). The alternative to campus police acquiring rifles and such equipment is to depend solely on the community police in the case of an active shooter at a school like movie theaters and other public and commercial venues do. Campus police departments, which still plan to take advantage of the 1033 program can implement policies to reduce the amount of mistrust felt among community members by banning their use during parades or student protests (Chokshi, 2014) and against students.

Another piece of controversial equipment in the school setting is the Taser. Often seen as a positive alternative to firearms because they are less lethal, Tasers provide an electrical shock in order to stop a noncompliant or attacking subject. Their presence in schools is contested, because they jeopardize student safety while creating an uncomfortable learning environment. The Taser instruction manual recommends against its use on children, warning of the risk of death or serious injury (Klein, 2016). The jolt of electricity can send the developing body into cardiac arrest, and the psychological consequences of deploying a Taser on a child include a diminished trust in authority figures and a decreased self-image (Klein, 2016). Despite these warnings and consequences, SROs are increasingly armed with Tasers. In 2013, a 17-year-old male suffered serious neurological injuries after falling backwards when a school-based officer deployed a Taser during a fight between students, leading to a lawsuit and a so-far failed call for the banning of Tasers in public schools (McKenna & Pollock, 2014). Tasers are already banned in Texas' juvenile detention facilities (Klein, 2015).

The level of public support for surplus military equipment, firearms, and Tasers in schools is pegged to parents' fears about violence and crime on campus. An accurate perception of the crime rate on K–12 and college campuses is difficult to achieve due to a lack of standard categorization of crimes used by law enforcement, no centralized tracking system or agency responsible for data collection, media sensationalism, and personal bias. The lack of data collection and tracking creates a lack of accurate information. For example, public perception is affected when reputable news agency reports are contradictory for instance, a rise in physical attacks on teachers (Bidwell, 2014), and a decline in school crime in nearly every category (Brown, 2016). In order to provide a more sensational view of the situation, some reports focus on short-term crime trends, such as a rise in violent crime from one year to the next, even if over the longer term, such crime has steadily fallen (Williams, 2016).

The main source for school-based crime statistics in the U.S. is the annual Indicators of School Crime and Safety report, published by the National Center for Education Statistics. The 2014 report shows that violent deaths at schools rose from the 2010–11 school year to the 2011–12 school year (Robers, Zhang, Morgan, & Musu-Gillette, 2015). This could lead to a concerning headline and public fear of school violence and a call for more school police officers to be hired. However, until that one year, violent deaths at school had been on a steady decline since the 2006–07 school year.

Dilemma 3: Off Campus Patrol: Protecting Students Beyond School, or Inviting Fatal Encounters?

Law enforcement agencies chartered to serve a particular college campus or school district often have police powers outside of the campuses they directly serve. About 88% of public and 63% of private campuses had a memorandum of understanding or other formal written agreement with outside law enforcement agencies. More than half conducted joint patrols with local law enforcement (Reaves, 2015). This ensures that campus police officers can respond to threats in nearby areas that could impact the campus. On the other hand, increasing patrol and operations beyond the campus likewise increases the likelihood of a controversial encounter with a member of the public. This, in turn, negatively affects students, and the entirety of the university-community relationship. This was the case in the Samuel DuBose incident, described in the introduction to this chapter.

Some students at the University of Cincinnati felt unsafe in their own learning environment and even considered not continuing their education at the university (Knight, 2015).

On the other side of the dilemma, a campus police department can play a role in revitalizing near-campus commercial and residential areas, while restoring trust in the institution of policing. The campus police department at Wayne State University in Detroit, in partnership with the city police department, expanded its service zone to include the entire off-campus Midtown area. A diverse group of business owners in Detroit's Midtown district credit this partnership with revitalizing the area close to the school, by drawing new residents and businesses to the district and increasing student comfort and safety (Cowley, 2015).

CONTRADICTIONS

In this section we explore situations in which multiple opposing realities seem to exist as to the purpose of the American system of education.

Education as Site of Equal Access and Racial Stereotypes

The U.S. Department of Education's (n.d.) mission is to "promote student achievement and preparation for global competitiveness by fostering educational excellence and ensuring equal access" (para. 1). The Department of Education does not directly administer the nation's locally governed school districts; however, this mission statement is useful in examining contradictions, however, the educational setting is both influenced by and perpetuates negative racial stereotypes, and security-based incidents such as school shootings amplify this.

The existence of police on campus is contextualized within the fear of school shootings, combined with the perpetual framing of young, racialized minorities as the antithesis of safety. Throughout American history, Black men have been described as brutish beasts capable of inflicting great harm (Bouie, 2014). This tendency to assign superhuman traits to Black men has been observed in implicit bias studies, as has the observed phenomenon of White people reporting that Black people perceive less pain while withstanding physical punishment (Waytz, Hoffman, & Trawalter, 2015). This tendency was in full display in Officer Darren Wilson's description of juvenile Michael Brown as "Hulk Hogan" and a "demon" (Bouie, 2014), and has had deadly consequences in that and other situations. Of all racial groups who experienced death at the hands of U.S. police in 2015, Black victims were the most likely to have been falsely perceived to be armed when they were not actually carrying a weapon (Hirschfield, 2015).

Media portrayals perpetuate stereotypes of racialized minorities. First, media over-represent the proportion of violent crime to total crime, and overemphasize the race of non-White offenders (Gilliam & Iyengar, 2000). For example, during coverage of the Virginia Tech massacre, which was perpetrated by a Korean immigrant, a third of the news articles implicated his ethnicity as a factor in his actions. Ironically scant mention of race was made in the Columbine massacre, carried out by two young, White males (Park, Holody, & Zhang, 2012). The racialization of the perpetrators of school shootings is significant. When school shooters are members of a racial outgroup, as was the case with Virginia Tech, members of the racial majority, in this case White Americans are more likely to attribute the shooter's race as a cause of the crime (Chen, Purdie-Vaughns, Phelan, Yu, & Yang, 2015).

Education as Liberation and Social Control

Educational institutions are inherently contradictory when considering their mission to educate, develop, and inspire students, and their goal of social control through standardization, discipline, and surveillance. Students are more likely to learn and achieve in a "safe, healthy and supportive environment, which develops mutual compassion and respect" (Kentucky Department of Education, 2015, para. 4). The contradiction in having police on campus is in the effect police have on learning and safety. Police officers do not make all students feel safe. Police, and the security cameras and metal detectors that often accompany them, especially in schools serving underprivileged students, can create a prison-like feel in school, distracting students from learning (Mallett, 2016).

Can a campus maintain a climate of openness when police elicit fear in some students? In the college setting, imagery of officers equipped with military gear could affect freedom of speech if students fear they would be confronted by officers during demonstrations (Bauman, 2014) or simply speaking out in class. Examples of this could be seen at University of California campuses during a spate of protests in 2010 and 2011 over tuition increases and in support of the Occupy Wall Street movement. University police officers dressed in full riot gear were recorded pepper spraying seated students and beating students with batons (Gabbatt, 2013). This incident ended with financial consequences to the university as well; University of California paid out $1 million in a lawsuit filed by demonstrators and $38,000 in worker's compensation to the officer. Such penalties can divert funds from student-centered programs and agitate student discontent over university finances. The University of California has seen student protests across the past decade against tuition increases and student food insecurity, homelessness, and debt (Watanabe, 2016), so situations where students feel threatened by police and then see the school's money spent on resolving those situations, instead of student services, is not ideal.

Education as Equalizer and Oppressor

Another inherent contradiction in American education is the system's reputation for being an equalizer among peoples, while simultaneously performing functions that maintain the status quo in terms of oppression of minorities. Education has been referred to as the "great equalizer" in America since that term was coined in 1848 (Rhode, Cooke, & Ojha, 2012), and today, equal access, diversity, and cross-cultural understanding are the core mission of educational districts at the federal, state, and local levels (Kentucky Department of Education, 2015; U.S. Department of Education, n.d.). Despite this perception and focus, the numbers tell a different story. One 25-year study of 790 Baltimore schoolchildren, for example, found that only 4% of the disadvantaged students obtained a college degree by age 28 (Badger, 2014). Students being removed from their schools by arrests is only one factor in a complex system of disadvantage and oppression, but it is a significant, direct way in which the school system perpetuates and reinforces the racial and class bias of American society at large and supports the school to prison pipeline. In the 2011–12 school year, federal data show that Black students made up 16% of public school enrollment, but 31% of students who were arrested in schools (Blad, 2016). In McKinney, Texas, Black students make up 13% of the school population but 39% of campus-based arrests and 61% of disorderly conduct citations (Anderson, 2015). In Chicago, the arrest rates of Black and White students is disproportionate with a 30 to one ratio (Anderson, 2015).

Some less critical observers are likely to infer from this data that Black students are more disruptive at school than White students. Others will realize that there are often different consequences for the same behaviors between White and non-White students. The system ensures disparities in a number of ways. First, schools with majority nonwhite students and/or a high percentage of students in poverty tend to be more likely to have security personnel, including police officers, on premises in the first place, increasing the likelihood of an enforcement encounter (Anderson, 2015). Data from 2005–2010 show that the more non-White students a school has, the more likely it is to have security personnel stationed full time (Robers, et al., 2015). This statistic includes private security guards, without arrest powers and often unarmed, as well as SROs. For example, in 2009–10, 13.6% of schools with fewer than 5% non-White students had full time security personnel, while 41.3% of schools with more than 50% of non-White students had the same. However, this correlation does not exist when examining armed security, including SROs, specifically. In each year studied, schools with 20–50% non-White students had more armed guards than schools with more than 50% non-White students (Robers et al., 2015). Second, the subjective and discretionary nature of the school disruption laws discussed earlier in this chapter contribute to higher arrest rates for minority children (Blad, 2016).

The New York City school police have taken steps to address racial disparities in school arrests. During training, rookie officers are tasked with reflecting on racial disparities in campus-arrest data, discussing the often hidden costs of arrests and summonses on students, and engaging in conflict resolution through role play. Since the trainings commenced in 2012, Bronx schools have seen a significant fall in arrests and summonses (Anderson, 2015). In addition to the racial disparity, there are concerns about the treatment of students with disabilities. Advocates of this population claimed that the behaviors which caused a student to be arrested were often "manifestations of their disabilities, and therefore legally required to be handled therapeutically, rather than through law enforcement" (Thurau & Wald, 2010, p. 981).

Police Officers as Protectors and Punishers

The original intent of the SRO program was to build positive relationships between students and law enforcement (Anderson, 2015). SROs can act as counselors, and teach classes on crime prevention, substance-abuse education, and safety (Kennedy, 2001; Weiler & Cray, 2011). SROs have also been referred to as "surrogate parents, counselors, coaches, and an extra pair of hands for school administrators" (Thurau & Wald, 2010, p. 978). Greatly different outcomes for students can result depending on which of these conflicting roles an SRO is primarily operating. In a scenario where a student swears at a teacher, they say, an officer operating from the law enforcement perspective would see no dilemma while deciding to arrest the student for disorderly conduct, but one operating through the mentorship lens would more heavily consider the maintenance of the relationship between the student and school law enforcement.

Some SROs are trained to de-escalate conflict and to understand the relationship between students' brain development and misconduct (Childress, 2016). However, 38 states do not require any specialized training for school resource officers (Childress, 2016). Students arrested by SROs "face humiliation and stigma from classmates and teachers after being led from the school in handcuffs" (Theriot, 2009, p. 280). Taking into consideration these negative consequences of school-based arrest, SROs who do not exercise appropriate discretion or who underplay the educational role can have the effect of teaching mistrust of law enforcement from a young age, contradicting the intent of the program to build positive relationships.

Contradictions in the Assessment of School-Based Policing

Published information addressing what impact the influx of police officers in schools has had on crime in schools is in and of itself a contradiction. Most government research and evaluation of SROs focus on satisfaction surveys rather than objective data concerning crime statistics (Merkwae, 2015). A review of SRO programs revealed that very few conduct useful or valid assessment (Myrstol, 2010). Studies do not use a representative sample of schools nor are there studies directly comparing schools with and without SROs in the same time period (Na & Gottfredson, 2011). Depending on study location and types of data collected, criminal charges against youth have gone both down and up in correlation with an increase in school resource officers (Sneed, 2015). Different districts may experience different results depending on the training and hiring procedures used (Sneed, 2015) and relationship with school personnel. Theriot (2009) found, much to his surprise and ours, that fewer students were arrested for assault and weapons charges in schools with SROs. It is possible that SROs can have a positive effect through the deterrence of criminal behavior.

Making a value judgment as to the benefit of police in schools is challenging because the idea of police productivity—such as arrests—is counterintuitive. A productive SRO can remove the most threatening students from campus and these arrests simultaneously increase the rate of reported crime at the school. A SRO's productivity then contributes to the narrative that police at school arrest too many students. Students at schools with SROs are more likely to be referred to law enforcement for every type of infraction, as opposed to the prohibited behavior being dealt with administratively by school officials (Spencer & Hooper, 2016). Reductions in arrests can be met by the criticism that the school district police force makes too few arrests to justify its budget (Ray, 2016).

IMPLICATIONS FOR EDUCATIONAL LEADERSHIP

Educators at the K–12 and college levels are faced not only with the responsibility of simultaneously providing for the safety and the fair treatment of students on school grounds by police, but also with the educational challenge of students struggling to process the national narrative surrounding policing and social justice. When 500 students at Princeton University participated in protests in response to the nonindictments of the police officers responsible for the deaths of Michael Brown and Eric Garner (Taylor, 2015), administrators were required to make tough calls about how to maintain order and provide a learning experience.

In July of 2016, Carmen Farina, chancellor of the New York City school system, issued the following statement, during a particularly tumultuous week where civilians and officers were killed:

> Last week's killings of two black men by police in Louisiana and Minnesota, and the tragic shooting deaths of five police officers in Dallas, have shaken the nation. We are all still hurting over these and other recent heinous acts. As painful as these events are, I strongly believe that as New York City educators and parents, we have a moral obligation to address the difficult questions about race, violence, and guns, and to engage students in the critical work of healing our country. We must not avoid these tough conversations—they are necessary if we hope to build a just society for all. I am writing to ask you to partner with us on this important work. I encourage you to come together in our offices, classrooms, teacher prep rooms, principals' offices, cafeterias, playgrounds, and auditoriums—and start a conversation. Discuss the recent events, and help each other process the anger that is gripping our communities. Listen to and support one another. The goal should be to open up lines of communication, build bridges, and foster respect. (Farina, 2016, para. 1)

Chancellor Farina indicates that addressing these topics in school and with students is a responsibility of educators and parents. While educators and parents tackle issues surrounding racism and violence in society, the issue of law enforcement's relationship to the community also must be addressed by parents, teachers, and law enforcement. Next, we profile some of the programs currently in schools and colleges.

The Case of Liberation Diploma Plus High School

An experimental elective course at Liberation Diploma Plus High School in Coney Island called Junior Citizens Police Academy is pairing students who have negative experiences with the police with police officers as teachers. Most of the students at Liberation Diploma Plus have had negative police encounters; some have already been incarcerated. The class is a chance for the students to hear from police officers about their own troubled youth and the stress experienced on the job as an officer, resulting from dangerous situations and constant disrespect (Taylor, 2016).

During class discussions, students are not immediately willing to accept the perspectives of the police officers. Simulated policing scenarios were more successful in helping students understand tense encounters from the officers' point of view. In these simulations, it was common for the students to end up shooting at unarmed suspects (Taylor, 2016). Future iterations of the program will entail field trips, hands-on activities, and tours of local police precincts (Taylor, 2016).

Exercises Promoting Multiple Perspectives, Dialogue, and Deliberation in Miami

Florida International University (FIU) emphasizes diversity, collaboration, and problem solving as part of its *Global Learning for Global Citizenship* initiative (Landorf & Doscher, 2015). As a majority-minority, Hispanic serving institution, most FIU students identify with historically underrepresented populations (Landorf & Doscher, 2015). In order to position these students to bring their voices from the margins to the mainstream, FIU uses democratic deliberation, a process which values a multitude of opinions and perspectives when solving problems and making decisions (Landorf & Feldman, 2016). One undergraduate course developed as part of this initiative at FIU includes Comparative Criminal Justice Systems. Students in this class examine the issues facing law enforcement by looking at what is happening in other countries. Some sections of the course include an in-class visit from German police officers, and others include a week-long trip to London to visit local police stations (Feldman, 2015).

Student-led and community-based global learning activities have also directly addressed the issue of policing and police in schools utilizing principles of democratic deliberation. Democratic deliberation is a process that has "equal participation, respect for the opinions of others, the adoption of a societal perspective on the issue, and reasoned justifications of one's opinions" (De Vries, Stanczyk, Wall, Uhlmann, Damschroder & Kim, 2010, p. 1891). By virtue of discussion, the process of deliberation transforms preferences to "other regarding, not just self-regarding" (McAfee, 2012, p. 24).

Connecting Police With Minority Youth

The FIU Police-Youth Dialogues are a series of sit-down talks between local high school students and police officers. Both parties agree to voluntarily participate in the discussions, which take place in a neutral venue. Moderated by an FIU professor with conversation starters and discussion points, all in the room are invited to share their perspectives and concerns around crime and policing. Antione Hardy, the inaugurator of the program, "respected the police as a young man of color growing up, but too often saw individual officers who did not earn that respect" (FIU Department of Communication Arts, 2015, para. 1). Hardy saw two sides that need to be brought together which inspired the creation of the community dialogues: "young people who feel strongly about their right to assemble and to exercise free speech" and "the police tasked with maintaining order" (para. 1). During one of these dialogue sessions, students were able to express concerns about officers' "heavy handed approach" directly to the police, and officers were able to vocalize the anxiety of experiencing "unknown situations" (FIU Department of Communication Arts, 2015, para. 4).

FIU's Global Learning initiative has also reached out into the community to mend police-youth relations through the university's Haitian Mentorship Program. Each summer, middle school students of Haitian background participate in a summer camp led by FIU undergraduate mentors. Each year, one of the sessions focuses on the students' anxieties and concerns regarding police officers. Open discussions among the students and mentors are encouraged, and police officers from several local agencies are invited to participate in the conversation.

DISCUSSION AND IMPLICATIONS

In the preceding sections, we have laid out dilemmas and contradictions facing educators as it pertains to the presence and utilization of police officers in the K–12 school and the college campus. We have also presented the case that educators can and should engage students at all levels in structured learning experiences including in and outside of the classroom which include conversation, deliberation, and processing of personal experiences in order to assist students with making sense of the national conversation around policing and police brutality, issues which are partly manifested locally in their own school setting. Throughout this chapter, we have intermingled our discussion of K–12 schools and institutions of higher education. This is intentional, as there is significant overlap in the sorts of questions and concerns about the expansion and ubiquity of officers in these settings.

Similarities and Differences Between Policing in K–12 and College Institutions

Policy. In both the K–12 and higher education settings, police departments justify their presence as necessary should a school shooting or other similar worst case threat occur. In both settings, critics fear that students of the institution, rather than being protected by the police, are more likely to end up with criminal records as the result of engaging in behavior which is prohibited by law, but which could be considered in line with that student's age and stage of development and not require criminalization. While both K–12 and college educators should prefer educational over punitive responses to student behavior, the same strategies that K–12 schools may implement to limit interactions with police officers may not be directly transferable to the college setting. College classrooms are made up of students of all ages and it is usually the case that they do not contain children. Disruption and misbehavior are less expected and less understandable in the college setting. A recent study by the Yale Child Study center indicates that teacher bias regarding sex and race lead to expectations that students will behave in certain ways. Teachers watch until they see these behaviors in Black male preschool children and punish the behavior (Gilliam, Maupin, Reyes, Accavitti, & Shic, 2016). Thus the school to prison pipeline is begun (Pane & Rocco, 2014).

Pedagogy. When it comes to classroom conversations about policing, a topic which often goes hand in hand with violence, racism, and oppression, there is no clear line to be drawn between K–12 and college students. High school freshmen and college freshmen alike want to talk about their complaints and concerns about how the community is policed. As evidenced by the several programmatic examples from the previous section, very similar dialogue exercises have been held with middle school, high school, and college. Deliberative exercises help students, including at the K–12 level, to develop the ability to take on the perspectives of others and to explain and understand events and experiences in their own lives (Alfaro, 2008).

Though pedagogy is often used to mean teaching strategies even at the college level, the word specifically refers to the instruction of children. The practice of teaching adults, which is also known as andragogy, focuses on the construction of meaning of the learners' prior experiences as opposed to the discovery of terms and concepts in a sequentially ordered curriculum (Pratt, 2016). Because older learners have more life experience, this can be leveraged in the college setting by relying even more heavily on participant experience and by inviting college students to be responsible for facilitating dialogues with their peers or with K–12 students. K–12 students may require more background information and guidance in order to have a productive conversation on the topic.

CONCLUSION

While frontline educators do not directly make decisions about the size and scope of campus policing, it is important that educational professionals and administrators develop well-informed positions on the role of police in schools and advocate for policies that are most appropriate for their students. This chapter provides only the smallest glimpse into the number of stories that exist in news articles across the Internet about students being handled with great force and arrested for minor transgressions which posed no threat to the safety of teachers or fellow students. We cannot make the case that police officers should be entirely removed from school settings. There have been 11 school shootings in the U.S. in the one year this chapter has been under production, resulting in nine deaths (List of school shootings, n.d.). This only includes incidents where a firearm was discharged, and does not count other incidents and threats including students who have brought prohibited deadly weapons to campuses without using them, or assaults with other types weapons including knives. Police officers also work to root out gang activity and drug deals on and near campus. Under the present system and circumstances and with a lack of data on the effects of police in schools, it is not clear that the net benefit of police officers removing truly violent and dangerous students from the school setting is greater than the net consequence of the numerous other students who end up with criminal records, injuries, and a lifelong distrust of law enforcement resulting from unnecessary interactions with officers.

Efforts should be made to limit the types of situations, which result in officer entry into the classroom. Schools can limit students' unnecessary exposure to the criminal justice system by ensuring a consultation between the police officer, teacher, and principal occurs before arresting a student on disorderly conduct charges (Theriot, 2009). In Hinds County, Mississippi, for example, the local Sheriff has called for teachers and parents to work more cooperatively to resolve issues of student discipline and to make the calling of his department a last resort (Spencer & Hooper, 2016). Another example, in Broward County, Florida, an agreement between the school board, police departments, the local judicial circuit, and civil rights groups was reached which limits when police officers should become involved in school misconduct cases (Sneed, 2015). A law passed in Denver, Colorado similarly limits when police officers should respond to school misconduct (Sneed, 2015). Finally, school-based dialogue and deliberation programs, a number of which we have profiled, which bring together students, police officers, administrators, and elected officials, can have an impact both within and beyond K–12 and higher education classrooms.

REFERENCES

Alfaro, C. (2008). Reinventing teacher education: The role of deliberative pedagogy in the K–6 classroom. In J. R. Dedrick, L. Grattan, & H. Dienstfrey (Eds.), *Deliberation & the work of higher education*. Dayton, OH: Kettering Foundation Press.

Anderson, M. D. (2015). When schooling meets policing. *The Atlantic*. Retrieved from http://www.theatlantic.com/education/archive/2015/09/when-schooling-meets-policing/406348/

Badger, E. (2014). What your 1st grade life says about the rest of it. *The Washington Post*. Retrieved from https://www.washingtonpost.com/news/wonk/wp/2014/08/29/what-your-1st-grade-life-says-about-the-rest-of-it/

Bauman, D. (2014). Campus police stash armored vehicles at M-16s just in case. *The Chronicle of Higher Education*. Retrieved from http://www.chronicle.com/article/On-Campus-Grenade-Launchers/148749

Bidwell, A. (2014). Report: School crime and violence rise. *U.S. News and World Report*. Retrieved from http://www.usnews.com/news/articles/2014/06/10/incidents-of-school-crime-and-violence-on-the-rise-for-students-and-teachers

Blad, E. (2016). State laws that can lead to school arrests targeted for change. *Education Weekly*. Retrieved from http://www.edweek.org/ew/articles/2016/01/27/state-laws-that-can-lead-to-school.html

Bouie, J. (2014) Michael Brown wasn't a superhuman demon. *Slate*. Retrieved from http://www.slate.com/articles/news_and_politics/politics/2014/11/darren_wilson_s_racial_portrayal_of_michael_brown_as_a_superhuman_demon.html

Brown, E. (2016). School crime rates are down in almost every category—except sex crimes at colleges. *The Washington Post*. Retrieved from https://www.washingtonpost.com/local/education/school-crime-rates-down-in-most-every-category--except-sex-crimes-at-colleges/2016/05/03/94f578f2-114d-11e6-93ae-50921721165d_story.html

Chen, C. Y., Purdie-Vaughns, V., Phelan, J. C., Yu, G., & Yang, L. H. (2014). Racial and mental illness stereotypes and discrimination: An identity-based analysis of the Virginia Tech and Columbine shootings. *Cultural Diversity and Ethnic Minority Psychology, 21*(2), 279–287.

Childress, S. (2016). Do cops in schools know how to police kids? *PBS Frontline*. Retrieved from http://www.pbs.org/wgbh/frontline/article/do-cops-in-schools-know-how-to-police-kids/

Chokshi, N. (2014). School police across the country receive excess military weapons and gear. *The Washington Post*. Retrieved from https://www.washingtonpost.com/blogs/govbeat/wp/2014/09/16/school-police-across-the-country-receive-excess-military-weapons-and-gear/

Cowley, S. (2015). How Wayne State Police helped breathe life into a blighted Detroit strip. *The New York Times*. Retrieved from http://www.nytimes.com/2015/02/26/business/smallbusiness/how-wayne-state-police-helped-breathe-life-into-a-blighted-detroit-strip.html?_r=2

De Vries, R., Stanczyk, A., Wall, I. F., Uhlmann, R., Damschroder, L. J., & Kim, S. Y. (2010). Assessing the quality of democratic deliberation: A case study of public deliberation on the ethics of surrogate consent for research. *Social Science & Medicine, 70,* 1896–1903. doi:10.1016/j.socscimied.2010.02.031

Donagan, A. (1996). Moral dilemmas, genuine and spurious: A comparative anatomy. In H.E. Mason (Ed.), *Moral dilemmas and moral theory* (pp. 11–23). New York, NY: Oxford University Press.

Farina, C. (2016). Letter from Chancellor Farina on Recent Events. *NYC Department of Education*. Retrieved from http://schools.nyc.gov/Offices/mediarelations/NewsandSpeeches/2016-2017/Letter+from+Chancellor+Fari%C3%B1a+on+Recent+Events.htm

Fausset, R., Perez-Pena, R., & Blinder, A. (2015). Race and discipline in spotlight after South Carolina officer drags student. *The New York Times*. Retrieved from http://www.nytimes.com/2015/10/28/us/spring-valley-high-school-sc-officer-arrest.html?_r=0

Feldman, E. (2015). German police visit 'comparative criminal justice' classroom. *FIU Global Learning*. Retrieved from https://goglobal.fiu.edu/2015/06/04/german-police-visit-comparative-criminal-justice-classroom/

FIU Department of Communication Arts. (2015). Miami-dade police & youth community dialogues. *CARTA News*. Retrieved from http://cartanews.fiu.edu/miami-dade-police-youth-community-dialogues/

Gabbatt, A. (2013). UC Davis pepper spray officer awarded $38,000 compensation. *The Guardian*. Retrieved from https://www.theguardian.com/world/2013/oct/23/pepper-spray-cop-uc-davis-compensation

Gilliam, F. D., & Iyengar, S. (2000). Prime suspects: The influence of local television news on the viewing public. *American Journal of Political Science, 44*(3), 560–573.

Gilliam, W.S. Maupin, A. N., Reyes, C. R., Accavitti, M., & Shic, F. (2016). Do early educators' implicit biases regarding sex and race relate to behavior expectations and recommendations of preschool expulsions and suspensions? A Research Study Brief. Retrieved from http://ziglercenter.yale.edu/publications/Preschool%20Implicit%20Bias%20Policy%20Brief_final_9_26_276766_5379.pdf

Hanks, D. (2018). Miami-Dade Schools wants $30 million to protect against mass shootings. *Miami Herald*. Retrieved from http://www.miamiherald.com/news/local/education/article201097404.html

Hirschfield, P. J. (2015). Lethal policing: Making sense of American exceptionalism. *Sociological Forum, 30*(4), 1109–1117.

Jacobsen, S. K. (2015). Policing the ivory tower: Students' perceptions of the legitimacy of campus police officers. *Deviant Behavior, 36*, 310–329.

Kennedy, M. (2001). Teachers with a badge. *American School & University, 73*(6), 36–38.

Kentucky Department of Education. (2015). *Characteristics of highly effective teaching and learning*. Frankfort, KY: Author.

Klein, R. (2015). Kids in Texas are more likely to get Tasered in school than in jail. *The Huffington Post*. Retrieved from http://www.huffingtonpost.com/entry/texas-tasers_us_563a5524e4b0b24aee487be1

Klein, R. (2016). Set to stun. *The Huffington Post*. Retrieved from http://data.huffingtonpost.com/2016/school-police/tasers

Knight, C. (2015). UC students press for solutions after DuBose shooting. *Cincinnati Enquirer*. Retrieved from http://www.cincinnati.com/story/news/2015/09/21/dubose-rally-uc-sept-21/72594074/

Landorf, H., & Doscher, S. (2015). Defining global learning at Florida International University. *Diversity & Democracy*. Retrieved from http://www.aacu.org/diversitydemocracy/2015/summer/landorf

Landorf, H., & Feldman, E. (2016). Using democratic deliberation in an internationalization effort in higher education. In R. Mizzi, T. Rocco, & S. Shore (Eds.), *Disrupting adult and community education: Teaching, learning, and working in the periphery*. Albany, NY: SUNY Press.

Lee, J. (2016). Issues of oversight of police on campus. *WISCAPE*. Retrieved from https://wiscape.wisc.edu/wiscape/home/blog/wiscape-blog/2016/04/22/issues-of-oversight-of-police-on-campus

List of school shootings in the U.S. (n.d.). *Wikipedia*. Retrieved from https://en.wikipedia.org/wiki/List_of_school_shootings_in_the_United_States#2010s

Mallett, C. (2016). The school-to-prison pipeline: A critical review of the punitive paradigm shift. *Child & Adolescent Social Work Journal, 33*(1), 15–24.

Mason, H. E. (1996). Introduction. In H. E. Mason (Ed.), *Moral dilemmas and moral theory* (pp. 3–10). New York, NY: Oxford University Press.

McAfee, N. (2012). Three models of democratic deliberation. In W. M. Barker, N. McAfee, & D. W. McIvor (Eds.), *Democratizing deliberation: A political theory anthology* (pp. 21–37). Dayton, OH: Kettering Foundation Press.

McGreal, C. (2012). The US schools with their own police. *The Guardian*. Retrieved https://www.theguardian.com/world/2012/jan/09/texas-police-schools

McKenna, J. M., & Pollock, J. (2011). Law enforcement officers in schools: An analysis of ethical issues. *Criminal Justice Ethics, 33*(3), 163–184.

Merkwae, A. (2015). Schooling the police: Race, disability, and conduct of school resource officers. *Michigan Journal of Race and Law, 21*(1), 147–181.

Murphy, K. (2016). UCPD's most aggressive cop? Ray Tensing. *Cincinnati Enquirer.* Retrieved from http://www.cincinnati.com/story/news/2016/06/08/tensing-ucpds-most-aggressive-cop/85591810/

Myrstol, B. A. (2010). Police in schools: Public perceptions. *Alaska Justice Forum, 27*(3), 5–8.

Na, C., & Gottfredson, D. (2011). Police officers in schools: Effects on school crime and the processing of offending behaviors. *Justice Quarterly*. Retrieved from https://ccjs.umd.edu/sites/ccjs.umd.edu/files/pubs/Police%20Officers%20in%20Schools-Effects%20on%20School%20Crime%20and%20the%20Processing%20of%20Offending%20Behaviors.pdf

Pane, D. M., & Rocco, T. S. (2014). *Transforming the school-to-prison pipeline: Lessons from the classroom*. Rotterdam, the Netherlands: Sense.

Park, S., Holody, K. J., & Zhang, X. (2012). Race in media coverage of school shootings: A parallel application of framing theory and attribute agenda setting. *Journalism & Mass Communication Quarterly, 89*(3), 475–494.

Peak, B. J. (2015). Militarization of school police: One route on the school to prison pipeline. *Arkansas Law Review, 68*(1), 195–229.

Pratt, D.D. (2016). The Research Lens. In D.D. Pratt & D. Smulders (Eds.), *Five perspectives on teaching: Mapping a plurality of the good* (2nd ed.). Malabar, FL: Krieger.

Ray, K. (2016). Do local school districts need their own police departments? *WFTV 9*. Retrieved from http://www.wftv.com/web/wftv/news/9-investigates/do-local-school-districts-need-their-own-police-departments/294106931

Reaves, B. A. (2015). Campus law enforcement, 2011-12. *Bureau of Justice Statistics*. Retrieved from http://www.bjs.gov/content/pub/pdf/cle1112.pdf

Rhode, D., Cooke, K., & Ojha, H. (2012). The decline of the 'great equalizer.' *The Atlantic*. Retrieved from http://www.theatlantic.com/business/archive/2012/12/the-decline-of-the-great-equalizer/266455/

Rivas, J. (2016). How high school teens got a police department to get rid of its military equipment. *Fusion*. Retrieved from http://fusion.net/story/309666/high-school-students-get-police-drop-1033-guns/

Robers, S., Zhang, A., Morgan, R., & Musu-Gillette, L. (2015). *Indicators of school crime and safety: 2014*. (NCES 2015-072). Washington, DC: National Center for Education Statistics. Retrieved from http://nces.ed.gov/pubs2015/2015072.pdf

Sneed, T. (2015). School resource officers: Safety priority or part of the problem? *U.S. News & World Report*. Retrieved from http://www.usnews.com/news/articles/2015/01/30/are-school-resource-officers-part-of-the-school-to-prison-pipeline-problem

Spencer, K., & Hooper, A. (2016). Bullied by the badge. *The Huffington Post*. Retrieved from http://data.huffingtonpost.com/2016/school-police/mississippi

Taylor, K. (2016). Minority youths mistrust police. A Brooklyn high school has a plan. *The New York Times*. Retrieved from http://www.nytimes.com/2016/09/11/nyregion/minority-youth-mistrust-police-a-brooklyn-high-school-has-a-plan.html

Taylor, K. Y. (2015). Black lives matter on campus too. *Al Jazeera America*. Retrieved from http://america.aljazeera.com/opinions/2015/11/black-lives-matter-on-campus-too.html

Theriot, M. T. (2009). School resource officers and the criminalization of student behavior. *Journal of Criminal Justice, 37*, 280–287.

Thomsen, J. (2015). Campus or city police? *Inside Higher Ed*. Retrieved from https://www.insidehighered.com/news/2015/07/30/prosecutor-calls-u-cincinnati-police-force-be-disbanded-and-replaced-city-police

Thurau, L. H., & Wald, J. (2010). Controlling partners: When law enforcement meets discipline in public schools. New York Law School Law Review, *54*, 977–1020.

U.S. Department of Education. (n.d.) Mission. *U.S. Department of Education*. Retrieved from http://www2.ed.gov/about/overview/mission/mission.html

Watanabe, T. (2016). UC students disrupt regents' meeting with protests against possible tuition hike. *Los Angeles Times*. Retrieved from http://www.latimes.com/local/education/la-me-ln-uc-regents-tuition-20161117-story.html

Waytz, A., Hoffman, K. M., & Trawalter, S. (2015). A superhumanization bias in Whites' perception of Blacks. *Social Psychological and Personality Science, 6*(3), 352–359.

Weiler, S. C., & Cray, M. (2011). Police at school: A brief history and current status of school resource officers. *The Clearing House: A Journal of Educational Strategies, Issues, and Ideas, 84*, 160–163.

Williams, T. (2016). Whether crime is up or down depends on data being used. *The New York Times*. Retrieved from http://www.nytimes.com/2016/09/28/us/murder-rate-cities.html?_r=0

Yale University. (n.d.). History of the YPD. *It's Your Yale*. Retrieved from http://your.yale.edu/community/public-safety/police/history

CHAPTER 6

CENTERING CULTURAL RESPONSIVENESS IN THE EVALUATION OF COMMUNITY-BASED EDUCATION

Towards Genuine Accountability

Thomas Archibald, Natalie E. Cook, and Rodney Hopson

ABSTRACT

The "era of accountability," with its emphasis on "evidence-based" education, privileges technical rationalistic program planning and evaluation, effacing the historical precedent of education as a liberatory force for social justice and ignoring the fundamental intertwining of evaluation, culture, and values. Culturally responsive evaluation (CRE) offers a remedy to these acts of erasure and neglect. CRE is the nexus where validity and social justice meet, dialogically providing genuine accountability not only to funders and administrators, but also to diverse learners. We present a conceptual framework of CRE praxis to center culture and values in the evaluation of community-based education to promote social justice.

Convictions of Conscience: How Voices From the Margins Inform Public Actions, and Educational Leadership, pp. 97–117

INTRODUCTION

Evaluation is, or should be, a fundamental part of any educational endeavor. Evaluation is frequently defined as "the act of judging the value, merit, worth, or significance of things" (Schwandt, 2015, p. 1). Within the broader field of education, evaluation tends to carry two related but distinct meanings: In formal, classroom-based educational settings, "evaluation" (often called "assessment") pertains to the evaluation of student learning outcomes; whereas, in nonformal and informal settings, the term refers to what is more properly called "program evaluation." Program evaluation, which is the primary focus of this chapter, consists of "the systematic collection of information about the activities, characteristics, and outcomes of programs to make judgments about the program, improve program effectiveness, and/or inform decisions about future programming" (Patton, 2008, p. 39). Educational organizations are typically required to evaluate their programs. Funding agencies—be they governmental or nongovernmental—often include program evaluation as a key stipulation of the provision of funds. This more general emphasis on program evaluation is couched within what has been called the "era of accountability" (Barnett, Shoho, & Bowers, 2013; Chouinard, 2013), whereby educational practitioners are increasingly expected or obliged to use "evidence-based" practices and programs.

In this chapter, we present a conceptual analysis of the risks posed when accountability-based and evidence-based approaches exert undue influence on the evaluation of educational programs. Then, we offer culturally responsive evaluation (Hood, Hopson, & Frierson, 2005, 2015; Hopson, 2009) as a framework to steer educators away from and through those risks. Like other contributors to this volume, we focus specifically on urban educational contexts. Urban settings are often characterized by diverse, diverging, and varied agendas which can provide dynamic yet challenging contexts for evaluation. An analysis of the effects of technical rationalistic accountability regimes on urban educational evaluation thus becomes essential, especially when evaluation "aims both to respect the multiplicity and diversity of life experiences and values that comprise urban communities, as well as to encourage and promote meaningful engagement with experiences, activities, and policies that serve democratic values of voice and empowerment, justice and equity" (Hopson, Greene, Bledsoe, Villegas, & Brown, 2007, p. 894). We focus on community-based nonformal education rather than on formal classroom education, since the effects of the era of accountability on evaluation in community-based education has, to date, been less thoroughly studied than those in the formal education domain. However, we posit that the issues we address below are ubiquitous across many educational and social contexts.

EDUCATIONAL EVALUATION IN THE ERA OF ACCOUNTABILITY

Broadly speaking, the era of accountability is a response to the perceived lack of effective and efficient government oversight of social programs and other governmental expenditures of the 1970s and 1980s. It began with efforts undertaken by the U.S. federal government to adjure greater accountability at the federal agency level, which subsequently affected the way governmental offices in the U.S. worked at state and local levels. In the educational domain, the United Kingdom (Biesta, 2004; Hursh, 2005), Australia (Kimber & Ehrich, 2011), and other nations (Kamens, 2013) experienced similar shifts towards increased accountability during the same time period. More recently, the tenets of the era of accountability have been taken up with fervor by multilateral international development organizations, large philanthropic organizations, and other institutions whose reach extends across the globe, thus exporting the accountability movement internationally.

Although precursors to the era of accountability in the U.S. can be noticed as far back as Lyndon Johnson's Great Society, perhaps the inaugural moment in the history of this era was the enactment of the Government Performance and Results Act (GPRA) (Public Law 103-62) in 1993. GPRA was followed in 2002 by the Program Assessment Rating Tool (PART), an initiative of the Office of Management and Budget (OMB) under President George W. Bush. PART was introduced "to more rigorously, systematically, and transparently assess public program effectiveness and hold agencies accountable for results by tying them to the executive budget formulation process and program funding" (Heinrich, 2011, p. 123). At the same time, the debates around accountability heated up within the fields of education and evaluation following the passage of the No Child Left Behind (NCLB) Act of 2001 (Public Law 107-110), which contains over 100 references to "scientifically based research" and effectively mandates randomized controlled trial (RCT) designs for the research and evaluation of federally funded education programs (Carlson & Levin, 2005; Feuer, Towne, & Shavelson, 2002).

In these debates raging around the proper place of RCTs in program evaluation and social research, RCTs were discursively positioned as the "gold standard" for research and evaluation. The debates represent in effect a rekindling or new iteration of the "the science wars" about the (contested) relationship between "hard" and "social" sciences (Parsons, 2003) and "the paradigm wars" about the (contested) relationship between quantitative and qualitative research methodologies, especially as pertains to validity and quality (Moss, Phillips, Erickson, Floden, Lather, & Schneider, 2009). All of these "wars" and debates are similar in that they are centered on questions of what counts as credible knowledge. They have to do with knowledge hierarchies, and thus too with the politics of knowledge, an inherently value-laden concern.

The social scientific debates around "evidence-based" practices, programs, and policies followed after similar debates within medicine and health care, pertaining to evidence-based medicine (EBM). In a paper drawing on Deleuze and Guattari and evoking Orwellian "newspeak," Holmes, Murray, Perron, and Rail (2006) presented the EBM movement as "outrageously exclusionary and dangerously normative with regards to scientific knowledge ... a good example of microfascism at play in the contemporary scientific arena" (p. 181)—a "regime of truth" in the Foucauldian sense. According to Holmes and colleagues, "Such a hegemony makes inevitable the further 'segmentation' of knowledge (i.e., disallowing multiple epistemologies), and further marginalize[s] many forms of knowing" (p. 181).

In the era of accountability, evaluation is valued for its perceived scientific and technical authority, and is portrayed as a way to legitimize government activities, ensure cost-effectiveness, and enhance managerial decision making—essentially a model of New Public Management (NPM) (Chouinard, 2013, p. 238). In NPM regimes, efforts to improve the efficiency and performance of public sector entities are derived from private sector techniques focused on benchmarking and performance management. However, equating program evaluation with the private sector management techniques that comprise NPM risks transfiguring evaluation into a professional activity that "functions less like a critical voice weighing in on the value (or lack thereof) of public programs and policies and more like a technology that operates with well-defined procedures and indicators" for constant checking and verification—an audit society (Schwandt, 2015, p. 96).

In essence, NPM is an embodiment and application of technical rationality in inquiry for social management, or, as some would say, for social engineering (Erickson & Gutierrez, 2002). Technical rationality refers to a positivist epistemology of professional knowledge and practice in which "professional activity consists of instrumental problem solving made rigorous by the application of scientific theory and technique" (Schön, 1983, p. 21). It is, according to Schön (1983), the dominant epistemology of practice, "the view of professional knowledge which has most powerfully shaped both our thinking about the professions and the institutional relations of research, education, and practice" (p. 21).

Approaches to program planning and evaluation that are guided (implicitly or explicitly) by the technical rationalistic tenets of NPM contain a number of problematic assumptions that compress and flatten *both* the inquiry (i.e., the evaluation) *and* the object of inquiry (i.e., the educational program). Specifically, we highlight some of the ontological and praxeological assumptions that emerge regarding what education *is*, along with some of the epistemological and axiological assumptions about what evaluation *is*. Against this backdrop of managerialism and technical rationalistic accountability procedures, we then present CRE as an alternative framework which has the potential to foster genuine accountability in the evaluation of community-based nonformal education programs.

CONSTRUCTIONS OF NONFORMAL EDUCATION

Generally, in order to evaluate something (i.e., an "evaluand"), one must have a fairly clear idea of what that thing is, or is supposed to be. What is education? More specifically, what is community-based nonformal education? Nonformal education has been defined as "any organized, systematic, educational activity carried on outside the framework of the formal [educational] system to provide selected types of learning to particular subgroups in the population, adults as well as children" (Coombs & Ahmed, 1974, p. 8), nonformal education includes, but is not limited to: science, technology, education, and math (STEM) outreach; after-school youth development initiatives; literacy education; adult basic education; entrepreneurship training; agricultural extension; community-based rural schools; and more (Eshach, 2007; Rogers, 2005). However, despite the relatively well-established nature of this definition, upon closer examination, it becomes evident that nonformal education is something of a contested construct.

For example, in Archibald's (2015) qualitative study of the epistemological politics at play in the practices of the "evidence-based program" movement, he found that, in essence, his interlocutors were working with and talking about two fundamentally different nonformal educations. In one version ("Mode 1"), nonformal education is an infrastructure for the dissemination of scientific information; in the other ("Mode 2"), it is a site of grassroots knowledge sharing. Program planning and evaluation decisions are campus- or scientist-driven in Mode 1, while they are community-driven in Mode 2. In Mode 1, the essential unit of educational interaction is a "program," meaning a tightly bounded and scripted curriculum; in Mode 2, it is a set of practices and processes. In Mode 1, which focuses on content delivery (especially delivery of scientific knowledge and techniques) and specific, quantifiable outcomes, behavior change is assumed to be simple and linear. Mode 2 is more focused on process facilitation and general outcomes, remaining more open to the complex, nonlinear nature of behavior change. Each of these approaches to education represents and manifests starkly different assumptions about the nature of evidence and knowledge and about how they are supposed to influence professional practice.

Wilson and Cervero (1997) use Foucauldian discourse analysis to historicize the ascendency of technical rationality in the professionalization of adult education, asking, "So where does this theoretical hegemony of technical rationality come from? How has this received tradition become so orthodox as to be beyond question?" (p. 88). They then trace the origins of these aspirations to scientific practice in adult education to the emergence of the professionalization movement in the 1920s—a harbinger or even precursor to the accountability and managerialism movements in contemporary education, what Biesta (2004) refers to as the "current hegemony of the technical-managerial approach" (p. 236). This echoes Schön (1983), for whom many occupations seeking professionalized status in the 20th century attempted to achieve it through the scientific legitimization of practice, predicated on what Forester (1989) calls the ideal "rational-comprehensive" depiction of scientific inquiry.

At what cost, though? The late social justice educator Phyllis Cunningham "has charged that adult educators have lost their vision of the impact they could have on society precisely because they have opted for focusing on professional technical interests rather than emancipatory ends" (Wilson & Cervero, 1997, p. 100). Brookfield (2000) foregrounds critical reflection in adult education for the very same reason; by focusing the attention of adult educators, as critical inquirers, into their own and others' practice, critical reflection

> asks that they examine both the social functions of adult education (particularly the extent to which the field and its workers leave unchallenged dominant cultural values and social systems) and the way their own practice reproduces existing patterns of inequity. (p. 33)

Thus nonformal education is awash in (often tacit) conflicts about ontology (i.e., what education *is* and who educators and learners *are*) and praxeology (i.e., how we understand human action, especially with regards to behavior change). Biesta (2010) has addressed both of these conflicts. In the ontological domain, "talk about 'what works' ... operates on the assumption of a mechanistic ontology that is actually the exception, not the norm in the domain of human interaction" (p. 497). However, in a demonstration of extreme technical rationality, some proponents of evidence-based education express their desire to replicate the impact that RCTs had on agriculture and medicine. This ontological conflation overlooks the ways in which "the dynamics of education are fundamentally different from the dynamics of, say, potato growing or chemistry" (Biesta, 2010, p. 497). This is what Biesta (2010) refers to as the "efficacy deficit" of the evidence-based education movement, "indicating that in the social domain interventions do not generate effects in a mechanistic or deterministic way, but through processes that ... are open so that the connections between intervention and effect are non-linear" (p. 497).

In the praxeological domain, Biesta (2010) decries the "application deficit" that inheres the notions of evidence-based and evidence-informed practice. The application deficit results from thinking of the impact of modern science on society in terms of the application of scientific knowledge. Such a view

> at least misses important aspects of what makes the application of such knowledge possible (particularly the work that is needed to transform the outside world so that knowledge becomes applicable) and perhaps even serves as an ideology that makes the incorporation of practices into particular networks invisible. (p. 499)

This analysis of the ontological and praxeological assumptions of the evidence-based education movement highlights the selective organization of community-based nonformal education as a purely technical rationalistic endeavor. It emphasizes that when technical rationalistic, Mode 1 enactments of nonformal education become the norm, the emancipatory, social justice potential of adult education risks being lost.

CONSTRUCTIONS OF EVALUATION: THE IMPORTANCE OF VALUES

Just as there are multiple perspectives on—or multiple versions of—nonformal education, program evaluation is also characterized by a diversity of forms and functions. There exists a multiplicity of evaluations. As indicated above, in the section on debates about what constitutes credible evidence in evaluation and applied social science research, epistemological politics are one important point around which diverging constructions of evaluation pivot. Yet another point of divergence is the way in which values can, should, or do inform evaluation practice, a concern which is fundamentally axiological in nature.

Perhaps ironically, despite the fact that the word "value" resides at the heart of the word "evaluation," program evaluation practitioners and scholars are far from a consensus regarding the proper place of values and valuing in evaluation. In the first instance, the discussion on this topic occurs on a philosophical level that is more epistemological or even methodological in tone. For example, one of the founders of the field of evaluation, Michael Scriven, has consistently engaged with this topic, most recently in his discussions of "an evaluation specific methodology"

(Scriven & Davidson, 2013) and "the logic of evaluation" (Scriven, 2016), where he (like others) problematizes the fallacious "value-free doctrine" of the social sciences—a vestige of positivism—to emphasize the obvious yet frequently ignored primacy of values and valuing in evaluation. Scriven (2016) laments the ironic "phenomenon of valuephobia" in evaluation (p. 29), seeing many of the major schools of thought in evaluation "as a series of attempts to avoid direct statements about the merit or worth of things" (Scriven, 1993, p. 8). For Scriven, the question of valuing in evaluation is a fundamental epistemological and methodological one at the core of the discipline.

For many other evaluation scholars, the values question is more explicitly axiological, in that it pertains to ethics, and to the ethical imperative of evaluators in pursuit of a good and just society. In this vein, the work of the evaluation professional is not simply to apply scientific evaluation theories to problems of practice: "training in technique in evaluation must be wedded to education in both the disposition and the capacity to engage in moral, ethical, and political reflection on the aim of one's professional undertaking" (Schwandt, 2015, p. 9). Regarding the axiology or ethical imperative of evaluation, many prominent evaluation scholars explicitly center a normative mission for social justice and human rights at the heart of their evaluation practice and scholarship. Ernie House (1990) describes well the paradigmatic shift that occurred within evaluation through which the dominant technical rationalistic tradition gave way to or at least made room for the realization that, given the central place of values in evaluation, evaluation is inherently and inevitably political:

> Philosophically, evaluators ceased to believe their discipline was value-free and realized their practice entailed promoting the values and interest of some groups over others, though they were by no means clear on what to do about this discovery. They struggled with the seemingly conflicting demands of being scientific on the one hand and being useful on the other. Politically, evaluators moved from a position in which they saw themselves as technical experts opposed to the evils of politics to a position in which they admitted evaluation itself was an activity with political effects. (p. 25)

This type of reflection is what Mertens and Wilson (2012) have characterized as the Values Branch of evaluation. As Greene, Millet, and Hopson (2004) write, nicely summarizing the values branch:

> Evaluation is not only, or even most importantly, a matter of method and design. It is also inherently and fundamentally a matter of politics and values. This is because evaluation is politically located in social contexts; it is both shaped by the *political* relationships and power dynamics that

> characterize a given context and, in turn, influences the contours and future character of these relationships. (p. 97, emphasis in the original)

Going further towards an explicit commitment to social justice and human rights, Mertens and Wilson (2012) also describe what they refer to as the Social Justice Branch of evaluation, closely associated with the transformative paradigm of evaluation. According to Mertens (2009), the transformative paradigm "offers a meta-physical umbrella" (p. 4) that brings together various theoretical and methodological traditions such as participatory methodology, Marxism, feminist theory, critical theory, and critical race theory, among others. In social justice-oriented and transformative evaluation, important axiological assumptions include respect for cultural norms, promotion of social justice, furtherance of human rights, and addressing inequities. The ontological assumptions of these evaluation approaches have some roots in historical realism yet also include an openness to the multifaceted nature of our world and to the possibility of ontological plurality. Epistemologically, it thus follows that in transformative and social justice evaluation, knowledge is seen as constructed within a context of power and privilege. This evaluation paradigm, as developed and articulated especially by scholars such as Stafford Hood, Rodney Hopson, Henry Frierson, Karen Kirkhart, Hazel Symonette, and Katrina Bledsoe, is what is known as culturally responsive evaluation.

AN INTRODUCTION TO CULTURAL RESPONSIVENESS IN EVALUATION

Cultural responsiveness—a construct that has also been referred to as cultural relevance, cultural competence or competency, multicultural competence, and other similar terms—pertains to "an ethical imperative [that] represents the intentional effort of the evaluation team to produce work that is valid, honest, respectful of stakeholders, and considerate of the general public welfare" (American Evaluation Association, 2011). It is important to note that while these related terms are often used interchangeably, there carry slightly different meanings and implications. For example, cultural competence suggests an end-point of a process of development, a teleological point at which one can arrive. It also hints at a sort of minimal acceptable standard, akin to "tolerating diversity," a frequently used but rhetorically questionable phrase. To combat this some authors have intentionally defined cultural competence as inquiry "that employs culturally and contextually appropriate methodology; and that uses stakeholder-generated, interpretive means to arrive at the results and further use of the findings" (SenGupta, Hopson, & Thompson-Robinson, 2004, p. 5). The American Evaluation Association (2011) also suggests that a

> culturally competent evaluator is prepared to engage with diverse segments of communities to include cultural and contextual dimensions important to the evaluation. Culturally competent evaluators respect the cultures represented in the evaluation throughout the process. (p. 1)

In the fields of education and evaluation, a preference for the term "cultural responsiveness" has emerged, since it signals the need to continually respond to the ongoing, dynamic phenomenon that is culture in/and human interaction.

Although culture has become an increasingly prominent topic of discussion in the evaluation community, "as a fairly new and emergent construct, there remain many gaps in our knowledge about how to integrate notions of culture and cultural context into evaluation theory and practice" (Chouinard & Cousins, 2014, p. 457). As a shared goal in the community of professional evaluators, cultural responsiveness is a constantly revisited construct with multiple layers (American Evaluation Association, 2011).

The American Evaluation Association's Core Concepts

The American Evaluation Association (2011) issued a public statement on cultural competence, which outlines "several core concepts [that] are foundational to the pursuit of cultural competence" (p. 1). The first core concept is that since culture "is central to economic, political, and social systems as well as individual identity, ... all evaluation reflects culturally influenced norms, values, and ways of knowing—making cultural competence integral to ethical, high-quality evaluation" (p. 1). Secondly, since the United States is comprised of a diversity of cultures, cultural responsiveness is fluid, such that "an evaluator who is well prepared to work with a particular community is not necessarily competent in another" (p. 1). The third core concept "requires that evaluators maintain a high degree of self-awareness and self-examination to better understand how their own backgrounds and other life experiences serve as assets or limitations in the conduct of an evaluation" (p. 1). Finally, the fourth concept is that "culture has implications for all phases of evaluation—including staffing, development, and implementation of evaluation efforts as well as communicating and using evaluation results" (p. 1).

Cultural Responsiveness as an Integral Part of Evaluation Work

While not all evaluation scholars and practitioners agree, and although there remains significant work to further operationalize the construct of cultural responsiveness, there is a growing recognition that concern for culture is a necessary part of evaluation work. According to SenGupta, Hopson, and Thompson-Robinson (2004),

> culture is an undeniably integral part of the diverse contexts of evaluation, and therefore an integral part of evaluation. Culture is present in evaluation not only in the contexts in which programs are implemented but also in the designs of these programs and the approach, stance, or methods evaluators choose to use in their work. *A common thread between culture and evaluation is the concept of values*. Culture shapes values, beliefs, and worldviews. Evaluation is fundamentally an endeavor of determining values, merit, and worth. (p. 6, emphasis added)

Further, the American Evaluation Association (2011), asserts that there is "universal influence of cultural values and perspectives" and that "to draw valid conclusions," evaluation ought to

> consider important contributors to human behavior, including those related to culture, personal habit, situational limitations, assimilation and acculturation, or the effect of the evaluand. Without attention to the complexity and multiple determinants of behavior, evaluations can arrive at flawed findings with potentially devastating consequences. (p. 2)

Thus, regardless of a specific evaluation project or a particular approach to evaluation, culture is always, necessarily, a relevant matter in evaluation work.

Principles of Cultural Responsiveness in Evaluation Practice

Hopson (2004) describes five foundational principles involved in culturally responsive evaluation. The first principle is that "the social location of the evaluator matters," capturing the significance of the evaluator's own background in the lens through which s/he works, implying that positionality is important on the part of the evaluator (p. 12). The second tenet is that "evaluators play a role in furthering social change and social justice," as "evaluators 'are more than technicians' " and have the ability, if not the obligation "to recognize asymmetric power relations to challenge systems and mechanisms of inequity and injustice in hope of dismantling oppression against cultural groups on the fringes of our larger society" (p. 12). This suggests that regardless of evaluators' own paradigms, the *work* of evaluation is critical and transformative in nature.

The third principle is that "avoiding ethnocentricism means embracing multiple cultural perspectives" (p. 12). Hopson (2004) articulates that "the culturally competent evaluator is able to shift between diverse perspectives, recognizes the limits of narrow culturocentric standards and ideas, and values reciprocal cultural understanding" (p. 12). Thus, through reflexivity, an evaluator may recognize ethnocentricism present in her or his own work. The fourth tenet is that "culture is central to the evaluation process" because of "the profound way in which culture (including racial and ethnic identity, social origin, class background, etc.) shapes worldview, values and norms, and thereby impacts the uses of, reactions to, and legitimacy of, any evaluation" (p. 13).

The fifth principle is that "culturally and ethnically diverse communities have contributions to make in redefining the evaluation field" (p. 13). It is crucial to recognize that "the contributions of these diverse and often marginalized groups ultimately triggers alternative ways for responding to evaluative processes of change and transformation both locally and globally" (Hopson, 2004, p. 13). As attention to the concept of cultural responsiveness rises in the field of evaluation, these elements of cultural responsiveness in the field can help evaluators pursue this goal in their work.

Hopson (2004) adds to this discussion the notion of the sociocultural perspective. He explains that

> those who attempt to study and advance knowledge of multicultural and culturally competent evaluation inevitably find that the central issue is to move beyond narrow culture-bound assumptions toward diverse sociocultural perspectives and experiences. (p. 1)

Hopson's attention to the benefit of a more *socio*cultural perspective is noteworthy and calls us to recognize that culture captures diverse social experiences, not just limited "cultural features," which may at times, contribute to the development and reproduction of stereotypes. Further, as evaluators engage in the "process of learning, unlearning, and relearning," which is part of the ongoing work of cultural responsiveness in evaluation, evaluators must acknowledge that

> competence in one context is no assurance of competence in another. The culturally competent evaluator (or evaluation team) must have specific knowledge of the people and place in which the evaluation is being conducted—including local history and culturally determined mores, values, and ways of knowing. (American Evaluation Association, 2011, p. 2)

Further, an important theoretical and historical achievement of CRE is in forwarding alternative epistemologies that are socially active and critical (Hopson, 2009), such that alternative ways of knowing are respected as valuable and valid rather than deviant or illegitimate.

While it may not be immediately obvious given the sensibility of attention to culture in evaluation work, cultural responsiveness has not been a priority in all evaluation endeavors. Ironically, some of the most "rigorous" evaluation work, such as that which is associated with the "evidence-based" education movement, may completely disregard culture, or may only include it as just another variable. Such evaluations may assert that culture was "controlled" for, or that cultural responsiveness was achieved by translating program materials in multiple languages and including pictures that "looked like" program participants. While these considerations are useful, they are more surface-level cultural accommodations than they are intentional considerations towards the cultural responsiveness for which the American Evaluation Association advocates and the ethical imperatives of evaluation work demands.

Culturally Responsive Evaluation for Genuine Accountability: A Practice Example

As stated above, CRE is important not only because it produces more just evaluation, but also because it produces higher quality evaluation. The relationship between cultural, context, validity, and quality provides the rationale for CRE's salience in the quest for genuine accountability. For example, Symonette (2009) describes how ethical practice and excellence in inquiry "are intimately intertwined with orientations toward and responsiveness to diversity, and most importantly, one's boundary-spanning capacities for authentically engaging with diversity" (p. 279). Kirkhart (2005) describes the need to think in terms of multicultural validity (MCV), citing five dimensions that direct "attention to different types of evidence to support or challenge validity" (p. 22)—interpersonal, consequential, experiential, theoretical, and methodological. Citing Kirkhart, Hopson (2009) writes, "Methodological threats to MCV occur when research designs are in violation or conflict with cultural norms or when evaluation questions are framed within narrow perspectives that hold little or no meaning to communities or populations" (pp. 442–443).

Yet beyond questions of design, from an even broader perspective informed by and sensitive to the conflicting sets of epistemological, praxeological, ontological, and axiological assumptions that characterize different ways of perceiving or doing education and evaluation, CRE emerges as a prerequisite for high-quality and valid evaluation of urban community education programs—at the center, not the margins. In other words, if community education consists of a set of technical procedures whereby scientific facts are transferred to participants, then standard technical conceptualizations of "rigorous" evaluation can apply, and value-oriented and culturally-responsive approaches may not be necessary for good evaluation. But, if what we present above holds true, and if nonformal education is actually a relational coconstruction of new knowledges and new realities in highly political contexts laden with values and power relations, then CRE and related evaluation approaches take on a special importance.

To further illustrate this point, we briefly present a handful of vignettes—adapted from real nonformal education and evaluation contexts—to demonstrate what is at stake as educators and evaluators negotiate the multiple perspectives and tensions related to the epistemological, praxeological, ontological, and axiological assumptions that inhere their work. Imagine there are three organizations working to provide family and youth support services through nonformal, community education in a medium-sized U.S. city. These three organizations are described very briefly below:

Christian Youth & Family Resource Center. The Christian Youth & Family Resource Center, established in 1967, leverages resources from Christian churches, volunteers, and donors to support families and individuals in need. The center serves about 30 families in the Southeast region of the city. A major part of the Youth & Family Resource Center's work is its afterschool program for youth. The center's afterschool program provides youth from 3rd to 12th grade with ongoing academic support, service learning opportunities, counseling, and spiritual guidance.

Youth Enrichment Center. The Youth Enrichment Center was established by a community coalition in 1979 to buffer children from the issues of poverty, crime, and drug use in the city. Today, the Youth Enrichment Center serves about 200 youth by offering programming around academic enrichment, leadership skills, nonviolence education, and fitness and nutrition education. The center also provides seasonal support, such as back-to-school supplies and holiday gifts.

Social Justice Mission. The Social Justice Mission is part of an international organization that works to assist those in need by providing food, clothing, financial assistance, shelter, spiritual support, and case management. It also runs special seasonal programs, such as back-to-school drives and Christmas drives to provide children in need with gifts. On a case-by-case basis, the Social Justice Mission also provides emergency assistance and disaster relief. In addition, the organization offers special programs for youth and seniors.

Imagine these organizations were planning, implementing, and evaluating activities and programs from a technical rationalist perspective, as if careful application of science-based principles to societal problems is what matters, and as if rigorous application of science-based methods is the best way to assess success. Here is what we might see.

In order to receive grant money to continue offering their programs, the Christian Youth & Family Resource Center and the Youth Enrichment

Center both apply for a federal grant being administered by the state. About 20 years ago, two psychology researchers at a university in another state did a series of RCTs of various afterschool enrichment programs. Then, another researcher, hired by the federal government, conducted a systematic review of the literature on afterschool programs and found that the four curricula the original researchers studied and published on had been evaluated with a rigorous methodology and had been found to, on average, show that the program was effective in making positive changes among youth on the three main quantitative variables of interest. As a result, these four curricula earned the honorific label of "evidence-based" nonformal education programs. The federal government was seeking accountability, so in this new funding cycle, it created the funding program such that community organizations would be required to choose from among those four programs. Unfortunately, the curricula were developed and tested in a predominately white university town in the Midwest, whereas the population served by the Christian Youth & Family Resource Center and the Youth Enrichment Center is characterized by considerably more racial, ethnic, and linguistic diversity than that Midwest town. Yet because of city budget cuts, both programs felt they had to pursue this grant. Luckily, they both were funded.

After they began implementing the curricula, they were also required to complete implementation checklists to ensure that their community educators were following the scripted delivery methods prescribed in the curriculum. The educators and administrators often felt a need to adapt some elements of the activities and case examples used in the curricula, because they noticed that their normally highly-engaged youth participants seemed to be losing interest in the activities and lessons. But, they were also wary of being sanctioned by the state for not respecting the obligations of the funding agreement. They wondered whether or not their youth participants were benefiting from this curriculum, but were told by the state representative that they did not need to do an outcome evaluation on the program, since its effectiveness had already been scientifically proven.

Meanwhile, after a staff meeting one day, the educators of the Social Justice Mission—which was able to weather the city budget shortfalls by relying on support from their international headquarters—began informally discussing how the hard economic times were affecting their community. Each staff member could recount at least one story of a neighbor or friend struggling to make mortgage and car payments, and it was looking like it was going to be a cold winter. As a holistic community education and development organization, the Social Justice Mission felt fairly well-prepared to intervene and respond to their community's needs. Yet before doing so, one educator suggested conducting a rapid, culturally responsive action inquiry needs assessment and program evaluation. They formed a coalition of local leaders and educators, and invited a community organizer that had studied CRE and critical race theory in evaluation to come guide their design of the inquiry. They created "listening posts" at community gathering spaces such as the grocery store, the bus stop, and a pedestrian mall near downtown; there, they gave away coffee and muffins as they chatted with people about their hopes, fears, needs, and wants. Each station had people fluent in Spanish and English, and participant feedback was gathered in people's own handwriting on a large sheet of paper set up on an easel, or was noted by an inquiry team member if the person was unable to write on her or his own. Based on their inquiry, the Social Justice Mission quickly adapted its programmatic offerings to better meet the educational and material needs of their constituency.

In all three cases, nonformal urban educational programs were planned, implemented, and evaluated. For the Christian Youth & Family Resource Center and the Youth Enrichment Center, technical rationalism, scientific evidence, and accountability to federal and state funding agencies drove their work. Their pedagogy and their evaluative inquiry became mechanistic, compliance-based, and unresponsive to the cultures, values, and lived realities of their learners. For Social Justice Mission, program planning and evaluation were guided by culturally responsive and community-centered inquiry, which allowed them to respectfully engage with context and actively respond to their learners' needs.

As much as we evaluators would perhaps like to (over)promise, one evaluation study will not necessarily meet the needs of all stakeholders. It is incumbent upon the evaluator to seek consensus on evaluation priorities, to invoke an arbitrator role among competing priorities (including their own), and avoid undermining the quality of the evaluation by trying to be all things to all people (Greene, 1986). There is very often a distinction between evaluation that meets the needs of the communities and evaluation that meets the needs of funding bodies, between evaluation for purposes of learning and social change and evaluation for accountability and managerial control. Often, the distinction highlights fissures of mutual exclusivity; "Paradoxically, certain accountability requirements can hinder organizational learning, and it is thus important to differentiate among factors that enable and impede learning," especially when "resource dependence plays a central role in shaping relationships of accountability (Ebrahim, 2005, pp. 56–57). As discussed above in terms of Mode 1 and Mode 2 education, the fundamental epistemological, ontological, and axiological assumptions that constitute the dominant (hegemonic) paradigm of community education presuppose particular methodologies of accountability which in turn create a positive feedback loop to make some realities more real and others less so, further marginalizing individuals and communities that the social programs are purported to serve.

CONCLUSION

Divergent education*s* and evaluation*s* are on display in these vignettes. And though the cases may seem like caricatures—exaggerated to make a point—they are not too far from many actual examples of education and evaluation in the era of accountability. But in this dominant framework, the question arises, "accountable to whom?" The abiding irony is that, as we have presented above, CRE and related evaluation approaches are not just "right" because they cater to participants' identities and feelings. Rather, they are *needed* because the dominant approach to accountability risks producing ineffective programs and inconclusive or erroneous evaluations.

This is why epistemological politics matter for true accountability. As Scriven (2008) so eloquently wrote in his critique of the RCT design, "This issue is not a mere academic dispute, and should be treated as one involving the welfare of very many people, not just the egos of a few" (p. 24). That is why we see CRE as the nexus where validity and social justice meet, dialogically providing genuine accountability not only to funders and administrators, but also to diverse learners in urban communities and other contexts. In light of the myriad philosophical tensions that arise for program planning and evaluation in community-based urban educational contexts vis-à-vis technical rationalistic accountability paradigms, we urge administrators, educators, and evaluators to seriously consider centering CRE praxis in the evaluation of community-based education to promote social justice.

Of course, this is easier said than done. In an effort to offer some suggestions and guidelines, however tentative, to those educational administrators and other leaders in nonformal urban education programs who seek to enhance the evaluation of their programs via cultural responsiveness, we conclude by presenting some practical implications of the analysis presented in this chapter. Overall, the most important approach is to identify and question the tacit assumptions that undergird educational programs and their evaluations. What is the program trying to achieve? How? Who decided? Who identified "the problem" being addressed? Who was at the planning table? Who is the evaluation for? What is the evaluation for? Who decides what counts as credible, valid knowledge?

In the domain of adult education, Stephen Brookfield provides practical ways to work critically with assumptions, focusing on in particular on causal, prescriptive, and paradigmatic assumptions (Brookfield, 2012). In the domain of evaluation, Donna Mertens and Amy Wilson offer a framework for analyzing epistemological, ontological, axiological, and methodological assumptions that imbue both program planning and evaluation (Mertens & Wilson, 2012), while Archibald, Cook, and colleagues have merged the work of Brookfield, Mertens, and others to develop a facilitated intervention to promote "evaluative thinking" as a way to unpack the critical assumptions in a program's theory of change (Archibald, Sharrock, Buckley, & Cook, 2016). They present hands-on activities that program administrators can use to help the educators with whom they work better identify and question assumptions. Such efforts to analyze assumptions can help administrators and educators explicitly elucidate what "type" of education is (supposed to be) enacted. They can also reveal cultural assumptions about the learners or purported beneficiaries. Similarly, Hopson and his colleagues created a practical framework for embedding CRE into program evaluation (Hood, Hopson, & Kirkhart, 2015). Educational program leaders can apply that framework in commissioning, planning, implementing, and using program evaluation.

It is important to note that all of these practical steps must be handled with care. While they are practical, they are not simply technical fixes to technical problems. Even without broaching the subject of culture, which can be sensitive and can lead to defensiveness, leaders must be very intentional about "scaffolding" their efforts to unearth and question the assumptions under which they and their colleagues operate on a day-to-day basis, since doing so tends to be unsettling. "Safe space," which may be difficult to foster, is required. Leaders must be aware of and work with power differentials around the room. Nevertheless, we posit that confronting the risks involved in questioning assumptions and centering culturally responsiveness in education far outweigh the alternative. We hope that this chapter will help educational leaders engage in this difficult yet crucial work.

REFERENCES

American Evaluation Association. (2011). American Evaluation Association Public Statement on Cultural Competence in Evaluation. Fairhaven, MA: Author. Retrieved from www.eval.org

Archibald, T. (2015). "They just know": The epistemological politics of "evidence-based" non-formal education. *Evaluation and Program Planning*, *48*, 137–148.

Archibald, T., Sharrock, G., Buckley, J., & Cook, N. (2016). Assumptions, conjectures, and other miracles: The application of evaluative thinking to theory of change models in community development. *Evaluation and Program Planning*, *59*, 119–127.

Barnett, B., Shoho, A., & Bowers, A. (Eds.). (2013). *School and district leadership in an era of accountability*. Charlotte, NC: Information Age Publishing.

Biesta, G. J. (2004). Education, accountability, and the ethical demand: Can the democratic potential of accountability be regained? *Educational Theory*, *54*(3), 233–250.

Biesta, G. J. (2010). Why "what works" still won't work: From evidence-based education to value-based education. *Studies in Philosophy and Education, 29*(5), 491–503.

Brookfield, S. (2000). The concept of critically reflective practice. In A. Wilson & E. Hayes (Eds.), *Handbook of adult and continuing education* (pp. 33–49). San Francisco, CA: Jossey-Bass.

Brookfield, S. (2012). *Teaching for critical thinking: Tools and techniques to help students question their assumptions*. San Francisco, CA: Jossey-Bass.

Carlson, J. S., & Levin, J. R. (2005). *The No Child Left Behind legislation: Educational research and federal funding*. Greenwich, CT: Information Age Publishing.

Chouinard, J. A. (2013). The case for participatory evaluation in an era of accountability. *American Journal of Evaluation, 34*(2), 237–253.

Chouinard, J. A., & Cousins, J. B. (2009). A review and synthesis of current research on cross- cultural evaluation. *American Journal of Evaluation, 30*(4), 457–494.

Coombs, P. H., & Ahmed, M. (1974). *Attacking rural poverty: How nonformal education can help*. Baltimore, MD: Johns Hopkins University Press.

Ebrahim, A. (2005). Accountability myopia: Losing sight of organizational learning. *Nonprofit and Voluntary Sector Quarterly, 34*(1), 56–87.

Erickson, F., & Gutierrez, K. (2002). Comment: Culture, rigor, and science in educational research. *Educational Researcher,* 31(8), 21–24.

Eshach, H. (2007). Bridging in-school and out-of-school learning: Formal, non-formal, and informal education. *Journal of Science Education and Technology, 16*(2), 171–190.

Feuer, M. J., Towne, L., & Shavelson, R. J. (2002). Scientific culture and educational research. *Educational Researcher, 31*(8), 4–14.

Forester, J. (1989) *Planning in the face of power*. Berkeley, CA: University of California Press.

Greene, J. C. (1986, April). *Participatory Evaluation and the Evaluation of Social Programs: Lessons Learned from the Field.* Paper presented at the Annual Meeting of the American Educational Research Association, San Francisco, CA.

Greene, J., Millet, R., & Hopson, R. (2004). Evaluation as democratizing Practice. In M. Braverman, N. Constantine, & J. K. Slater, (Eds.), *Putting evaluation to work for foundations and grantees*. San Francisco, CA: Jossey-Bass.

Heinrich, C. (2011). How credible is the evidence, and does it matter? An analysis of the Program Assessment Rating Tool. *Public Administration Review,* 72(1), 123–134.

Holmes, D., Murray, S. J., Perron, A., & Rail, G. (2006). Deconstructing the evidence-based discourse in health sciences: Truth, power and fascism. *International Journal of Evidence-Based Healthcare, 4*(3), 180–186.

Hood, S., Hopson, R. K., & Kirkhart, K. E. (2015). Culturally responsive evaluation. In K. A. Newcomer , H. P. Hatry, & J. S. Wholey (Eds.), *Handbook of practical program evaluation* (4th ed., pp. 281–317). Hoboken, NJ: Jossey-Bass.

Hood, S., Hopson, R., & Frierson, H. (Eds.) (2005). *The role of culture and cultural context: A mandate for inclusion, the discovery of truth, and understanding in evaluative theory and practice*. Greenwich, CT: Information Age Publishing.

Hood, S., Hopson, R., & Frierson, H. (Eds.) (2015). *Continuing the journey to reposition culture and cultural context in evaluation theory and practice*. Greenwich, CT: Information Age Publishing.

Hopson, R. K. (2004). *Overview of multicultural and culturally competent program evaluation: Issues, challenges and opportunities.* Woodland Hills, CA: California Endowment.

Hopson, R. K. (2009). Reclaiming knowledge at the margins: Culturally responsive evaluation in the current evaluation moment. In K. E. Ryan & J. Bradley Cousins (Eds.), *The SAGE international handbook of educational evaluation* (pp. 429–446). Thousand Oaks, CA: SAGE.

Hopson, R. K., Greene, J. C., Bledsoe, K. L., Villegas, T. M., & Brown, T. A. (2007). A vision of urban educational evaluation. In. W.T. Pink, & G. W. Noblit (Eds.), *International Handbook of Urban Education* (pp. 893–914). Dordrecht, The Netherlands: Springer.

House, E. (1990). Research news and comment: Trends in evaluation. *Educational Researcher, 19*, 24–28.

Hursh, D. (2005). Neo-liberalism, markets and accountability: Transforming education and undermining democracy in the United States and England. *Policy Futures in Education, 3*(1), 3-15.

Kamens, D. H. (2013). Globalization and the emergence of an audit culture: PISA and the search for 'best practices' and magic bullets. In H. D. Meyer & A. Benavot (Eds.), *PISA, power and policy: The emergence of global educational governance* (pp. 117–139). Oxford, England: Symposium Books.

Kimber, M., & Ehrich, L. C. (2011). The democratic deficit and school-based management in Australia. *Journal of Educational Administration, 49*(2), 179–199.

Kirkhart, K. E. (2005). Through a cultural lens: Reflections on validity and theory in evaluation. In S. Hood, R. Hopson, & H. Frierson (Eds.), *the role of culture and cultural context: A mandate for inclusion, the discovery of truth, and understanding in evaluative theory and practice* (pp. 21–39). Greenwich, CT: Information Age Publishing.

Mertens, D. M. (2009). *Transformative research and evaluation*. New York, NY: Guilford Press.

Mertens, D. M., & Wilson, A. T. (2012). *Program evaluation theory and practice: A comprehensive guide*. New York, NY: Guilford Press.

Moss, P. A., Phillips, D. C., Erickson, F. D., Floden, R. E., Lather, P. A., & Schneider, B. L. (2009). Learning from our differences: A dialogue across perspectives on quality in education research. *Educational Researcher, 38*(7), 501–517.

Parsons, K. (Ed.). (2003). *The science wars: Debating scientific knowledge and technology*. Amherst, NY: Prometheus Books.

Patton, M. Q. (2008). *Utilization-focused evaluation* (4th ed.). Beverly Hills, CA: SAGE.

Public Law No. 103-62. Government Performance and Results Act of 1993.

Public Law No. 107-110. No Child Left Behind Act of 2001.

Rogers, A. (2005). *Non-formal education: Flexible schooling or participatory education?* Hong Kong: Comparative education Research Centre, University of Hong Kong.

Schön, D. A. (1983). *The reflective practitioner: How professionals think in action*. New York, NY: Basic Books.

Schwandt, T. (2015). *Evaluation foundations revisited: Cultivating a life of mind for practice*. Stanford, CA: Stanford University Press.

Scriven, M. (1993). *Hard-won lessons in program evaluation. New Directions for Program Evaluation, 58*.

Scriven, M. (2008). A summative evaluation of RCT methodology: An alternative approach to causal research. *Journal of Multidisciplinary Evaluation, 5*(9), 11–24.

Scriven, M. (2016). Roadblocks to recognition and revolution. *American Journal of Evaluation, 37*(1), 27–44.

Scriven, M., & Davidson, E. J. (2013). Evaluation specific methodology. Workshop facilitated at the American Evaluation Association Conference, Washington, DC.

SenGupta, S., Hopson, R., & Thompson-Robinson, M. (2004). Cultural competence in evaluation: An overview. *New Directions in Evaluation, 102*, 5–19.

Symonette, H. (2009). Cultivating self as responsive instrument. In D. M. Mertens & P. E. Ginsberg (Eds.), *The handbook of social research ethics* (pp. 279–294). Thousand Oaks, CA: SAGE.

Wilson, A. L., & Cervero, R. M. (1997). The song remains the same: The selective tradition of technical rationality in adult education program planning theory. *International Journal of Lifelong Education, 16*(2), 84–108.

CHAPTER 7

STANDING WITH THE DEMONIZED

Empowering Gang-Labeled Latino Youth

César A. Cruz and Tracey Benson

ABSTRACT

Most national studies find that less than 5% of youth ever join gangs, however every city in the United States with a population above 250,000, and 92% of the largest cities, reported the presence of active youth gangs (Stinchcomb, 2002). Historically, young people who are affiliated with gangs are often dismissed, ignored, or seen as disposable. This contemporary "demonization" of gang-involved youth comes from historical and present-day narratives that continually stigmatize an already marginalized group of young people. In this chapter, we examine how these portrayals perpetuate narratives that Latino, gang-involved youth are a problem in need of a solution. We continue by introducing Homies Empowerment, a youth development program, which employs a developmental framework that recasts gang membership to serve as a foundational asset on which to build young leaders of tomorrow.

Convictions of Conscience: How Voices From the Margins Inform Public Actions, and Educational Leadership, pp. 119–140

INTRODUCTION

Decades of research, Hollywood films, and news reports have created a narrative that gangs are terrorizing our society and must be stopped. Mass media, in particular, accounts for most of what we may learn about other people. According to Ericson, Baranek, and Chan (1991), the vast majority of people spend more time interacting with media compared to human beings. Television shows, like *Law and Order,* often bombard viewers with a view of gangs and their communities (Ericson, Baranek, & Chan, 1991) that pits their communities against law enforcement officers, reinforcing the narrative of noble public servants who struggle with tough emotions in service of justice and peace by protecting neighborhoods rife with crime, violence, and gangs. This extreme emphasis on crime and violence in television shows and on the news "not only influences public attitudes and opinions toward crime and criminals, it also helps to maintain crime as a salient political issue" (Suerette, as cited in Thompson, Young, & Burns, 2010, p. 410). The excessive attention given to focusing on crime and gangs has created a massive culture of fear and this fear has "seriously eroded the quality of life among American urban dwellers" (Suerette, as cited in Thompson et al., 2010, p. 410).

Within this context, we focus on Latino immigrants because of their high rates of gang affiliation in the United States. According to the National Gang Center (1996–2011), Latinos make up 47% of all gang affiliated U.S. citizens, followed by Blacks at 38%, and Whites at 11%. Sociologist, Alfredo Miranda, highlights the importance of focusing on immigrant gang affiliation because they are "especially vulnerable (due to a) lack (of) resources and (a) familiarity with the justice system. Immigrants also report fewer instances of abuse because of fear of deportation" (Miranda, as cited in Duran, 2013, p. 58). Brown (2002), in her book *Gang Nation,* writes about the creation of Latinos as *delinquent citizens*. According to Brown, the adjective "delinquent" precedes the term "citizen" because "this sense of Latino gang members and perhaps all Latino Americans precedes all conceptions of citizenship within mainstream rhetoric" (p. xxiii). Duran (2009) suggests that stereotyping Mexican American communities as *gang infested,* and equating gangs as synonymous with crime allows for differential policing that no longer emphasizes criminal acts, but rather perpetual criminal people.

CREATING THE LATINO DELINQUENT

The Office of Juvenile Justice and Delinquency Prevention has declared that police officers across the nation have ethnically and racially labeled gang members as Latino (47%) and Black (31%) (Egley, as cited in Duran, 2009). The *New York Times* suggested labeling youth as gang-members has, in essence, applied the label of gang member to an entire racial and ethnic group, especially males (Duran, 2013). Duran (2013) theorizes that gang labeling is important for at least three reasons: (1) It is overly broad in definition but specific in terms of whom the label is applied to; (2) it allows for selective and aggressive law enforcement; and (3) it responds to groups formed from racial oppression with neutral-sounding code words to perpetuate a cycle of increased oppression. Since the 1980s, in response to this image of the gangster as the new urban predator, a larger number of cities have created specialized gang units to support a war on gangs that will eliminate this alleged threat. The image of the urban terrorist lurking in neighborhoods at night was bolstered not only by pseudo-scientific research dating back to the 1920s, but also mainstream media controlling the public image and narrative of Latinos literally into the living rooms of people.

Hollywood Gangsters

During the infamous Zoot Suit riots of the 1940s, Mexican American youth banded together in gangs to defend themselves against sailors who came in drunk into Los Angeles and tried to beat them up (Franco, 2018). In the mid-1950s gangs became "primarily characterized as nonwhite, immigrant, violent, criminal, remorseless, and more dangerous than the past" (Duran, 2009, p. 11). *Delinquent Boys: The Culture of the Gang* by criminologist Albert Cohen's (1955) was one of the seminal books written in this time-period that characterized gangs as defying middle-class norms by exhibiting behavioral acts that were malicious, negativistic, and nonutilitarian, with no real purpose-acts committed just for the hell of it. Other researchers followed in its ideological footsteps. Hollywood took their turn at creating the character of the bandido and the Mexican bandit, who would eventually become the prison and barrio gangster from books crafted from pseudo-scientific criminal research.

Rita Moreno, a veteran Latina actress, featured in the documentary, *The Bronze Screen: 100 Years of the Latino Image in American Cinema*, comments "Hollywood is very influential in placing in the minds of people images of what we Latinos are ... many of those images deal with gangs" (De Los Santos, Racho, & Domínguez, 2002). Playwright, Luis Valdez (*Zoot Suit*), further adds in the documentary that, "Hollywood deals in stereotypes in every movie that it makes." Director, Gregory Nava (*Mi Familia*), theorizes that a lot of stereotypes come about out of "guilt in order to justify something that people deep down, unconsciously know is unfair, and not right, but they want to somehow compensate for it" (De Los Santos, Racho, & Domínguez, 2002).

It was during this same golden era of Hollywood film classics that researchers were depicting Mexicans as violent, lawless criminals. Various influential films that introduced the idea of the Mexican to the national consciousness, including *The Mask of Zorro* (1940), *Neptune's Daughter* (1949) and *Touch of Evil* (1958) either depicted the Mexican as a bandido, a buffoon, or a lesser class citizen. According to Hollywood actress, Elizabeth Peña, images were "sown on the big screen" in the public's imagination (De Los Santos, Racho, & Domínguez, 2002). "If u talk like deeees," with a Spanish accent, you are seen as a moron," Peña added (Domínguez & De Los Santos, 2002).

Films like *Boulevard Nights* (1979), *Colors* (1988), *Blood In, Blood Out* (1993) and *Mi Vida Loca* (1993) perpetuated popular, negative Latino stereotypes for decades. Even with the civil rights and Chicano (Mexican American) power movement of the 1960s, the popular images in the mainstream media of Mexican Americans did not change in the decades of the 1960s, 70s, 80s, or 90s. According to film director, Luis Valdez (La Bamba), "the urban gang film was the training ground for a self-perpetuating image" (Valdez, quoted in *The Bronze Screen* by De Los Santos, Racho, & Domínguez, 2002, Chapter: Urban Greaser). Actor Danny de la Paz, who starred in the gang film *Boulevard Nights* (1979), adds that these negative stereotypes are merely for the "purpose of making money at the movies" (de la Paz, quoted in *The Bronze Screen* by De Los Santos, Racho, & Domínguez, 2002, Chapter: Urban Greaser).

Creating a Moral Panic

Pseudo-documentaries such as *Gangland* on the History Channel, *Lock-up* on MSNBC, and others, have made a career out of "displaying violent, criminal images of how gangs organized syndicates designed to make money or prey on the innocent" (Duran, 2013, p. 3). This is what researchers McCorkle and Miethe (2002) have identified as creating a *moral panic*. Sociologists Thompson, Young, and Burns (2010) published a 5-year, in-depth study in which they found that the news "not only presents information, it also articulates ideological messages concerning the meaning and definition of gangs" (p. 410). In essence, the news is one of the major vehicles that helps people construct reality. Duran (2013) states that people generally construct reality from four sources: personal experience, other individuals, social groups and institutions, and the mass media. Moreover, Altheide and Surette (as cited in Thompson et al., 2010) argue that most individuals rely heavily on mass media to form their sense of reality. This, they found is especially true of their beliefs and attitudes related to crime and criminal justice because most individuals have limited personal contact and experience with crime.

It is not enough that media sells violence, but researchers like Ibarra and Kitsuse (as cited in Thompson et al., 2010) argue that newspapers are major contributors to the public discourse and perception of social problems. The primary job of news writers is to create vivid images in our heads so that stories stick with the reader. These graphic images of the monsters, the mass murderers, rapists, and the urban terrorist gangsters all create a new reality for us where it is no longer safe to come outside because of the perceived violence of these street gangs (Thompson et al., 2010). Profit, viewership, and readership drive the content of publications and television broadcasts, not a moral compass. (Thompson et al., 2010). With these alarming images, well ingrained through a period of at least six decades, intentional or unintentional harm to the societal perception of large groups of people has occurred. We bear witness that seeing Mexican youth through this lens, turns them into perpetual criminals, and that perception, for many, will become their reality.

Our Perception Becomes Their Reality

According to Duran (2013) "both Latinos and Blacks are three times as prevalent on gang lists as compared with their proportion of the population in the U.S., whereas whites are underrepresented by twelve times" (p. 11). Contrary to popular opinion, the overrepresentation of Latinos and Blacks on gang lists is because gang members are racially profiled and labeled in police department controlled gang databases, not because they are more prone to join gangs (Duran, 2013). Researcher Malcolm W. Klein (as cited in Duran, 2013) made some key findings regarding the overrepresentation of Black and Latino gang membership.

> Gang officer perceptions of gangs often did not match research findings. Most gang crime is minor; most gang activity is non-criminal; street gangs are social groups; street life becomes a part of gang culture; and the community context in which gangs arise is often ignored. The police, on the other hand, portrayed gangs as violent criminal enterprises, fundamentally different from other social groups and divorced from local community problems. (p. 54)

Criminologists Baglivio, Jackowski, Greenwald, and Howell found in their 2013 study *Serious, Violent, and Chronic Juvenile Offenders*, that both "Blacks and Hispanics are less likely than Whites to be in the severe 5% of offenders" (p. 85). The fact that Whites disproportionately represent the most severe criminal offenders does not match popular social consciousness that Latinos and Blacks commit the most heinous crimes and are the biggest threat to the social order. While social entrapment is most certainly a factor in Latino youth gang involvement, there are also contextual factors that play a role within a very complex reality that they are living in U.S. society.

Barrera (as cited in Duran, 2013) argues that "the ongoing segregation of people of color from whites allowed for certain neighborhoods to create the conditions for a barrio internal colony: indigenous populations dominated by foreigners" (p. 11). Barrera describes colonialism as

> a structured relationship of domination and subordination, where the dominant and subordinate groups are defined along ethnic and/or racial lines, and where the relationship is established and maintained to serve the interests of all or part of the dominant group. (p. 12)

Most Americans, in theory, would not want to live in a society that has internment camps or internal colonies, however, violation of people's rights become much less of a concern as barrios and ghettos are "equated with breeding grounds for gangs and criminality—the two terms were used interchangeably" (Barrera, as cited in Duran, 2013, p. 11).

Blacks and Latinos are contained and profiled at a young age. By the time they turn 20, they have a criminal record, are labeled as gang members, lose the right to vote because of felonies, and struggle to find a job or housing due criminal records. This becomes an effective way to maintain the status-quo where certain people are kept in their place (hood, barrio, jail cell, class stratification) (Duran, 2013) and creates a vicious social cycle of containment that functions for generations as children grow up in communities where these patterns are their daily reality. "Along with suppression by the criminal justice system and poor living conditions, firearm production and the attractiveness of the gang image led many into unfortunate outcomes, which only enhanced a colonial design of indigenous self- destruction and self-hate" (Duran, 2013, p. 12). A combination of societal factors, criminalization of Latino populations, lore of gang life, and a general acceptance labeling Latinos as criminals are all contributing factors to gang participation among Latino youth.

Gangs and Protection

Latinos in U.S. barrios are often caught between nations. Brown (2002) argues that Latinos are caught between a U.S. narrative that says "this ain't your country" and "viva mi barrio [long live my neighborhood]" (p. 40). Duran (2013) affirms the work of Dr. Acuña, who writes about the impact of colonization in his book, *Occupied America: A History of Chicanos,* by noting that colonization in hoods and barrios has "structured the life chances for youth of color in several ways:

1. by providing reasons for joining neighborhood groups created for physical and psychological protections;
2. by creating the conditions that encourage gang rivalries; and
3. by allowing the dominant majority to frame gang behavior and create a suppression response" (p. 13).

According to this theory, marginalized groups have created gangs as a source of social control and community empowerment. Duran argues that

> ignoring the current and past experiences of racial and ethnic oppression hides the significance placed on the social construction of race and keeps racism masked and perceived as an illusion, yet it is issues of race, class, and identity that fuel gang membership. (Duran, 2013, p. 13)

Cruz (2010) in his book, *Bang for Freedom,* departs from the perspective that oppression is the key factor that has led youth into gangs and asserts that it is a failure to acknowledge that gangs may also serve other purposes that have always been positive, as the overarching factor influencing gang membership. In his book, Cruz writes about the formation of two major Mexican gangs, the Mexican Mafia and Nuestra Familia. He details the history of *mutualistas* or mutual aid societies that many communities used to support each other for generations. The narrative Cruz provides is gangs as not just a response to oppression, but as second family units and fraternities. Cruz's book incorporates his life-long research, experience living and teaching in barrios, and becoming a research-based practitioner that has worked directly with gang involved youth. Cruz, along with several grass-roots community workers, cofounded a youth development organization, *Homies Empowerment,* that views young people in gangs as kin, connected, and resilient.

CHANGING THE LENS: CRIMINALS TO DEVELOPING YOUTH

"Every city in the US with a population above 250,000 and 92% of the largest cities, reported the presence of active youth gangs" (Stinchcomb, 2002, p. 27). This reality is presenting itself in many urban cities such as Los Angeles (East L.A., South-Central), San Francisco (Mission district), Chicago (La Villita, Barrio Pilsen), East Boston (Chelsea, Roxbury, Mattapan, Dorchester), New York (Bronx, Queens, Harlem), and even in places such as South Omaha, Nebraska. The mere sound of the word *gang* causes many to scramble for solutions to this phenomenon that is seen as a generational epidemic. Therefore, when people think about gangs, the first thought that comes to mind is how we can intervene and cure this societal ill. It is then that a series of programs, or proposed remedies, are created and projects are undertaken. However, gangs, by the definition found in the Merriam-Webster Dictionary (n.d.), are not inherently negative, yet when this label is imposed on poor Latino youth, they go from being "a group of persons having informal and usually close social relations" to "a group of persons working to unlawful or antisocial ends; especially: a band of antisocial adolescents" (definitions 2 & 1a).

Programs and projects are often funded and implemented claiming or seeking to be the solution to this problem, but with very little thought, as to the root causes of gang involvement, and only the symptoms are treated, result in ineffective Band-Aid programs as opposed to real healing. Contemporary solutions rarely consider actual gang-members and the circumstances that drive them to join. Therefore, most of the emphasis has traditionally been on gang prevention, not on youth development and empowerment, or seeing gangs as asset-based organizations for young people. There is an overwhelming need for youth development programs that incorporate best practice as identified by empirical research, build upon assets of gangs, and promote asset-based strategies for empowering gang involved youth.

Diagnosing the Problem: Macro and Micro Factors and Root Causes

The environment serves as a macro factor that contributes to gang involvement. Although many believe that youth choose to join a gang, the reality is that there is a wide range of factors causing them to be involved with gangs, some positive, and some for mere survival. The combination of poverty, unemployment, and racial segregation that plague many communities of color create the perfect conditions for gangs as we currently know them. Several of the major factors that tend to increase the likelihood of gang involvement are discussed by Klein (as cited in Stinchcomb, 2002) who focuses on Black communities but whose findings are comparable to those of any person growing up in a predominantly minoratized" (oppressed) urban area. Klein (as cited in Stinchcomb, 2002) states the major factors for gang involvement are the "loss of industrial jobs, out migration of the middle class, growing residential segregation of the inner-city, increasing failure of schools to prepare inner-city children for a service economy, and the resulting strains on family life" (p. 28). Stanton-Salazar (2001) describes minority-based urban neighborhoods and their geographical and segregated manifestations as invisible social prisons in which youth have to function when living within them. Youth in these communities that become involved with gangs, are generally fleeing rough childhood experiences and are looking to feel accepted, loved, and protected; they are in search of a sense of belonging, a sense of family, which albeit often conditionally contingent upon loyalty and obedience, is provided by gangs.

Micro factors such as the Latino's youth experiences also function as a contributor to gang involvement. The adolescent youth experience is a phase of life filled with difficult physical, emotional, and psychological changes for the average person. During adolescence, young people are shaping their sense of self, and are thus very susceptible to influence. It is also during this time that youth, especially those youths that experience multiple psychosocial risk factors such as low self-esteem, exposure to trauma, hopelessness, and relationships with negative peer groups, are expressively more likely to take part in antisocial behavior such as drug use, violence, early sexual activity and delinquency (Flannery, Singer, & Wester, 2001; Jessor, Van Den Bos, Vanderryn, Costa, & Turbin, 1995). It is not uncommon for gang-involved youth to carry the scars of childhood experiences and to have them manifest via their decision-making process at this stage in life. This is also the stage in life where youth often first become affiliated with gangs.

Schooling experiences can help to mediate the adolescent experience but for many gang involved youth, it becomes a type of oppressive schooling experience that is implemented in most U.S. public schools throughout adolescence. Gang involvement is often paired with high push-out rates and both are found in communities with the above mentioned conditions. School hours are critical for youth because during this time, they stay away from influences that can be negative as well as gain the knowledge necessary to shape their value systems. But, when youth find themselves in educational settings where the information being taught is uninspiring and irrelevant to their lives, many steer away (or are being pushed away) from schools and the pull from the streets becomes stronger and much more attractive. Even though education is a powerful tool, when youth are not taught to value their own history, culture and indigenous languages, it can also be seen as contributors to gang involvement.

Some youth resist the negative experiences in school instead turning to gangs as a form of resistance. What is seen as rebelliousness may actually be a reasonable opposition to "a schooling process that disrespects them; they oppose not education, but schooling" (Valenzuela, 1999, pp. 7–8). Within a great majority of schools, as in the general society, the young people who are affiliated with gangs are often dismissed, ignored or seen as disposable. Rather than receiving an empowering education, this population whose ancestors experienced a forceful integration into U.S. society through slavery, colonization and conquest are taught a history that not only ignores the rich culture and their people's contributions to society, but it also emphasizes the need for assimilation (Ogbu, 1974). Thus, it should come as no surprise that these youths who have been robbed of their empowering history consciously or unconsciously oppose the cultural practices and discourses associated with the dominant group including schooling (Fordham & Ogbu, 1986).

Regardless of the angle one chooses to analyze gangs, "from both a macro-based, socioeconomic opportunity perspective and a micro-based, personal psychological perspective, gangs are essentially meeting the unfulfilled needs of their members" (Stinchcomb, 2002, p. 29). These young people who have been brought up in cycles of violence, including poverty, abuse, and neglect, are in search of a sense of belonging, a sense of power, and/or a sense of safety, all versions of which they often find in gangs. Payne (as cited in Rios, 2010) goes further and describes gang life as "a space of resistance, comfort, and fortitude developed by Black men to move and negotiate through the throes of inadequate educational and economic opportunity" (p. 26).

CASE STUDIES AND PROGRAM ASSESSMENTS

Gangs are not a new phenomenon and therefore, there have been a multitude of programs that have been developed in search of a solution to this perceived problem. These programs, while possibly well-intentioned, primarily approach their mission from a deficit-model, "defin[ing] participants by their problems and [seeking] to 'fix' them" (Bloom, Irvy, Thompson, 2010, p. 13). Organizations often attempt interventions with the goal of eliminating gangs altogether, while ignoring pervasive social ills that plague the communities in which gangs thrive such as poverty, racism, and inequality. It is because of a multitude of contributing factors that "evaluating youth gang interventions is a complex undertaking" (Howell, as cited in Loeber & Farrington, 1998, p. 285). According to Howell (as cited in Loeber & Farrington, 1998) the difficulty in measuring the effectiveness of gang interventions lies primarily in three areas; first, establishing the formation and membership of a gang; second, verifying the dissolution of a gang; and third, locating evidence of a reduction in delinquent behavior directly related to decreased gang involvement. However, a challenge greater than the multitude of measurement issues is that "very few rigorous evaluations of youth gang programs have been undertaken" (Howell, as cited in Loeber & Farrington, 1998, p. 285). Therefore, a review of the existing literature for evidence of best practice is extremely complex.

Assessment of Youth Gang Programs

There has only been one national survey assessing youth gang prevention programs conducted (Spergel & Curry, 1993). In the sole national study of gang prevention programs, Spergel and his colleagues surveyed 254 respondents, 45 communities, and 6 special program sites (Spergel & Curry, as cited in Loeber, 1998). The following are the findings of this assessment along with the programs that have historically shown the most promise.

Chicago Area Project, Chicago, IL

The Chicago Area Project (CAP) established in the 1930s created by Clifford Shaw "was designed to implement the community organization theory ... 'on social disorganization,' proffering the notion that community organization could be a major tool for reducing crime and gang problems" (Howell, as cited in Loeber & Farrington, 1998, p. 286). Among the strategies implemented by CAP was the "curbside counselor" which consisted of members of the community, including reformed ex-convicts, who were able to speak with gang-involved youth and "effectively advise the boys in local language and manner to pursue paths to appropriate legitimate behaviors" (Spergel, as cited by Bates & Swan, 2013, p. 131). Although this project was headed in the right direction as it "emphasized local community responsibility for addressing the delinquency problem, ... it did not address external citywide, governmental, and commercial factors that might have created conditions responsible for local problems" (Spergel, as cited by Bates, 2013, p. 131). While CAP did not undergo any substantive evaluation process, they claim to have been a successful gang intervention model (Klein, as cited by Loeber & Farrington, 1998).

House of Umoja, Philadelphia, PA

The House of Umoja, created in the 1960s, was formed with the goal of reducing youth gang violence in Philadelphia. Their approach consisted of "provid[ing] for black gang youths altruistic, extended-family values based on African culture" (Fattah, 1987, p. 37). Although this organization tapped into culture, a critical component of identity and self-esteem, it failed to create "a model to work in different settings, ... [with] underlying principles and techniques that do not rely on the charisma of a particular individual" (Fattah, 1987, p. 41). This program had many success stories. However due to the heavy influence and reliance on a specific charismatic leader, there were questions about the replicability and sustainability of expanding this model.

Project BUILD, Chicago, IL

Project BUILD (Broader Urban Involvement and Leadership Development) established in the mid-1980s incorporated schools in their model. They believed that including school was essential because youth who are gang-affiliated spend a large part of waking hours there. Project BUILD provided gang prevention curriculum and after-school programming that addressed the issues behind the youth's involvement with gangs. This program was "evaluated rigorously, and shown to have promise" (Stinchcomb, 2002, p. 33). The evaluation of the program incorporated a "nonequivalent comparison group" design, in which three pairs of public middle schools were matched on the basis that the same gang actively recruited members from both schools in a pair. One school in each pair was randomly assigned to be an experimental school, and the other was designated as a comparison school. Although the evaluators found that youth enrolled in the program were less likely to join a gang than non-included youth, the evaluation pool was very small, and the evaluation period was only short-term (Thompson & Jason, as cited in Loeber & Farrington, 1998).

Roca, Chelsea, MA

Roca, based in Chelsea, Massachusetts is a youth development organization that has been deemed successful in large part because it has created a "theoretical shift that emphasizes engagement over social control" (Morrison, as cited by Rosenfield, Quinet, & Garcia, 2010, p. 100). According to a paper commissioned by The Bill & Melinda Gates Foundation, there are four major aspects of Roca's framework that have enabled this organization to continue their work with gang-involved youth. Through their "relentless outreach," Roca is determined to target and actively recruit gang-involved youth via their presence in the streets. They have implemented a "highly individualized, youth-centered support [intake] process" and go beyond "establishing credibility" and creating a "safe-haven with strong, caring relationships" (Bloom et al., 2010, p. 14). Once these young people, who are considered "high risk" are recruited and brought into a safe haven from the streets, Roca implements "wraparound services as part of a clearly articulated plan," which in essence means that youth set goals for themselves, identify the support they will need and are closely monitored by an adult advocate within the organization (Bloom et al., 2010).

Shortcomings of Previous Programing

These case studies show that addressing gangs through the "implement[ation of] theoretical interventions that rely exclusively on intuitive, emotional, political, or fiscal support" (Knox, as cited in Stinchcomb, 2002, p. 37) is like putting a Band-Aid on a deep, open wound, as it would not be providing for the necessary treatment to heal. Thus, even if counselors, culture and schools are involved as seen in the previous cases, without both the youth and their micro and macro needs and contributions being acknowledged, these programs cannot be successful.

For programs to be successful at reaching and having a profound effect on the lives of Latino gang-involved youth, they must address the social and economic conditions that surround them. There have been many publications written about gangs and youth involvement in them, yet there is not much information available focusing on the proposed target population. Of the 1,170 journals, 1,010 were empirical articles, less than 30% included Latino youths living in the United States or Puerto Rico, only approximately 6% reported results for Latino youths, and less than 3% focused exclusively on Latino youths (Rodriguez & Morrobel, 2004). Although 1,010 empirical articles were published in six youth development journals, only 62 reported results for Latino youths, less than half of which focused on issues related to Latino youths exclusively. In addition, the studies in the youth development journals that were Latino youth-centered were overwhelmingly deficit oriented. The articles were largely reporting issues related to sexual activity (23%), substance use (17%), depression (17%), and issues related to negative peer pressure or deviant peers (17%). This means that a great majority (74%) of the studies were unable to address and/or evaluate the assets that youth, their communities, and obviously, gangs can contribute.

BEST PRACTICES IN INTERVENTION

Youth development differs from intervention because it seeks to empower young people and its goal is to use a participatory youth-driven process to help young people strengthen positive attitudes, behavior, and skills to assist their functioning in life (Jennings, Parra-Medina, Messias, & McLoughlin, 2006; Wong, Zimmerman, & Parker, 2010). Youth development shifts the focus from that which blames youth for what seems like poor choices being made, such as becoming affiliated with gangs, to that which recognizes a young person's individual and his/her community's experience and contributions and seeks to provide the support that is lacking. This results in empowerment rather than alienation, accusation, and punishment.

If popular research resists criminalizing the youth who are involved with gangs but instead frames the gangs as centers of youth development, researches may recognize the assets that gangs could potentially contribute to our society. There are several desirable assets that gangs possess. Gangs generally operate within an organized structure that provides safety to its members; as many young people "become gang members as a way of avoiding victimization by family members, acquaintances, and others in their community" (Melde, Taylor, & Esbensen, 2009, p. 567). Gang memberships also requires high levels of discipline and commitment, which are highly desirable characteristics in adulthood.

In principle, gangs operate as most nations do, yet this society criminalizes the youth who join street gangs but turns a blind eye to the example that its leaders provide. "Great nations engage in national wars for almost identical reasons [that gangs do] ... personal honor, prestige, and defense against perceived threats to one's homeland" (Miller, as cited by Howell, n.d.). The same attributes we celebrate in great soldiers are shared by great gang-members. Helping guide these youths who inhabit these strong principles would create not only a stronger individual but would benefit and strengthen an entire society.

Become Familiar With the Community

Before organizations attempt to create a program that will effectively engage youth involved with gangs, they must familiarize themselves with the community that the youth grew up in, and in most cases, is all they know. If service providers are unaware of the existing conditions causing youth to feel the need to become involved with gangs, then they will be unable to completely understand what the real needs of the community are. Stinchcomb (2002) recommends service organizations

> analyze community needs [and strengths], develop an appropriate conceptual framework, incorporate[e] macro and micro strategies into a comprehensive program design, and review the results of preceding research in order to identify what relevant approaches that have demonstrated success elsewhere might be applied locally. (p. 37)

Through following this strategy organizations can develop a better understanding of the broader context of the community before delving into intervention strategies.

When getting to know a physical community that the youth grew up in, abandoning the "seriously limited" deficit model thinking is key because it does not account for the assets that these young people possess, and can lead to a diagnosis that merely treats symptoms, and not root causes. Many of the positive attributes and core values that guide most gangs go beyond the physical space and are deeply rooted in their cultural background. Thus, in order to fully understand a young person's motivations for becoming affiliated with gangs, one should study both the youth's ethnic background, not to stereotype and overgeneralize, but to appreciate the community cultural wealth that it possesses.

Community Cultural Wealth and Ethnic Identity

Identity is largely defined by one's ethnic and cultural background and when valued and properly taught, it can be used as a tool for empowerment and resiliency. It has been argued that understanding Latino youth development cannot be understood without first considering ethnic identity (Neimann, Romero, Arredondo, & Rodriguez 1999; Oboler, as cited in Rodriguez & Morrobel, 2004). Phinney (cited in Rodriguez & Morrobel, 2004) states that adolescents with positive ethnic identities more effectively handle negative stereotypes and prejudice instead of internalizing negative self-perceptions.

One's ethnic background is directly linked with one's culture. According to Yosso (2005), when assessing an individual's assets, his/her community cultural wealth must be properly accounted for. Yosso states "Community Cultural Wealth is an array of knowledge, skills, abilities, and contacts possessed and utilized by Communities of Color to survive and resist macro and micro- forms of oppression" (p. 77). In this model, there are six forms of capital that are presented as wealth: aspirational, navigational, social, linguistic, familial, and resistant. They are defined as follows:

- *Aspirational*: Ability to hold onto hope in the face of structured inequality and often without the means to make such dreams a reality.
- *Linguistic*: Intellectual and social skills attained through communication experiences in more than one language and/or style.
- *Familial*: Community history, memory and cultural intuition. "Extended family," which may include immediate family (living or long passed on) as well as aunts, uncles, grandparents and friends who we might consider part of our *familia* (family) [or tribe]. [The extensive] funds of knowledge within Mexican American communities.

- *Social*: Networks of people and community resources. *Mutualistas* or mutual aid societies are an example of how historically, immigrants to the U.S. and indeed, African Americans even while enslaved, created and maintained social networks [including gangs, tribes, and kinships].
- *Navigational*: Skills of maneuvering through social institutions; resilience that has been recognized as "a set of inner resources, social competencies and cultural strategies that permit individuals to not only survive, recover, or even thrive after stressful events, but also to draw from the experience to enhance subsequent functioning."
- *Resistant*: refers to the knowledge and skills fostered through oppositional behavior that challenges inequality [such as youth rebellion] (Yosso, 2005, pp. 77–79).

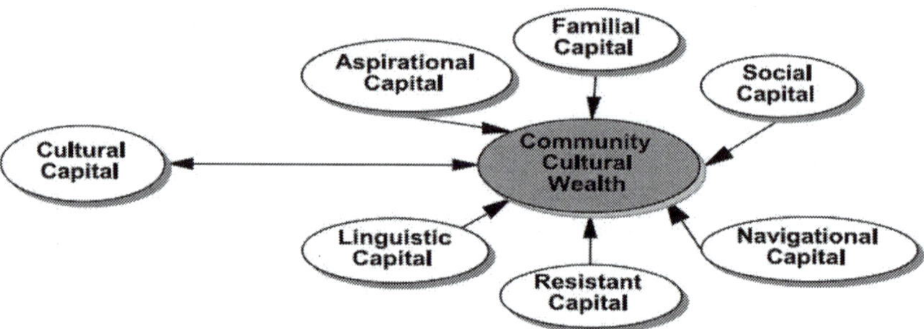

Source: Adapted from Oliver & Shapiro, 1995 as cited in Yosso, 2005.

Figure 7.1. A model of community cultural wealth.

Studying the model of community cultural wealth (Figure 7.1) enables us to better understand the decision-making process of these youth, and the wealth of resources they carry. We can see where the need for a family bond comes from as well as locate where the motivation and determination to struggle or rebel against oppressive structures (Pizarro, 1998; Villenas & Deyhle, 1999). Currently, many Latino youth are taught that they are mere criminals, deviants or hoodlums that must be reformed because they carry few assets that will help them in society. However, a fostering of an understanding of community cultural wealth would help to raise the self-esteem and sense of self-worth among these youths.

Homies Empowerment: A Youth Development Strategy for Schools

Homies Empowerment is an example of the community cultural wealth model in action. It is an organization that develops gang involved/impacted

Latino youth in Oakland, CA guiding them towards their life's purpose; taking gang strengths as assets including family, a sense of belonging, safety, discipline, commitment, and resistance. This model incorporates a youth development strategy pairing gang involved/impacted high school aged youth with role models (Homie Mentors) who have either been in gangs or can understand the need to be in gangs and the resources that young people get out of gangs, such as a second family unit, a sense of belonging, protection, and camaraderie. These Homie Mentor teams serve many roles from best practices research including the "curbstone counselor" (CAP) as a Homie Counselor, the Homie Educator (*Umoja*), with a paradigm shift (*Roca*) that values gang involved youth and does not demonize or pathologize them. This after-school community-based program provides wrap-around services where students are involved in Ethnic Studies, self-care and the Leader Within classes, Young Womyn/Men's Circle, civic engagement with paid internships, Homies Study Table, Homies Counseling, and Unity Dinners. In all of these spaces, there is home-grown, grassroots study hall for students in and out of school that focuses on their development and growth.

Figure 7.2 and Table 7.1 are learning opportunities as a part of this model.

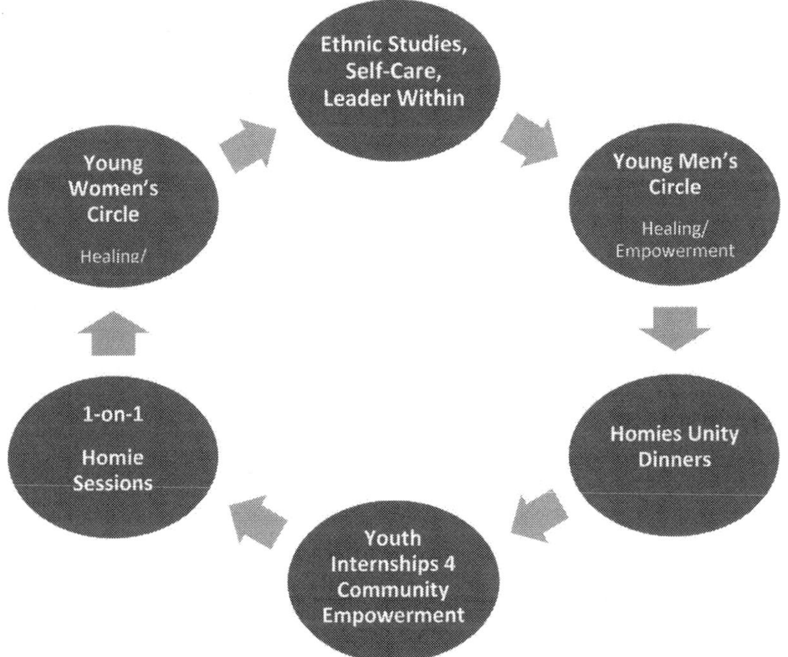

Figure 7.2 Homies Empowerment Learning Spaces.

Table 7.1.
Homies Empowerment Strategies

Programs	Target Audience	Purpose	Measurable Outcomes
Ethnic Studies, Self-Care and the Leader Within Course (Best practices research, Umoja cultural roots) *12 week cycles	Middle, High-school age youth at various sites, average class size 15–30, ages 14–24	– Learn history – Develop socio-emotional skills – Find sense of purpose	1. Knowledge of Self 2. Increased Self-Esteem* 3. Creating Goals 4. Academic plan*
Gender-Based Violence Workshops *6 week cycles	High-school age youth at various sites, average class size 15–30	– Analyze gender-based violence, human and child trafficking, prostitution, suicide amongst queer youth of color, as well as teen pregnancy, domestic violence, and rape.	1. Address sexism/ patriarchy 2. Create action plans to address prostitution* 3. Reduce hate crimes*
Homies Unity Dinners *weekly	All ages, 100–150 in local rec center	A weekly gathering where youth from rival neighborhoods come together to break bread with various guest speakers of all backgrounds.	1. Gang unity 2. Tutoring-improve grades* 3. Job skills 4. Less crime involvement*
Jornalero (Day-Laborer) Breakfast Program *weekly	High-school age youth at various sites, average group size 15-30	– Gang members as leaders, giving back – Opportunity to show initiative in a civic engagement program	1. Job/Career Skills* 2. Develop responsibility 3. A way to give back
Youth Internships 4 Community Empowerment *daily	High-school age youth at various sites, average class size 15-30	– Develop various career skills – See the purpose of education	1. Job/Career Skills* 2. Develop responsibility 3. A way to give back

(Table continues on next page)

Table 7.1. (Continued)

Programs	Target Audience	Purpose	Measurable Outcomes
The Homie Counselor Sessions (Best practice research, CAP "Curbside Counselor") *daily	1-on-1 sessions, case load 15 students per counselor	Daily check-ins with youth in the program, especially focusing on those who are going through difficult situations	1. Increased self-esteem 2. Increased trust and commitment to the program
Homie Study Table *daily basis	High-school age youth at various sites, average class size 15–30	– Develop study habits – Receive needed academic support – Practice appreciating the process of learning	1. Consistent attendance 2. Increased assignment completion 3. Increase in grade point average

The Homies Empowerment model serves as a pedagogical strategy for school leaders who are struggling to find programming to effectively serve gang-involved youth. Unlike traditional trauma informed practices, which merely scratch the surface by treating the symptoms of abuse, neglect, feelings of powerlessness, this youth empowerment model is centered on helping young people find resiliency within by developing knowledge of self and fostering a strong sense of critical hope. Because many gangs serve as a protective factor, this learning model fosters a sense of *familia* through employing a cohort approach to creating a community of kinship and support for academic and life success. The personalized learning approach of the Homies Empowerment model creates a hand-in-hand relationship between the student, academic advisor, and mentor which sustains a secure base of support while the empowered youth build their own personalized road map to success.

The Homies Empowerment model subscribes to a specific, asset-based theory of action. Homies Empowerment believes that if gang involved/impacted Latino youth (1) are shown respect, love and are honored as part of a warrior society; (2) are taught their history, their contributions to this society; (3) are not given up on, but supported at every stage of their development; and (4) are given a way to channel their energy towards self and community improvement projects or outcomes, then gang involved/impacted Latino youth will feel a sense of community, purpose and will take the necessary steps to chart a course for their life path and for their involvement in their own communities in a positive way.

Quantifiable measures of success of the impact of the Homies Empowerment model include (1) enrollment in school/vocational programs, (2) improved attendance, (3) reduction in the amount of suspensions/expulsions in school, (4) increase in grade point averages, (5) increase in graduation rates from high school, (6) higher acceptance rates into college, and (7) reduction in involvement with the criminal justice system. This approach seeks to create measurement tools that can assess a young person's self-esteem before they enter the program and after various intervals such as after one semester, one year, and three years as well.

The Homies Empowerment model brings together multiple services (career vocational and technical education, truancy support, academic services, dropout prevention, therapy, career, and college counseling) within one program to support gang-involved youth. While school and district leaders continue to search for solutions to gang problems, the Homies Empowerment model is a strategy that does not seek to fix the problem, but instead builds upon the many strengths and assets gang-involved youth carry with them to school every day.

CONCLUSION

The historical demonizing of Latino gangs through television, the news media, and Hollywood films has created a moral panic and social consciousness that gang membership is a problem to be solved or eradicated. This deficit-based perspective overlooks the positive attributes associated with gangs and gang membership. This oversight forgoes opportunities to build upon the assets Latino gangs instill within their members. With most contemporary intervention programs attempting to "correct" the gang problem, Homies Empowerment offers a youth development model for schools and school districts to better serve gang-involved, Latino youth. Departing from traditional frameworks, the Homies Empowerment model centers around building a sense of belonging, ethnic pride, and community commitment. Through the implementation of this community-based model of youth development, gang membership is no longer seen as a barrier to progress, but instead as a foundation on which to help youth build the necessary skills and mindsets to be productive citizens.

ACKNOWLEDGMENT

The chapter title "Standing With the Demonized" derives itself from a phrase that Father Gregory Boyle uses to depict the work of Homeboy Industries.

REFERENCES

Baglivio, M., Greenwalk, M., Howell, J., & Jackowksi, K. (2014). Serious, violent, and chronic juvenile offenders. *Criminology & Public Policy, 13*(1), 83–116.

Bates, K., & Swan, R. (2013). Juvenile delinquency in a diverse society. Thousand Oaks, CA: SAGE.

Bloom, D., Irvy, R., & Thompson, S. L. (2010). Building a learning agenda around disconnected youth. *MDRC, Bill and Melinda Gates Foundation*, 1–41.

Brown, M. (2002). *Gang nation: Delinquent citizens in Puerto Rican, Chicano and Chicana narratives*. Minneapolis, MN: University of Minnesota Press.

Cohen, A. (1955). *Delinquent boys: The culture of the gang*. New York, NY: Free Press.

Cruz, C. (2010). *Norteños/Sureños: Time to 'bang' for freedom, brief history of Mexican Mafia & Nuestra Familia*. Oakland, CA: Making Changes Press.

De Los Santos, N. (Director), Racho, S. (Director), & Domínguez, A. (Director) (2002). *The bronze screen: 100 years of the Latino image in American cinema* [Documentary]. United States: Questar.

Duran, R. (2009). Legitimated oppression: Inner-city Mexican American experiences with police gang enforcement. *Journal of Contemporary Ethnography, 38*(2), 143–168.

Duran, R. (2013). *Gang life in two cities: An insider's journey*. New York, NY: Columbia University Press.

Ericson, R., Baranek, P., Chan, J., & Ericson, R. (1991). *Representing order: Crime, law, and justice in the news media*. Toronto, CN: University of Toronto Press.

Fattah, D. (1987). The House of Umoja as a case study for social change. *Annals of the American Academy of Political and Social Science, 494*(1), 37–41.

Flannery, D., Singer, M., & Wester, K. (2001). Violence exposure, psychological trauma, and suicide risk in a community sample of dangerously violent adolescents. *Journal of the American Academy of Child & Adolescent Psychiatry, 40*(4), 435–442.

Fordham, S., & Ogbu, J. (1986). Black students' school success: Coping with the "burden of 'acting white' ". *The Urban Review, 18*(3), 176–206.

Franco, A. (2018). Threads of the Zoot Suit Riots: How the initial explanations for the riots hold up today. *Voces Novae, 10*(4), 1–29.

Gang. (n.d.). In *MerriamWebster.Com*. Retrieved March 13, 2018, from https://www.merriamwebster.com/dictionary/gang

Howell, J. (n.d.). Youth gang drug trafficking and homicide: Policy and program implications. Retrieved from https://www.ojjdp.gov/jjjournal/jjjournal1297/gang.html

Jennings, L., Parra-Medina, D., Hilfinger-Messias, D., & McLoughlin, K. (2006). Toward a critical social theory of youth empowerment. *Journal of Community Practice, 14*(1–2), 31–55.

Jessor, R., Van Den Bos, J., Vanderryn, J., Costa, F., & Turbin, M. (1995). Protective factors in adolescent problem behavior: Moderator effects and developmental change. *Developmental Psychology, 31*(6), 923–933.

Loeber R., & Farrington, D. (1998). Serious and violent juvenile offenders: Risk factors and successful interventions. Thousand Oaks, CA: SAGE.

Melde, C., Taylor, T., & Esbensen, F. (2009). "I got your back": An examination of the protective function of gang membership in adolescence. *Criminology, 47*(2), 565–594.

McCorkle, R., & Miethe, T. (1998) The political and organizational response to gangs: An examination of a "Moral panic" in Nevada. *Justice Quarterly, 15*(1), 41–64.

National Gang Center. (2017). Demographics: Race/ethnicity of gang members. Retrieved from https://www.nationalgangcenter.gov/Survey-Analysis/Demographics.

Neimann, Y., Romero, A., Arredondo, J., & Rodriguez, V. (1999). What does it mean to be "Mexican"? Social construction of an ethnic identity. *Hispanic Journal of Behavioral Sciences, 21*(1), 47–60.

Ogbu, J. (1974). *The next generation: An ethnography of education in an urban neighborhood.* Orlando, FL: Academic Press.

Pizarro, M. (1998). 'Chicano power!': Epistemology and methodology for social justice and empowerment in Chicana/o communities. *International Journal of Qualitative Studies in Education, 11*(1), 57–80.

Rios, V. (2010) Navigating the thin line between education and incarceration: An action research case study on gang-associated Latino youth. *Journal of Education for Students Placed at Risk, 15*(1–2), 200–212.

Rodriguez, M., & Morrobel, D. (2004). A review of Latino youth development research and a call for an asset orientation. *Hispanic Journal of Behavioral Sciences, 26*(2), 107–127.

Rosenfield, R., Quinet, K., & Garcia, C. A. (Eds.) (2010). *Contemporary issues in criminological theory and research* (2nd ed.). Belmont, CA: Wadworth, Cengage Learning.

Spergel, I., & Curry, G. (1993). The national youth gang survey: A research and development process. In A. P. Goldstein & C. R. Huff (Eds.), *Gang intervention handbook* (pp. 359–400). Champaign, IL: Research Press.

Stanton-Salazar, R. (2001). *Manufacturing home and despair: The school and kin support networks of U.S.-Mexican youth.* New York, NY: Teachers College Press.

Stinchcomb, J. (2002). Promising (and not-so-promising) gang prevention and intervention strategies: A comprehensive literature review. *Journal of Gang Research, 10*, 27–45.

Thompson, C., Young, R., & Burns, R. (2010). Representing gangs in the news: Media constructions of criminal gangs. *Sociological Spectrum, 20*, 409–432.

Valenzuela, A. (1999). *Subtractive schooling: U.S. Mexican youth and the politics of caring.* New York, NY: State University of New York Press.

Villenas, S., & Deyhle, D. (1999). Critical race theory and ethnographies challenging the stereotypes: Latino families, schooling, resilience and resistance. *Curriculum Inquiry, 29*(4), 413–445.

Wong, N., Zimmerman, M., & Parker, E. (2010). A typology of youth participation and empowerment for child and adolescent health promotion. *American Journal of Community Psychology, 46*(1–2), 100–114.

Yosso. T. (2005). Whose culture has capital? A critical race theory discussion of community cultural wealth. *Race Ethnicity and Education, 8*(1), 69–91.

CHAPTER 8

LEARNING THROUGH PHOTO-ESSAY CREATION

Identity of Working-Class Immigrants

Kyung-Hwa Kay Yang

ABSTRACT

This chapter highlights the identity reconstruction of adult immigrants and its implication for their agency development. It draws on a photo-essay creation project conducted with a group of adult immigrants regarding their experiences of immigration to the United States. The chapter offers adult educators practical insight into the use of photo-essays for teaching and also reminds adult educators of the importance of recognizing and upholding diverse immigrants' identities.

INTRODUCTION

This chapter explores the process of creating a photo-essay (an essay accompanied by related photographs) as a tool for adult literacy education involving working-class immigrants and discusses this practice in relation

Convictions of Conscience: How Voices From the Margins Inform Public Actions, and Educational Leadership, pp. 141–160

to identity. It is based on a multi-session project, in which a group of adult immigrants shared their experiences through autobiographical writing combined with photography. The project was designed on the premises that autographic writing can enable adult learners to broaden their views of themselves and the world around them (Karpiak, 2000) and that participatory photography (photography of one's own experiences) is useful to helping language learners convey the meanings of their experiences and share them with one another (Gallo, 2001).

The questions that I ask in this chapter are as follows: What is the role that photography plays in the process of participants' writing? How does the creation of photo-essays influence the lives of adult immigrants? What does this approach suggest about their identities? I, first, locate my theoretical underpinnings in the discourse on arts-based approaches to transformative learning and examine the literature on the identities of adult immigrants who are language learners. I then provide an overview of the project and introduce the background to the project, and its participants and processes. My analysis of the project focuses on two parts: One is the ways in which photography helped the participants write, and the other, the type of experiences that they gained through the project. For my analysis, I draw on Rose's (2007) framework for visual methods, using the participant-created photo-essays, focus group, and individual interviews as three parts of data required for the framework. Based on this analysis, I discuss the implications of photo-essay creation for adult literacy education, specifically involving working-class immigrants who are also language learners, and its connection to the discourse on immigrant identity. Ultimately, I aim to contribute to adult education practice.

PHOTOGRAPHY AND ADULT LEARNING

The photo-essay project was conceptually informed by the literature on "imaginative" transformative learning. Mezirow (2000) defined transformative learning as:

> a process by which we transform our taken-for-granted frames of reference (meaning schemes, habits of mind, mindsets) to make them more inclusive, discriminating, open, emotionally capable of change, and reflective so that they may generate beliefs and opinions that will prove more true or justified to guide action. (p. 8)

For Mezirow, the goal of transformative learning is perspective transformation in a personal life. He argued that individuals can achieve the goal by critically reflecting on their assumptions and beliefs and questioning their behavior (Mezirow, 1991). His approach has been criticized for its narrowly defined transformative process, on the grounds that it downplays the importance of emotional, spiritual, and aesthetic aspects of learning (Merriam & Bierema, 2014). In this vein, calling for imaginative engagement, Dirkx (2001) contended:

> Transformative learning does not necessarily require extraordinary events in our lives, nor does it always require that we think deeply and analytically about our beliefs and assumptions. Dramatic opportunities for transformative learning reside in imaginative engagement with the everydayness of our lives. (p. 16)

As a medium for the imaginative engagement, Dirkx paid attention to visual images and underscored that emotionally laden images, in particular, can allow adult learners to give meaning to their emotions, such as joy, sadness, and anger. Through this process, as he argued, they become more fully aware of their experiences and consequently can experience transformative learning.

In the discourse on imaginative transformative learning, Lawrence and Cranton (2009) defined transformative learning as "coming to see ourselves and the world around us from a different and more open perspective" (p. 313). Photography took center stage of their discussion of transformative learning. As the authors explained, perspective transformation requires flexibility in locating vantage points. When learners begin to discover new aspects of an ordinary object through a camera, they can also learn to look at their lives from a different perspective, which lays the groundwork for transformative learning. Similar to Dirkx (2001), they argued that photography as a form of artistic expression can bring learners' knowledge "from the unconscious that can contribute to transformative learning" (p. 317).

The role that participatory photography can play in imaginative transformative learning has been discussed by Clover (2006), who saw that participatory photography can allow adult learners to become artists on their own right by encouraging them to use their imagination. This process, she argued, empowers them because it inspires them to "invent new lives, new spirits, new spaces, and new forms of social engagement" (p. 288), and thus can lead to transformative learning.

I, too, bore witness to the ways in which participatory photography can contribute to empowering adult learners (Yang, 2014). In a project that I initiated, a group of adult learners, who were socioeconomically marginalized, learned digital photography, took photographs of their experiences, and exhibited their work in public. In interviews, they suggested that the project afforded a space for them to develop a sense of agency, specifically the agency of intentions (Ortner, 2001), which emphasizes the capacity to organize one's life "within a framework of their own terms, their own categories of value" (p. 80). Although immediate consequences on their lives were unknown, the project suggests that participatory photography can contribute to empowering them, as the participants showed their intention to change their lives for the better. As Clover (2006) asserted, participatory photography is essentially "learning for empowerment, action, and agency" (p. 276) and can assist socially marginalized adult learners who seek transformation of their lives.

Gallo (2001) suggests that participatory photography can be particularly useful in promoting transformative learning among working-class immigrants who are also language learners. In her English teaching project, she observed that participatory photography offered them an additional means to convey the meanings of their experiences, which in turn enabled them to reflect on their experiences and engage in meaningful conversations with one another. Consequently, she argued, "learners are personally transformed and may begin to take actions that lead to external transformations as well" (p. 115). Her analysis, however, stops short of details on how individual learners used photographs as a source for identity construction. In this chapter, I aim to elaborate on this.

ADULT IMMIGRANTS AND IDENTITY

I situate my conceptual ideas at the intersection of language learning and identity. Based on the premise that language is critical to identity construction, Norton (2013) states:

> By extension, every time language learners speak, read or write the target language, they are not only exchanging information with members of the target language community, they are also organizing and reorganizing a sense of who they are and how they relate to the social world. As such, they are engaged in identity construction and negotiation. (p. 4)

In discussing how learners come to learn a target language, Norton contended that the psychological concept of "motivation," which is prevalent in the theory of second language learning, is inadequate because it disregards power relations in which the learners situated. Even highly motivated learners, she explained, may be unable to learn a target language in a racist, sexist, or other socially unjust environment and can be unfairly regarded as unmotivated. Norton, thus, used the concept of "investment" instead. It refers to the idea that individuals invest in language learning as they expect to gain from it. As she put it:

> If learners "invest" in the target language, they do so with the understanding that they will acquire a wider range of symbolic resources (language, education, friendship) and material resources (capital goods, real estate, money), which will in turn increase the values of their cultural capital and social power. (p. 6)

Norton (2013), informed by poststructuralist feminist scholarship, argued that the increased values and power allow the learners to reassess their sense of themselves. According to her, learning a language means a path to identity reconstruction for adult immigrants. Identity is a central tenet in poststructuralist feminist scholarship and often is used interchangeably with the word "subjectivity." Both indicate a sense of oneself in relationship with other people. St. Pierre (2000) asserts that individuals can have two types of subjectivity: one is persistent in social norms such that individuals are forced to take it, and the other, actively constructed by them. This type of subjectivity is regarded as a "precondition of agency" (Allen, 2002, p. 135). To adult immigrants, thus, learning a language means not simply being able to communicate in a target language, but more importantly reconstructing their identities and acquiring agency as well.

Still, the process in which immigrants who are also language learners acquire agency through language learning remains obscure. Miller (2010) offers a more nuanced account of this in the U.S. context. As she explained, because those learners act in "ideologically infused spaces" (p. 481), in which monolingualism is considered a norm, their desire to learn and capacity to act toward learning English are not necessarily individually mobilized, but socially constituted as a "normal or recognizable action for adult immigrants" (p. 484); because they may assume a socially and ideologically constructed subjectivity (that is, they are deficient English speakers who must learn English to survive in this country, learning English does not always lead to agency or empowerment, but rather conformity to an ideological norm. Miller contended that agency is "discursively" developed, in the sense that it requires conscious conversations between learners and educators so that the learners come to reject ideologically constructed identities while the educators urge them to aspire to more advantageous ones—actively constructed subjectivity, in St. Pierre's (2000) term. Miller suggests that educators need to intervene in adult immigrants' identity development deliberately in order to assist them in acquiring agency through language learning.

Taken together, Norton's (2013) construct of investment is helpful to understanding how adult immigrants learn a dominant language and brings to the fore the importance of creating an inclusive environment for their learning. Language acquisition is a useful act. It, however, does not necessarily lead to their agency development from a poststructuralist perspective insofar as learners hold an ideologically constructed identity as immigrants. To contribute to agency development, it is important for educators to help them unsettle the identity and consciously reconstruct their own with higher aspiration. Such deliberate identities can lead them to invest more in their language learning (Miller, 2010). At issue is how to effectively disrupt the ideologically fabricated identity. I tapped into this question by using photo-essays as a medium in the following project.

THE PHOTO-ESSAY PROJECT

The project was carried out as an extension of my long-term involvement in adult education research conducted in partnership with a local education program designed for low-income adults in a Midwest metropolitan area. Over the past few years, I organized photography and video production projects for graduates of the program and studied the implications of the media for adult learning. The photo-essay project was carried out in the context. For eight weeks, the participants convened together for two hours every week, took digital photographs related to their experiences on immigration, and wrote autographic essays. The final photo-essays were compiled in a book, and a copy of the book was distributed to each participant. This creative process was followed by focus group and individual interviews.

Participants

The participants were recruited from the current and former students of a course of the aforementioned education program, which was specifically designed for Spanish speakers. A flyer was circulated among the population via e-mail and also in class. To participate, they were asked to write a short essay (up to 500 words) about their immigration experiences in either Spanish or English. They were also informed that the project was part of my research, meaning that they would be interviewed individually and that their photo-essays would be analyzed. Their participation in my research, however, was not required to join the photo-essay project. They were given the opportunity to make a decision as to their participation in my research once they complete the project. The purposes of this setup were to encourage more people to participate in the creation of photo-essays without the obligation to participate in my research.

Those who submitted the essays were all invited to the project. Of the nine people who initially joined the project, six completed it. Those who completed all consented to participate in my research and granted me the permission to use their photo-essays as my data. Of the six participants, one was a U.S. born citizen married to a first-generation immigrant, and the others were first-generation immigrants. Because I focus on immigrants in this chapter, my analysis is limited to these five participants. The basic demographics of the participants are shown in Table 8.1. All the names are pseudonyms chosen by the participants or me to protect their privacy.

Table 8.1.
Demographic Information of Participants

Name	Gender	Age	Approx. number of years in the U.S.	Highest formal education (country)
Martin	Male	50s	25	Associate degree (U.S.)
Photo One	Male	50s	30	Some college courses (U.S.)
Diez	Male	30s	15	Some college courses (U.S.)
Juan	Male	30s	15	High school (home country)
María	Female	40s	15	Associate degree (home country)

The education level of the participants is secondary graduation or higher. Four finished secondary education in their home country, and four took the GED in the United States. As María explained, the reason why she took the test despite the fact that she had earned an associate degree in her home country was that taking the test was less expensive than proving her degree. Three of the five participants took some college courses in the United States. In self-evaluation, most of them marked "good" as their Spanish proficiency level and "adequate" as their English proficiency level. They all worked full-time and indicated their income class as either low or lower middle.

The Creation of Photo-Essays

The project culminated in the creation of a collective photo-essay book, which included six short essays each of which was accompanied by several photographs taken by the individual participants. All the essays were written in English (approximately 500 words each), and four of them were also written in Spanish by the authors. Detail on the production processes is as follows.

The project began with the participants' practicing photography and sharing their stories. Based on my previous participatory photography project (Yang, 2014), I gave a prompt each week, including: "Take photographs of a person who you know well or an object that is interesting to you," "take photographs of your neighborhood or a place that you like or is important to you," and "take photographs related to your immigration story." The prompts moved from general to specific to the topic of the project. Each week, the participants selected several from the photographs they had taken and sent them to me electronically. I then uploaded the photographs onto a secure web depository. The participants and I viewed them together in group sessions.

In parallel, the participants developed their essays gradually. They began by sharing the stories written in the process of recruitment and further brainstormed the topics of their essays. The participants then wrote essay outlines and shared them in pairs. This was to allow them to talk about their stories at an intimate level and also to have a chance to learn how to write from each other. This peer support was followed by a whole group discussion, in which the individual participants received feedback from the group. María, who had few opportunities to discuss in group sessions due to her illness, decided to use the essay she had written (in Spanish) in the process of recruitment as the basis of her final project.

The individual participants and I agreed that we would work together until we both would become happy with their essays. They sent their drafts to me via e-mail. I then offered individual feedback, and they revised their drafts. This iterative process continued a few times for almost every participant. Not all the participants, however, worked at the same pace. Those who completed their essays early were encouraged to write them in Spanish as well. This was to enable them to engage in literacy practice in their own language. Four of the five participants wrote their essays in both languages. María, who had written her essay in Spanish, wrote an English version through the iterative process.

Upon completion of the essays, the individual participants were asked to select several from the photographs they had taken and to design the layout of their pages in the final book. After having the essays proofread, I put the individual essays and photographs together in a digital file with reference to each participant's page layout and sent the file to a local printing company to produce multiple copies of a complied photo-essay book.

Focus Group and Interviews

Toward the end of the project, I facilitated an hour-long focus group discussion among the participants. The questions asked in the discussion included: (1) What was the best and the most challenging part of the project? (2) How did photography help you think and write? (3) If you gained anything you had not expected to gain, what is it? (4) Do you see any changes in your life after the project? In addition to the focus group, I conducted individual interviews with each participant for approximately 45 minutes to listen to their immigration stories in detail and gain a deeper insight into their photo-essays.

WRITING, PHOTOGRAPHY, AND ADULT IMMIGRANTS' EXPERIENCES WITH THEM

I turn to Rose's (2007) analytical framework for visual methods, which emphasizes the importance of analyzing images in relation to the contexts where they were created and interpreted. The foci of my analysis are the interplay between writing and photography and the participants' experiences with the creation of photo-essays. I use the focus group and individual interviews as key sources of data and refer to the participant-generated photographs and their interpretations as secondary data and see them together in Rose's framework.

Complex Relationship Between Writing and Photography

My analysis suggests that the essay writing offered the participants an opportunity to think about and express their feelings, thoughts, and experiences and was the most rewarding experience for many of them. This was prominent, in particular, to Juan, Diez, and Photo One, who felt challenged by writing during the project. Juan said, "To make a point of what I am writing was the most challenging. OK, I can say, talk about my experience in different ways, you know, but finding lines and expressions, and putting them into words [was difficult]." When I asked whether the Spanish language would make a difference, his answer was negative. Although the difficulty of writing was inevitably due in part to the English language, he ascribed the difficulty not so much to the language itself as to structuring his essay. As he commented: "I can describe so many things in so many ways, but you have this certain number of words and certain space you can share with other people. After reading the whole thing [feedback], I paid more attention [to my thoughts and finally] I put it in my way." Juan entered into an implicit dialogue with his immediate audience (that is, the other participants and me) while developing his essay. This allowed him to reflect on his experience and thoughts more clearly. His essay was an outcome of this negotiation process and brought him a fulfilling experience.

Writing an essay was the most challenging and yet the best part of the project for Diez. As he commented: "I like, even though it was a little difficult, working on my essay, giving my feelings of how hard it was moving from one place to another ... I really enjoyed and am proud of that essay." When I asked him whether photography helped him write his essay, Diez responded:

> Yes, yes, photography helped me write the essay. First I came with the idea what I wanted to write and then took pictures and then translated the pictures into the essay and words, saying this picture means this and at one point how I felt.

Diez completed his photo-essay by taking photographs according to his initial ideas about his essay and then articulating each photo in written words. Diez was engaged in a porous, interweaving process between photography and writing.

Juan underwent a similar process. As he commented: "Yes, I think images helped me to write, to describe what is seen. Writing was complementing pictures that I wanted to take." He added that the "ability to put images and words together" was an unexpected gain. For him, photography was not simply instrumental to writing, but a leading medium through which to express his thoughts. While there are subtle differences in the ways in which Diez and Juan handled images and words in the process of creating their photo-essays, it is clear that photography helped them advance their writing.

This tandem process, however, was not common to all the participants. Writing was the most rewarding experience to Photo One as well. "I tried to explain what I feel and how I feel about this country. I wanna express it, I want to, but you know, how? That's the hard part," he said. "[But] I got the first step [through the project]." Although his feeling of accomplishment gained through writing was immense, he did not think that photography helped his writing; he, instead, experienced difficulty finding photographic objects to accompany his essay. "Crossing the [U.S. national] border" was the first thing that occurred to Photo One regarding immigration, but he could not figure out how to express it through photography. To overcome this difficulty, he said, he used his "imagination." As he put it:

> I was working on my essay and said how I am gonna take pictures about immigration, like people who are crossing the border or something like that. [However] first of all, I don't have time. I don't have too much money to go to the border to take pictures. I said to me, "Use your imagination," and I started looking everywhere.

Using his imagination, Photo One started to pay attention to his surroundings. One day he saw his neighbor pulling wildflowers from his yard.

That scene inspired him to describe immigrants as wildflowers, and so he photographed them. As he explained:

> When spring comes, these flowers come out. My neighbors start burning and cutting them from the grasses because they don't want this kind of flowers. They don't want them in their grasses and their gardens because they don't like them. You know, when people talk about immigrants and everything, I thought this flower belongs to this land. When we look at it very carefully, this flower is amazing. I try to leave some flowers on the side of some places of my garden because they are part of natural life. We must have it. By natural life I mean this place in the Midwest. These flowers belong to this land. [But] we don't want it. Why? We have to accept it. There may be a reason. We need to accept it.

Photo One implied that immigrants are part of the U.S. society, but constantly being outcast. Using his *imagination*, he turned an everyday object into an artistic expression. Although he thought that photography did not help him write, it seems that the process of taking photographs did help him think about immigrants and articulate his view.

Martin and María also experienced difficulty finding photographic objects to accompany their essays, saying that taking photographs was more challenging than writing. Martin, who had the most advanced English proficiency among the participants, did not seem to experience difficulty expressing himself in writing. He completed his essay earlier than any other participant. His experience with photography, however, was a different story. As he commented:

> What I learned is, it is hard for me to take a photograph. To find an object to take a picture and express what I want to express, there were some points when I tried, but I couldn't find anything. I had an idea, but I didn't have any object to take a picture of. So, I don't know. I just couldn't. I realized that those are my learning experience that I cannot associate my ideas with pictures.

In a similar vein, María, whose essay focused on her memories of her hometown and family, talked about her experience of creating a photo-essay as follows:

> My story was ready. I wrote it already because I like to write.... In the place where I live, there are things that remind me of my town, my country because there are a lot of people who are from my country.... But the thing is not everything can give the message you want to give in pictures.

Challenges in identifying photographic objects prompted María to pay close attention to her immediate surroundings and familiar objects. She gathered ordinary items, such as bread, coffee, or books, and important personal belongs and spread them out on a table to take a photograph. Pointing each item of the photograph, she explained:

> This is Mexican sweet bread. You always can find this type of bread in my house and coffee. For us, life is coffee. I love books. I love to read. I love to write. These are some letters that my nephew sent me in the beginning after I came to Chicago. This is me when I was 20…. This is what my sister did for me. She knitted it. These are part of my life or remembering things in my life.

Putting familiar objects together to take a photograph offered her immense emotional comfort. In her words: "[They] internally give me a lot of things to make me feel better. So I don't get more money out of this course, but *inside* I feel much better."

Similarly, Martin began to look around his surroundings to find photographic objects that matched his essay. In the essay, he narrates his inner conflict or confusion as an immigrant. "Despite the years gone by I am still aside, living in my own world," he wrote. While looking for an object at home to express his feeling, Martin accidentally saw three candles that his wife had purchased. He placed the candles in a circle and lit them. He then turned the lights off and took a picture of the candles glowing in the dark. He selected this photograph to cover the first page of his essay and explained the reason:

> I took the picture and looked it up in my camera. Then, it looked like infinity. Everything around was black. It's never ending. That's what I was thinking [when I wrote the essay]…. The candles represent me [contemplating,] "in which way do I need to go?"

For Martin, the black space of the photograph signifies the universe, which is open in front of him. His feeling of being lost in the universe is expressed through the three candles positioned in a circle, with neither beginning nor end, in the middle of the darkness—as if being deserted in an invincible somber labyrinth. Martin used this visual metaphor to represent his feeling as an immigrant.

In summary, Diez and Juan attributed their rewarding experience of writing to photography. In contrast, Photo One, María, and Martin thought that photography did not help them write. Instead they pointed to difficulty finding photographic objects to complete their photo-essays. This difficulty, in return, however, prompted them to pay attention to their familiar milieus and daily experiences, which led them to reflect on their lives more explicitly. Based on my analysis, it is not clear whether photography necessarily helps immigrant adults write better. It is suggested, however, that the creation of photo-essays can be instrumental to their reflections on their experiences. I inquire into this in the next section.

IMPACT OF THE PHOTO-ESSAY CREATION ON THE PARTICIPANTS' LIVES

In response to my question about changes in their lives after the project, the participants pointed to (1) a new understanding of their lives and (2) appreciation of photographic images. The understanding was evident, in particular, to Martin. "You got me think," he said:

> [I] started thinking of me as an immigrant and seeing myself in another way, I would say. I never, for 20 some years, I never stopped to think what I am doing here or things that you asked us to do or write about it.

This thinking, initially, made him confused about his identity as an immigrant; in the end, however, it enabled him to discover something important to his life. As Martin commented:

> The best part was discovering things. For a month I started thinking about what I have done as an immigrant, what my life has been here, how about succeeding in something or failing in something. I have been thinking into that. So if I had an idea whether I had succeeded, I wanted to take a picture of it, but I couldn't find anything.... At some point, I realized that it [my family] was the only thing that I have succeeded in. Maybe not personally, but I have created it.

The project disrupted Martin's everyday life. When he began to think about his life experience, he first felt overwhelmed by negative thoughts and feelings as if staying in a dark tunnel. But once he started to look around his surroundings to take photographs, this lent clarity to what mattered most to him. Martin realized that his family was part of his life as an immigrant and provided meaning to the life. His view on his life as an immigrant shifted from negative to positive. In a similar vein, Juan commented on his experience in the project as:

> Personally it was a good experience because I've never, or sometimes don't think any more about how I was here in this country.... I've never talked about it. I just remember this part of my life that I did share with so many people for those years living in this country. It makes me proud of what I have done so far and what I can do in the future.

Like Martin, Juan had rarely reflected on his life as an immigrant until participating in the project. It led him to think about his precarious childhood, the reason why he had decided to take a journey to the United States, and finally a family that he had created in the country. When he reflected on his experience, it moved from the adversity of the past to the security of the present, which assured him that he would be able to achieve even more in the future. The project helped him develop his confidence in himself as an immigrant. Juan revealed a different sense of himself as a result of his participation in the project. Diez's experience in the project was similar to Juan's. As he put it:

> I liked the experience of, while taking pictures, going back a little bit to the first years when I came to the United States.... Going back, I remember, I focused on hardship. So going back to my neighborhood to take pictures made me remember not where I come from, but how hard it was. It's a little easier now, but there are still difficulties. It was good experience to go back to where I first started.

The workshop offered Diez an opportunity to think about his beginning years as an immigrant. Like Juan, Diez came to the U.S. in his early 20s. Adjusting to a cold winter and learning a new language were the most challenging. Yet, he made efforts to establish his new life by advancing his education and working hard. He got married and became the father of two children. His experience over the past 15 years is reflected in his photo-essay. Looking back at the changes in his life, Diez came to realize that he in fact possesses the capacity to persevere adversaries and control his life, which is prominent in the last sentence of his essay: "I still miss my family, friends, and culture, but I'm working to build all those in my new home in [this city]."

Martin, Juan, and Diez regarded reflection on their lives as a major outcome of the project and revealed different, more empowered senses of self. Meanwhile, Photo One and María underscored their appreciation of photographic images as a major outcome of the project. They talked about how much thought they now put into photographs when they see or take them. Photo One commented:

> The first thing that changed is that when I see a picture, [I think] oh, that's nice. I mean any picture is interesting to me. Pictures mean a lot. I pay a lot of attention to pictures.... I think any picture you take is how you feel and how you think. It changes life, too. You see one picture, one horrible picture of suffering people. It changes your life.

Photo One not only came to appreciate photographic images aesthetically, but also realized the power of photographic images as a tool for self-expression and social impact. Similarly, María came to think of photography as a purposeful act and medium through which she can convey a specific meaning. As she put it:

> I like to take pictures with my phone and camera. But I think when you take a picture [simply] because you like something, it is different from taking a picture purposefully. You want to say something in the picture. It is different. That's something I learned. You have to think about what you want to say when you take that picture.

Taking photographs purposefully mattered to María because she believed that "pictures give a face to a story." The project helped her realize the power of photography as a vehicle to expressing her ideas and thoughts.

In brief, two themes emerged from my analysis. First, the creative process disrupted some participants' daily lives and prompted them to reflect on their lives as immigrants anew, if not for the first time. This led them to find new meaning and move forward in their lives and to realize what they had achieved in their lives. This assured them that they had the capacity to control their lives to a certain extent and would be able to achieve even more in the future. A new sense of agency was implicit in their comments. Second, some participants came to regard photography as a tool for self-expression and suggested that they were now more capable of conveying their beliefs and feelings through the tool. These two themes are not exclusive, but overlap and complement each other to a large extent, in that they both implied the participants' heightened sense of agency. This was particularly evident in the interviews with Juan and Diez, who indicated that photography was crucial to their writing.

PHOTO-ESSAYS AND IMMIGRANT IDENTITY

My analysis of the interviews suggests that participatory photography may not necessarily help immigrant adults write autobiographical essays. Some may feel a disjunction between photography and writing. As implied in the interview with Martin, it can be more likely to occur when learners have advanced writing skills. "I wrote the essay and then took some pictures to associate the pictures to the essay," he said. For him, the creation process flowed from writing to photography, not vice versa, as happened to Diez and Juan. Even in that case, however, participatory photography prompted Martin to look around and pay attention to his daily experience, which led him to think of his life as an immigrant differently from his initial thought expressed at the outset of the project. Therefore, despite the disjunction

Martin felt, I believe that the photography helped him reflect on his life more deeply than writing could have done alone.

Photo One also indicated the disjunction. As he said, he had a story first and then searched for photographic objects. Unlike Martin, however, his story had not been written until he completed his photography. English might have created an obstacle for him. In my observation, however, there was more than that. Each time he struggled to write his story, I believe that he organized his sense of self and relationship with the world (Norton, 2013). He had an idea, albeit vague, to share with other people in the beginning of the project, but it took time for him to articulate the idea. As mentioned in the previous section, Photo One wanted to express how he felt about the United States, but was not able to give voice to his feeling for a while. This was not due to his lack of English writing skills, but rather to his need for time to think and organize his identity in the sense of positioning himself in relation to other people and the world (St. Pierre, 2000).

The time he spent writing his essay reflects his journey to reconstructing his identity. The process of his looking around to find photographic objects might have eased the journey. Thus, although Photo One did not see a clear interplay between his story and photography, I believe that there was a connection between his "writing" and photography and that the connection contributed to his writing and articulation of his thought. I argue therefore that the creation of photo-essays on their lives can afford a space for adult immigrants to contemplate their identities as immigrants on their own and that participatory photography can facilitate this process.

As María pointed out, participatory photography can also provide a "face" to learners' stories to supplement their expressions. Provided that literacy practice is seen as a purposeful act people take to achieve certain goals in their lives (Papen, 2005), participatory photography can expand learners' literacy practices by adding visual means to the practices. It can also contribute to adult learners' second language acquisition. According to Larrotta and Serrano (2011), adults learn English effectively when they draw on the body of knowledge they have developed socially, culturally, and historically. As the majority of the participants implied, participatory photography can prompt adult learners who are also language learners to turn to this body of knowledge to begin their writing. Through the process of writing, they can learn English and develop dominant literacy practice. Although participatory photography may not entail the development of dominant literacy practice directly, it can pave the way for adult learners to develop language and literacy capacities by evoking their experience-based knowledge.

As examined earlier, learning a dominant language plays a significant role in immigrants' identity development (Miller, 2010; Norton, 2013). Based on the premise that the photo-essay project helped its participants learn English (especially writing), here I discuss the implications of photo-essay for the identity development within the discourse on transformative learning. Some participants indicated that the project did change their perspectives on the world. Martin, for instance, commented, "It's interesting to see we, as immigrants, are not in the same level.... [After this project] when I see somebody from my country or other countries, I try to talk to them and try to learn about their lives and how they view [the society]." This suggests that the project enabled Martin to have a more open, empathetic mind toward other immigrants. It is not so clear, however, to what extent the creation of photo-essays results in perspective transformation discussed in the literature on transformative learning (Lawrence & Cranton, 2009; Mezirow, 1991). Perhaps this is because the interviews were conducted immediately after the project was done. It is also due in part to obscurity in how to determine "transformation" (Merriam & Bierema, 2014). What is clearer, though, is that the project offered the participants a space in which to reflect on their experiences as immigrants and reconstruct their identities on their own terms.

Illeris (2014) argued that identity is a core concept of transformative learning; as it is established through interactions between an individual and society, it covers multiple dimensions of self from cognitive through emotional to social. From his perspective, identity transformation is key to transformative learning. In ever-changing contemporary society, he contended, individuals need to create, maintain, and change their identities in order to become competent and make right choices in their lives, especially when they have limited social resources. His argument suggests that identities should not be rigid, but flexible and ready to change. For possible changes, they need to be revisited and reshaped frequently. Whether or not the project enabled the participants to make right choices in their lives in the long run would warrant further inquiry. However, as shown in Juan's comment ("It makes me proud of what I have done so far and what I can do in the future"), it seems that the project allowed the participants to stop amid their busy lives to think and reestablish their individual identities as immigrants.

Through the project, Juan and Diez came to define themselves as a husband and father who envisions a better future as a member of society. Martin, who was too shy to talk about his life and submerged with negative thoughts about him in the beginning of the project, became more outgoing and came to see himself as someone who nonetheless achieved something dear to him. Photo One became confident to see that he could express himself through words and pictures. In comparison, it is not so clear how the project affected María's identity construction. The reason might be the fact that she was not able to be as involved in the group discussions as the other participants. This is suggestive of the importance of having dialogue and developing ideas with other people and over time for identity reconstruction.

Their reconstructed senses of self allowed them to think of themselves not simply as immigrants who struggle desperately to speak English and earn a minimum wage, as connoted in a social norm (Miller, 2010), but as individuals who possessed the agency to overcome obstacles and improve their lives. In doing so, they implicitly disregarded a socially and ideologically defined immigrant identity. By reconstructing their identities on their own terms, they developed agency as individuals living in and contributing to this society. As an individual's identity is developed through interactions between the individual and the society (Illeris, 2014), I believe that agency can also grow over time through the interactions. Terming this "engaged agency," Tennant (2012) argued, "[Although] our selves are forged and sustained within a culture, we all have unique biographies and unique predispositions and potentials. This is the source of our independence and our capacity for agency" (p. 171). Even though we all, including immigrants and natives, live with socially and ideologically constructed norms of who we are (St. Pierre, 2000; Miller, 2010), there are ways to challenge the norms and reconstruct new ones. The project suggests that the creation of photo-essays can offer adult immigrants an opportunity to bring to light and give meanings to their unique experiences and thereby allow them to unsettle socially and ideologically forged identities as immigrants and reconstruct their own. This process can fuel the agency to control their lives.

CONCLUSION

Autobiographical writing accompanied by participatory photography is a useful exercise to carry out in adult literacy education, especially involving immigrants who are also language learners. It can help them learn a target language effectively and at the same time better their lives in a country they have adopted as a second home by allowing them to reconstruct their identities as immigrants. Their language skills and new sense of selves can contribute to their agency development. Participatory photography, in particular, can facilitate the process of identity reconstruction by prompting them to look at their daily experiences from a new perspective. It may even help them write better and expand their literacy practices.

The creation of photo-essays can also benefit educators and educational leaders. Because, like learners, they live in and act within ideologically informed spaces (Miller, 2010), when there is a lack of conscious and deliberate efforts to discern different types of identities that working-class adult immigrants can take, they might impose an ideologically constructed identity on them and consequently hamper their identity reconstruction. By naming individual learners working-class immigrants collectively, they might unintentionally disregard different senses of self and different aspirations among the immigrants. Categorizing a collective identity as such can be risky and oppressive because it "can overlook internal differences" within a diverse group (Medina, 2003, p. 65). Adult immigrants' identities suggested in the photo-essays that learners create can offer educators and educational leaders an opportunity to learn about their diverse lives and aspirations from their perspectives. This learning process can help them avoid the risk of generalizing immigrant identities and also lay the groundwork for entering into discursive interactions with adult learners to help them reconstruct their identities.

Educators and educational leaders can encourage adult learners living in the margin of our society to disrupt their externally based, ideologically constructed identities and bring to the fore consciously reconstructed ones. In doing so, they can provide learners with a healthier and more satisfied sense of selves and a heightened sense of investment to engage in learning. They can also have an impact on the efforts to create a more inclusive society, especially in a time when hostility toward racial minority immigrants is increasingly devouring our society.

ACKNOWLEDGMENT

My sincere thanks and appreciation go to Randee Lipson Lawrence, professor emeritus from National Louis University, for her incessant support from the inception of the research project to the completion of the chapter.

REFERENCES

Allen, A. (2002). Power, subjectivity, and agency: between Arendt and Foucault. *International Journal of Philosophical Studies, 10*, 131–149.

Clover, D. (2006). Out of the dark room: Participatory photography as a critical, imaginative, and public aesthetic practice of transformative education. *Journal of Transformative Education, 4*(3), 275–290.

Dirkx, J. (2001). Images, transformative learning and the work of soul. *Adult Learning, 12*(3), 15–16.

Gallo, M. (2001). Immigrant workers' journey through a new culture: Exploring the transformative learning possibilities of photography. *Studies in the Education of Adults, 33*(2), 109–117.

Illeris, K. (2014). Transformative learning and identity. *Journal of Transformative Education, 12*(2), 148–163.

Karpiak, I. (2000). Writing our life: Adult learning and teaching through autobiography. *Canadian Journal of University Continuing Education, 26*(1), 31–50.

Larrotta, C., & Serrano, A. (2011). Adult learners' funds of knowledge: The case of an English class for parents. *Journal of Adolescent and Adult Literacy, 55*(4), 316–325.

Lawrence, R., & Cranton, P. (2009). What you see depends upon how you look: A photographic journey of transformative learning. *Journal of Transformative Education,* 7(4), 312–331.

Medina, J. (2003). Identity trouble: Disidentifiation and the problem of difference. *Philosophy and Social Criticism, 29*(6), 655–680.

Merriam, S., & Bierema, L. (2014). *Adult learning: Linking theory and practice.* San Francisco, CA: Jossey-Bass.

Mezirow, J. (1991). *Transformative dimensions of adult learning*. San Francisco, CA: Jossey-Bass.

Mezirow, J. (2000). Learning to think like an adult: Core concept of transformation theory. In J. Mezirow & Associates (Eds.), *Learning as transformation: Critical perspectives on a theory in progress* (pp. 3–33). San Francisco, CA: Jossey Bass.

Miller, E. R. (2010). Agency in the making: Adult immigrants' accounts of language learning and work. *TESOL Quarterly, 44*(3), 465–487.

Norton, B. (2013). *Identity and language learning: Extending the conversation.* Clevedon, UK: Multilingual Matters

Ortner, S. B. (2001). Specifying agency: The Comaroffs and their critics. Interventions: *International Journal of Postcolonial Studies, 3*, 76–84.

Papen, U. (2005). *Adult literacy as social practice: More than skills*. New York, NY: Routledge.

Rose, G. (2007). *Visual methodologies: An introduction to the interpretation of visual materials*. London, England: SAGE.

St. Pierre, E. A. (2000). Poststructural feminism in education: An overview. International. *Journal of Qualitative Studies in Education, 13*, 477–515.

Tennant, M. (2012). *The learning self: Understanding the potential for transformation.* San Francisco, CA: Jossey-Bass.

Yang, K. (2014). Participatory photography: Can it help adult learners develop agency? *International Journal of Lifelong Education, 33*(2), 233–249.

CHAPTER 9

THE INFLUENCE OF NEOLIBERALISM AND NEW MANAGERIALISM ON ESL PROGRAMMING AND INSTRUCTION IN COMMUNITY COLLEGES

Raul W. Cantu and Ann K. Brooks

ABSTRACT

This chapter describes how a neoliberal economic and political ideology affects English as a Second Language programming, instruction, and immigrant students at community colleges. We explore why immigrant students attend community colleges, what they hope to gain, and the exclusions and challenges they face there. We draw on research literature, written policy at the national and state levels, grey literature produced by foundations and not for profit organizations, and observation and documents from a large urban community college in the southwest of the United States. We conclude with a discussion of the damage neoliberal policies bring to community colleges' programming and instruction and identify opportunities for moving forward.

Convictions of Conscience: How Voices From the Margins Inform Public Actions, and Educational Leadership, pp. 161–180

INTRODUCTION

This chapter examines the influence of neoliberal ideology and managerialist practices in community colleges on English as a Second Language (ESL) programming and instruction and explores some of the possible effects on immigrants and other English language learners attempting to acquire the language skills to compete in the workforce or continue in higher education. We begin with Raul's story as a young second language learner and current ESL instructor in a community college and then draw on the research literature and the practices in one community college in the southwestern United States.

RAUL'S STORY

It's true what they say about our memory; certain things can take us back in time. It happens to me every semester on the first day of class. As I look out at my students' faces I see myself almost 50 years ago. My memories flood back to me and sweep me to the first time I heard English. I was 6 years of age and it was raining on my first day of school. Being on the east-side of Houston that drizzly August morning all the other children looked like me. They had brown skin and dark hair like me, but I did not realize they were different. I had not realized another way of speaking existed until our teacher, a very nice White lady, began to speak. The children sat up and then laughed in unison as the teacher said something to the class and twirled an umbrella. In that moment, I realized I was alone with my language with no way to understand those around me nor any way to communicate with anyone. I did not realize it at the time, but I had instantly become "the other."

I just sat there because I had promised my mother, in Spanish of course, that no matter what happened that first day of school, I would be "good boy." I could not do what I really wanted, which was to run out of that little room and back to the only world I had ever known. I wanted to run back to the cotton fields and down the hard-packed dirt roads until I could not run anymore. So I just sat there with my little brown hands crossed as if I were in church praying. I had no words. I could not tell the teacher that I thought she was funny, too. Instead, I sat there at my little wooden desk and felt like I was someone seeing the classroom from a distance. I felt that although I was there in that little classroom, I was deaf, mute and invisible. Now, nearly 50 years later, I would describe that experience as surreal. To this day, I can clearly recall the cool misty wetness of the air of that early morning walk to school, alone. I remember the teacher's twirled umbrella, and the children's laughter. It all felt like I was living in a dream world reality. I did not cry or feel anxious. That moment, so early in my education, was not bad, or good for that matter, but only something that I expected to awaken from just as from a dream.

The problem for me and many second language learners is that living without English is not just a dream. It is reality. I was always aware of my isolation every time I stepped out of the house and away from my mother's protection and nurturing kindness which was all delivered in Spanish. My sense of alienation had been present to varying degrees throughout my education. Now, nearly half a century later I remember my very first day of school. Each semester, I recall that fall morning because I have sat where my students sit, in ignorance and hope. However, I have not always related to my students in this way. I began teaching ESL to adults in 2001, and I distinctly remember walking down the college's long shiny hallways with another faculty member, and I remember thinking to myself, "*now I'm not the other*."

As I grew as an instructor and felt more secure in my position, I was able to realize my students were just like that scared little kid who was suddenly thrown into a world without a language with which to communicate. Their goals became more than a function of my job. Their desire to learn English struck me deeply, and I realized students are not " 'objects' into which teachers pour prescribed knowledge" (Freire, 1998, p. 4), the understanding I had been conditioned to, but autonomous learners with valuable experiences (Freire, 1998), ways of knowing and hopes.

One fall day, I began to wonder. Are my students being served by our ESL program and whose interests are being served by the way ESL program planning is being done and instruction delivered? These questions began to surface like some trapped air bubble that has found its way to the surface. I was in my office working on some student essays and looking out the window as a late afternoon fog rolled in from the north when a student came to me for help with her abusive relationship. I realized in that moment that our students need more than just English grammar skills from me. They need cultural capital as well (Warriner, 2016). They need "an understanding of the way things work in the USA and contacts/networks that help them acquire information to reach their goals to deal with the difficulties of their daily lives" (Warriner, 2016, p. 504). However, recently, I became aware that the college may not be aware of the obstacles community college ESL students face every day and have seen the ways students can be seen as a commodity by a college.

NEOLIBERALISM AND MANAGERIALISM IN COMMUNITY COLLEGES

Community colleges have historically been the most viable educational option for students from lower socioeconomic backgrounds and from marginalized populations. They have been characterized as educational options with public support, open access, learning support and a commitment to teaching (Ayers, 2005). However, neoliberal ideology has become increasingly evident in community college discourse (Ayers, 2005) and in practices such as reconceptualizing students as consumers and faculty as service-providers, hiring increasing numbers of per course faculty, seeing higher education as a business rather than a public good (Connell, 2013; Couturier, 2005; Giroux, 2002; Levin, 2005), and using managerialist practices imported from business in response to calls for efficiency and shifts in funding.

Neoliberalism is an ideology with many supporters. Faculty can often see administrators as instruments of neoliberalism and the causes of the challenges faced by both faculty and students in higher education today. Posecznick (2014) suggested, speaking from his hybrid position as both faculty and administrator, "it seems unfair to impugn an entire class of person for the ills of the era. Clearly, more nuance is required" (p. 5). Nuance is required because such a position fails to capture the complexity of the impact the economic and political zeitgeist has on community colleges as systems in which students, faculty, leaders, and communities make daily choices to resist, comply with, or find ways to protect access and learning opportunities.

Neoliberalism has been interpreted in many ways (Jackson, 2011; Olssen, 2006; Schram, 2014). The term is enigmatic because it describes an ideology that is neither *neo* nor *liberal,* as most Americans would interpret the words (Brown, 2003). It is not a new ideology, but a return to certain pre-Keynesian ideas about the creation of wealth and how it should be dispersed (Brown, 2003). However, while Keynesian welfare economics calls for government intervention to support society (Brown, 2003), neoliberal economics demands a competitive market-driven society with less government intervention (Brown, 2003; Sterne, 2006). Paradoxically, while neoliberal ideology calls for liberating market mechanisms, in practice, it enacts intensive interventions on both individuals and institutions (Shear & Zontine, 2010).

For universities, not only in the United States, but in other Organisation for Economic Co-operation and Development (OECD) nations, too, neoliberal ideology has meant serving the interests of competition in the global economy (Peters, 2013). Three important tenets of this ideology are "privatization, efficiency, and personal responsibility" (Silva, 2016, p. 59). Privatization of public higher education in the U.S. typically emphasizes market-oriented capitalism, more philanthropic support, increased tuition, and more ways to generate revenue (Lambert & Callan, 2014). The tenet of efficiency and productivity pushes toward maximizing economic opportunity, while minimizing costs. In community colleges, this plays out, for example, as hiring more part-time faculty, maximizing enrollment, the use of technology, and partnering with business and industry (Levin, Kater, & Wagoner, 2006). The tenet of personal responsibility sees a person's success as the result of personal effort and choice rather than affected by structural conditions. For community colleges, where institutional funding is linked to enrollment numbers and low completion rates are linked to low income (Ma & Baum, 2016), this can mean prioritizing students more likely to complete a course of study over those more likely to struggle.

Linking national economic goals of substituting technology for labor, committing to global competitiveness, and bowing to the rule of market forces (Ayers, 2005) has had a profound impact on education across the lifespan. The purpose of education has shifted from developing citizens capable of participating in a democracy to producing human capital. In 1977, the president of the American Economic Association, made this point clear:

> Although it is obvious that people acquire useful skills and knowledge, it is not obvious that these skills and knowledge are a form of capital, that this capital is in substantial part a product of deliberate investment, that it has grown in Western societies at a much faster rate than conventional (nonhuman) capital, and that its growth may well be the most distinctive feature of the economic system. (Schultz, as cited in Ayers, 2005, p. 532)

Ayers (2005) identifies two prevalent discursive practices in community college mission statements based on a systematic sample of 144 colleges in the U.S. that were at the time members of the American Association of Community Colleges. The first is that of the learner as an economic resource educated by the institution to serve economic purposes. Typical is this example from a community college system in Massachusetts:

> The community colleges support the public system of higher education by ... developing partnerships with business and industry to provide job training, retraining, and skills improvement to ensure a workforce equipped to meet the needs of a changing economy. (p. 540)

The second discourse Ayers (2005) identified links the curriculum to a market function. This phrase from a mission statement from a community college in Maryland illustrates this: "That business, government and industry in the community have an opportunity to enhance their operations through specially tailored educational programs developed in consultation with the college" (p. 533). In other words, neoliberalism in community colleges has meant that economic competitiveness has become the accepted justification for decision making. An accountability system is being used to tie learning to economic goals and the measurement of student, faculty, and administrator outcomes has been implemented as a means of enforcing compliance. Nevertheless, while community college mission statements often espouse neoliberal principles, they also, in many cases, promote a community college as an institution committed to justice and democracy. This contradiction rests in the texts of community college mission statements (Ayers, 2005) and reflects the complexity of the context in which program decision-making takes place. These decisions affect ESL learners at community colleges

Managing higher education institutions according to neoliberal ideology is what has come to be called "new managerialism" (Deem & Brehony, 2005) or simply "managerialism." Managerialism, as we will use it here, refers to both the importation of management practices from business to higher education and practices aligned with furthering a neoliberal agenda. In higher education, according to Shepherd (2017), practices closely related to the ideology of managerialism are

- A greater separation of academic work and management activity
- Increased control and regulation of academic work by managers
- A perceived shift in authority from academics to managers and consequent weakening of the professional status of academics (p. 1)
- Those that "arguably have their roots in neoliberalism" (p. 1) are
- An ethos of enterprise and emphasis on income generation
- Government policy focused on universities meeting socioeconomic needs
- More market orientation, with increased competition for resources. (p. 2)

These management practices can be seen at work in the management of community colleges and affect both ESL students and faculty.

ADULT ESL LEARNERS IN COMMUNITY COLLEGES

The students registering for ESL classes at the Community College come from all over the globe, and many Asian immigrants come from "educated and elite families" (Teranishi, Suárez-Orozco, & Suárez-Orozco, 2011, p. 154). But the biggest number of immigrants in the U.S. are from Latin America and Mexico (Teranishi et al., 2011), and in fact, in 2014, there were approximately 17.9 million foreign born Latinos in the U.S. who had never graduated from high school (Migration Policy Institute, 2014). They vary by ethnicity, level of academic preparation, goals, and reasons for coming to the U.S. (Blumenthal 2002; Razfar & Simon, 2011; Stromquist,

2012; Teranishi et al., 2011). The typical community college ESL population ranges from individuals with a high amount of academic preparedness to those who may have little formal education (Blumenthal, 2002; Razfar & Simon, 2011; Stromquist, 2012; Teranishi et al., 2011).

The U.S. Census provides a list of the 17 languages spoken at home in U.S. households. In 2000, there were 47 million people living in the U.S who spoke a language other than English at home (Tucker, 2007), and of this population, 8.1% were considered to have limited English proficiency (LEP) (Ryan, 2013). However, by 2010, 59.5 million people in the U.S. spoke a language other than English at home, and of this number, 8.7% were classified as LEP (Ryan, 2013). ESL is the fastest growing area of study in the United States (Kim & Diaz, 2013; Tucker, 2007). Many students attending community college ESL classes do so as a first step to a postsecondary education and for better jobs. These learners "are a highly heterogeneous and complex group of students, with diverse gifts, educational needs, backgrounds, languages, and goals" (National Council of Teachers of English, 2008), and as one anthropologist, Weinstein-Shr noted, the reasons why adults want to become literate vary according to an individual's goal (as cited in Schalge & Soga, 2008). Most students are foreign-born, and a few are the children of immigrants, who have graduated from a U.S. high school, but attend community college ESL classes as they prepare "for *regular* college courses" (Razfar & Simon, 2011, p. 598, emphasis original) such as English composition and rhetoric.

Because all community college students taking ESL courses want to improve their English, they may seem like a homogeneous group. However, several differences exist within this student population. First, students vary in their reasons or goals for taking ESL courses (Becker, 2011; Blumenthal, 2002; Warriner, 2016). People enroll in community college ESL courses because they want to improve their lives (Becker, 2011; Bernstein, Hellmich, Katznelson, Shin, & Vinall, 2015; Kim & Díaz, 2013; Stromquist, 2012; Tucker, 2007). The three most common goals of ESL learners are to obtain college educations, improve their job experiences, and communicate better in their communities. These goals intersect for one group of ESL learners in community colleges, Generation 1.5 students. These ESL learners were brought to the U.S. as minors and then educated in the U.S. and have a combination of academic, workplace and social goals (Connerty, 2009). For many community college ESL learners, the goals are job-related and these students view ESL courses as a way to get a job quickly, get more pay or get a better work schedule (Razfar & Simon; 2011; Warriner, 2016). Other ESL learners' goals are social, such as wanting to improve their English enough to be able "to help their children with homework, and to communicate with the people in their community" (Larrotta, 2010, p. 200).

Many adult ESL learners are also a part of the U.S. workforce. A 2015 Bureau of Labor Statistics report estimated the number of foreign born workers in the U.S. as 26.3 million, making up 16.7% of the total U.S. workforce (U.S. Department of Labor, 2015). As Pimentel (2013) pointed out in her report for the U.S. Department of Education's Office of Vocational and Adult Education, strong English language skills are "essential to enabling adult learners to meet the real-world demands of postsecondary training and employment" (p. 3). Consequently, one reason many adult ESL learners attend a community college is to improve their opportunities for a better job or for advancement within their chosen career path.

NEOLIBERAL IDEOLOGY, MANAGERIALISM, AND ESL STUDENTS

In keeping with the current neoliberal economic and political discourse and managerial practices in higher education, an ideology of English language learning argues, "the user of English can, through effort and hard work, be transformed into a better form of human capital through increasing his/her formal or measurable competence in English" (Warriner, 2016, p. 495). The myth exists that learning English is enough for an immigrant in the U.S. to succeed even though there is evidence of "an immense gap in what immigrant learners intend to achieve and actual attainment of their academic and career goals" (Becker, 2011, p. 17). However, as Warriner (2016) points out, adult ESL students in the U.S. are routinely viewed through a deficit lens and:

> studying English in itself does not and cannot provide access to more than minimum-wage, entry-level employment. Disguised as self-improvement and self-sufficiency, the limited employment opportunities available to adult learners of English in the USA are aligned with the neoliberal goals of the state, its economy, and its educational institutions. (p. 498)

ESL learners are also affected by neoliberal economic legislation, which has meant for all higher education students less government funding per student and higher tuition costs (Mackay, 2014). And in line with the ethos of managerialism redolent of business, colleges and universities have increasingly moved away from being public spheres of learning to being marketed as competitive entities with financial goals (Fish, 2009). This has resulted in making international students very attractive to higher education institutions because they pay more to attend class, and so "Colleges and universities across the country heavily recruit international students to … in many cases, significantly add to the bottom line" (Allen, 2017, para. 13) and in our current global economy, U.S. institutions compete with universities worldwide for this additional revenue. In the United States, the Association of International Educators reported there were more than 1 million international students in 2016 supporting over 400,000 jobs and infusing roughly 32 billion dollars into the higher education labor market (Allen, 2017). At Community College for instance, an in-district state resident student pays $305 per ESL course while international nonresident students pay $1,184 per course.

In addition to providing a more robust revenue stream for community colleges, the academic backgrounds of international students often make them more academically prepared to take college classes than immigrant students (Teranishi et al., 2011), exploits these students' dreams of migrating to the United States, and contributes to the internationalization of the labor market. For instance, "an Indian national working in the Middle East said his 'lifelong dream' was to get an MBA in the United States and eventually settle after landing a good job" (Samee Ali, 2016, para. 28). International students enrolling in college ESL classes with a high school diploma from their native country and the challenges they face in college are different from the challenges faced by immigrant students (Teranishi et al., 2011). For international students, the challenges are acquiring English and learning about U.S. educational customs (Teranishi et al., 2011).

While immigrant ESL students are also challenged by the need to learn English and educational norms, their level of academic preparation varies more than international students because some immigrant students have had little exposure to formal schooling (Teranishi et al., 2011). A 2003 nationwide literacy survey revealed that 61% of the students entering adult ESL classes were below a basic literacy level (Tucker, 2007). These students take about 18 months to even become prepared enough to succeed in an ESL program since they must be taught basic academic skills such as the importance of doing homework first (Tucker, 2007). Collier (1995) reported it takes four to seven years for second language learners to develop academic language proficiency in English. Furthermore, even though some Asian students may be more academically prepared, they still struggle with the forms, styles, and uses of the English language (Tucker, 2007). Finally, undocumented immigrants between ages 25–64 are more likely to be poorly educated with 45% having less than a high school education (Passel & Cohn, 2009).

ESL students in community colleges vary in their legal status (Larrotta, 2010; Stromquist, 2012), and this may or may not affect their admission status. Many community colleges have an open-door admission policy, and the legal status of students is generally not a concern except in states that require colleges to verify their legal resident status before enrollment (Kim & Diaz, 2013). However, a student's resident status does affect their ability to receive federal financial aid, and this can pose a financial challenge for some students (Flores, 2016; Stromquist, 2012). Tuition costs for immigrants vary according to immigrant status and state policy. According to a report by the National Conference of State Legislatures, there are 20 states that provide in-state tuition rates for certain undocumented immigrants (Mendoza, 2015). In four of these states, the decision to provide in-state tuition for undocumented students was made by states' university systems while in the other 16 states, the in-state tuition for these students was mandated by the states' legislatures. State laws allowing in-state tuition for undocumented students have requirements that must be fulfilled, such as graduation from a local high school, acceptance to a public university and a promise to apply for legal citizenship when eligible. Six states, Alabama, Arizona, Georgia, Indiana, Missouri, and South Carolina, prohibit in-state tuition for undocumented students. Utah is the only state to provide mandates that permit privately funded scholarships for undocumented immigrant students at colleges and universities (Mendoza, 2015).

Current neoliberal economic ideology is felt in both the discourse and the national, state, and local policies affecting ESL learners. The focus on enterprise and entrepreneurship has led to a discourse of self-reliance in documents aimed at English language learners and immigrants and the reduction of public funding for education. ESL students are evaluated and treated differently in many community colleges according to their value as a revenue stream and potential as human capital for the labor needs of what is characterized as a globally competitive world. Colleges and universities worldwide are pitted against each other for international student enrollment.

A CLOSER LOOK AT ESL PROGRAMMING AND INSTRUCTION AT COMMUNITY COLLEGES

Programming and instruction at community colleges is affected by neoliberal ideology at the level of political and economic policy, managerial practices at the institutional level, and discourse at the level of socialization. Managerial strategies can affect ESL programming and instructional practices by increasing managerial control and regulation of academic work (Shepherd, 2017). The centralization of decision-making has been described as a "bureaucratic structure [that] has become more centralised and less democratic—in other words, more structured like a corporation" (Shear & Zontine, 2010, p. 38).

Colleges operating within the neoliberal paradigm do not necessarily aim to produce future public minded scholars (Giroux, 2014; Taylor, 2017), but individual entrepreneurs with credentials that can be marketed to corporations (Lynch, 2006). The discourse of students as budding entrepreneurs who "have full responsibility over their investment decisions and must aim to produce a surplus value" (Olssen, 2006, p. 219) for example, is an important element of the neoliberal cultural paradigm (Marttila, 2013), which is played out on multiple levels. We will use examples from Raul's teaching to illustrate these points.

Recently, one of Raul's students, a young woman from Thailand married to an American, asked how America can hope to become better if people like her cannot take English classes? She wanted to participate in and contribute to American society, but wondered how she could do that if the college does not let her learn English? She was referring, in this case, to the course schedules, which did not offer classes at times that she would be able to attend. When she said this, Raul recalled Teranishi et al. (2011) making this same point: "The barriers that immigrant students face in obtaining a postsecondary education have long-term economic and social consequences, not only for the students personally but also for the nation as a whole" (p. 157). In the end, Raul felt he did not have an answer, at least not a good one. He suggested to her that she ask to speak with the dean of student services to see if something could be done to help adjust the schedule. But he felt his answer was hollow, and he had to ask himself whether he is part of the solution or the problem.

The centralized control of functions like course scheduling means that they are often less responsive to the needs of students like the young woman from Thailand who spoke with Raul. For example, at Community College, the ESL department chair makes textbook selections for about 30 adjunct instructors. Adjuncts have little input into the selected text, and students often buy texts that their adjunct instructor does not actually use. At Community College for the semester Raul's student was referring to, a group of three faculty members scheduled all courses across eight campuses with limited to no input from adjunct or other full-time faculty. The result was that students were not able to get the courses they needed at their campuses and had to drive long distances and take curtailed course schedules due to driving time conflicts with class times. This is exemplified by a comment a student made to Raul last summer, one he has heard constantly repeated. This student, "Roxangel" (pseudonym), complained that the ESL schedule in the fall semester was not good because she would have to drive a round trip of about 60 miles to attend an available writing class. She stressed how if she did not take the class, she would not be able to apply for a job that required her completion of the English courses. She protested that the whole thing about schedules was unfair because she could not move forward in her life without English. She did not know what to do. She had arrived here from Cuba just two months earlier and was alone with her 6-year old daughter. ESL programming staff, in response to a tight budget, made the scheduling decision.

Decisions made for financial reasons with minimal input regarding the impact on people like Roxangel illustrates Levin's (2005) point that the decisions in line with a neoliberal ideology often impact the least powerful. Like the women who spoke with Raul, many adult ESL students work at minimum wage jobs in the fast food industry, as warehouse workers and drivers, in the informal economy as nannies, in lawn care, construction, and home and office cleaning. These jobs offer little hope for the future. Women adult immigrants, like adult women students in higher education generally, often lack support systems that enable them to attend classes, often having family responsibilities that preclude attending classes at distant campuses or at times when they need to attend to children or are at work (McGivney, 2004). As one of Raul's students recently pointed out,

> I have been studying ESL classes at this college for three years, and I have been working a local hamburger fast food restaurant the entire time. My work schedule is at night, so I can only come to school in the morning and only after I get my kids ready and take them to school.

The challenge Raul's students face is not unique to Community College.

> [T]he Office of Educational Research and Improvement found that "of the 3 million nonparticipating adults who were interested in taking ESL classes, most (58.8 percent) reported that they did not know of any classes they could have taken in the past twelve months." (Tucker, 2007, p. 32)

Limited or inappropriate course scheduling is not the only challenge ESL students face as a result of the shift of authority from academics to managers (Shepherd, 2017). International students face many academic, social, and cultural challenges when entering U.S. universities and colleges, many of which need to be addressed at the level of faculty (Wu, Garza, & Guzman, 2015). For ESL students at Community College, the administration of first day exams is mandated by the department chair and approved by the dean. Unfortunately, while this type of testing standardizes student placement in courses and contributes to administrative efficiency, it does not consider such things as students' cultural background, their language learning anxiety, or their previous formal schooling (or lack of). Some students become so anxious they do not return. Student characteristics and factors impacting learning are more likely to be taken into consideration in course placement by those focused on effective learning and teaching than those more attuned to efficient institutional management. Recent research found that faculty concern was a significant predictor of student persistence in community colleges (Nakajima, Dembo, & Mosler, 2012). The authors suggested that this can be attributed to the increase in part-time faculty, citing Jacoby (2006) who found an association between a rise in part-time faculty rates and lower graduation and retention rates. Similarly, the trend in higher education toward increasing the proportion of adjunct faculty has meant less faculty participation in both programming and textbook decisions in building a community of learners among students like Raul's ESL students. The large number of adjunct instructors reflects the effort of colleges to cut costs and increase revenue in response to diminished public funding. In 1969, 27% of faculty members at two-year colleges were part-time (Rogers, 2015); in 2007, the number had increased to 68.7% with some schools as high as 80% (Kezar & Maxey, 2012).

The shift in faculty governance over academic matters and increase in adjunct faculty can have profound consequences on the lives of ESL students, particularly adult immigrant students who may have additional factors affecting their ability to persist with classes (Becker, 2011). However, research on the persistence of ESL students is sparse (Razfar & Simon, 2011). Some studies have noted that second language learners with low levels of cultural capital and without enough personal intellectual interaction with instructors and other students struggle to persist with their college work (Chavez, 2015; Janis, 2013; Tirelli, 2014). Others have suggested that student success and persistence in both academic credit and noncredit ESL courses can be supported by community college learning environments that encourage opportunities for intellectual interaction among ESL students, peers, faculty, and staff (Chavez, 2015; Janis, 2013; Tirelli, 2014). Under the market fundamentalism of neoliberal ideology, efficiency implemented through limited course offerings and per course faculty work against interactive learning communities like this, leaves struggling students to be responsible for their own success.

Finally, while some community colleges have included serving the needs of immigrants in their strategic plans, such as those active in the Community College Consortium for Immigrant Education, many have not. Most community colleges distinguish between noncredit basic ESL and academic ESL courses. To qualify to take academic ESL courses (often called Intensive English Programs), students must pay to take a placement test such as the Test of English as a Foreign Language (TOEFL) or the International English Language Testing System (IELTS). Intensive English Programs requiring a level of English proficiency and academic accomplishment to enroll are most often directed toward international students, who pay out-of-state tuition and constitute a revenue stream. "Indeed, underpinned by neoliberal reforms and the prospect of increased revenue, higher educational provision[s] for foreign students have been created" (Perkins & Neumayer, 2014, p. 248). Often these courses can be taken concurrently with regular academic courses. Those courses directed at working adults without academic preparation are frequently offered under adult and continuing education divisions and are not offered for academic credit toward a degree.

The challenges of our current economic and political ideology are felt across the globe, often on the backs of international students, immigrant and refugee students, and ESL instructors and students in community colleges. While each of us can act as individual faculty, programmers, and administrators to mitigate the effects on our students, many of our current challenges can be traced to neoliberal ideology and the concomitant practices of new managerialism.

ESL LEARNERS: HOPES AND DREAMS

Looking back over his career, Raul remembers the first time he realized the drive ESL students possess, especially Latinas. He had just begun his second semester teaching adults as part of a community college's outreach program. At the time, he lived in the same community in which he had been hired to teach evening classes. One day he saw one of his students, an elderly Latina. She was waiting for the bus. The scene struck so deeply that he could not take it out of his mind, and the strangest part was he did not know why he kept visualizing this person on the side of a busy semirural road waiting as large 18 wheelers and other vehicles raced past her. All the while she stood there just a few feet from the side of the road as if to say, "*Here I am and I don't care what you think. I have somewhere to be.*" She had to have waited there for at least an hour since the buses in the area usually arrive at the bus stop every hour. It was then the realization came to him. The woman was amazing, and he knew why. It was her tenacity. If she was waiting for a bus, it was because she had no other way to get around. He realized then, she had been walking to the evening ESL class and probably walking on her return trip home at night.

From that day on, he always remembered that tough woman waiting by the road, and he has come to realize that many ESL students face tremendous obstacles just to get to community college ESL classrooms (Chavez, 2015). He realized that they are all expecting something better for themselves. As Warriner (2016) has pointed out, some ESL learners study English because they expect to make more money or to get a job with a better work schedule. Other ESL students have told Raul that they hope to get a Green Card and become legal residents of the United States. Many just simply hope to be able to navigate American society and to contribute to making the world a better place for themselves and their families. However, the neoliberal economic ideology that is increasingly present in community college missions, strategies, and management practices views students as consumers of language education because they are expected to develop their skills to become marketable. If they fail, economic forces will push them to the side, acting as if they do not exist.

IMPLICATIONS FOR LEADERSHIP

What are the implications of neoliberal policies for college leaders such as executive administrators, faculty, and students? First, neoliberal policies force college administrators to find ways to meet financial obligations with less revenue (Levin, Kater, & Wagoner, 2006; Saunders 2014). As colleges try to survive with less funds in the neoliberal paradigm, they mimic corporate style ideas centered on economic accountability and human productivity that affect both faculty and students (Giroux, 2002). At the instructional level at Community College for example, the financial pressure means that faculty develop the ESL curriculum which provides an instructional scope and sequence that prepares students for academic success. Full time faculty are also required to teach a minimum of five courses per semester at Community College and still deliver quality instruction to meet the college goal of increasing student academic completion rates. Neoliberal policies ask faculty take on heavier workloads which affects the amount of time available for planning lessons and providing valuable feedback to student work (Giroux, 2002). As colleges focus on ways to meet financial obligations with less revenue, neoliberalism dictates that they imitate corporate ideas of economic efficiency and productivity. Colleges ask teachers to take on more responsibilities instead of hiring more people. Increased workloads affect instructors' capacities to provide quality instruction and threaten student completion rates. In fact, only 22% of first time students who enroll in community colleges earn a degree or certificate (National Center for Education Statistics, 2017).

The Impact of Neoliberalism on Colleges: Synthesis of Ideas

Neoliberal policies have affected everyone in community colleges. But most importantly, they affect the most vulnerable students. All colleges are being pressured to improve completion rates. However, neoliberalism's influence on funding, policy, and programming seems to be working against that goal. Our most disadvantaged students, such as many ESL learners, face challenges with transportation, fitting classes around work and childcare responsibilities, and others lack familiarity with academic institutions. Decisions made based on economic concerns without being informed by how those decisions will affect students, work against the goal of increasing completion rates. Much has been noted about neoliberalism's economic impact on colleges including low student completion rates. Raising completion rates is a complex issue and we do not attempt to solve this problem here, but scholars have offered valuable ideas that envision the beginning of a path to a better future for colleges. First, colleges should avoid a neoliberal policy stance that reduces education to the transfer of training skills and promotes top down communication patterns that value speaking to instead of with individuals (Freire, 1998). Next, it is important to understand students' evolving views of a college education so that "we can begin to craft solutions that will enable us to regain control of our institutions and shape our educational world" (Saunders, 2007, p. 7). Additionally, scholars have asserted that colleges should be student centered democratic spaces that encourage student collaboration, teach social responsibility, and promote students' critical thinking about themselves and their place in society so that they may begin to understand how things operate in society (Harper, 2014). Another suggestion has been to lower the high number of adjunct faculty by offering full-time employment to these part-time faculty members (Harper, 2014). In sum, these suggestions for a more democratic and humanistic form of education offer a vision for a way forward for community colleges by connecting educational efforts with students and faculty (Apple, 2006).

CONCLUSION

Neoliberalism is alive and thriving in community colleges across the country. The detrimental effects of this economic ideology are disputed by those that see it as fundamental way of promoting business while investing in human capital. However, the neoliberal economic ideology has led to the prioritizing of the production of human capital over the provision of an education that promotes the democratic values of inclusion, justice, and equality for everyone. Since the largest growing sector of the U.S. population is its immigrants, now is the time for this nation to secure a better future through promoting social equality for all its people.

REFERENCES

Allen, R. (2017, March 25). Survey finds foreign students aren't applying to American colleges. *NBC News*. Retrieved from http://www.nbcnews.com

Apple, M. W. (2006). Understanding and interrupting neoliberalism and neoconservatism in education. *Pedagogies*, *1*(1), 21–26.

Ayers, D. F. (2005). Neoliberal ideology in community college mission statements: A critical discourse analysis. *The Review of Higher Education, 28*(4), 527–549.

Becker, L. A. (2011). Noncredit to credit transitioning matters for adult ESL learners in a California community college. *New Directions for Community Colleges, 155*, 15–26. doi:10.1002/cc.454

Bernstein, K. A., Hellmich, E. A., Katznelson, N., Shin, J., & Vinall, K. (2015). Introduction to special issue: Critical perspectives on neoliberalism in second / foreign language education. *L2 Journal*, 7(3), 1–14.

Blumenthal, A. J. (2002). English as a second language at the community college: An exploration of context and concerns. *New Directions for Community Colleges, 117*, 45–53.

Brown, W. (2003). Neo-liberalism and the end of liberal democracy. *Theory & Event*, 7(1). Retrieved from https://muse-jhu-edu.libproxy.txstate.edu/article/48659

Chavez, M. A. (2015). Community college journeys of Hispanic esl women. *Community College Journal of Research and Practice, 39*(3), 207–221.

Collier, V. (1995). *Promoting academic success for ESL students: Understanding second language acquisition for school*. Jersey City, NJ: NJTESOL-BE.

Connell, C. (2013). Tired of waiting, employers provide just-in-time education. *The Hechinger Report*. Retrieved from http://hechingerreport.org/tired-of-waiting-employers-provide-just-in-time-education/

Connerty, M. C. (2009). Variation in academic writing among generation 1.5 learners, native English-speaking learners and ESL learners: An argument for corpus study (Doctoral Dissertation). Retrieved from http://etheses.bham.ac.uk/274/1/Connerty09PhD.pdf

Couturier, L. K. (2005). The unspoken is being undone: The market's impact on higher education's public purpose. *New Directions for Higher Education, 129*, 85–100.

Deem, R., & Brehony, K. J. (2005). Management as ideology: The case of 'new managerialism' in higher education. *Oxford Review of Education, 31*(2), 217–235. doi:10.1080/03054980500117827

Fish, S. (2009). Neoliberalism and higher education. *The New York Times*. Retrieved from http://www.nytimes.com

Flores, A. (2016). Forms of exclusion: Undocumented students navigating financial aid and inclusion in the United States. *American Ethnologist, 43*(3), 540. doi:10.1111/amet.12345

Freire, P. (1998). *Pedagogy of freedom: Ethics, democracy, and civic courage*. Lanham, MD: Rowman & Littlefield Publishers.

Giroux, H. A. (2002). Neoliberalism, corporate culture, and the promise of higher education: The university as a democratic public sphere. *Harvard Educational Review*, 72(4), 425–463.

Giroux, H. A. (2014). *Neoliberalism's war on higher education*. Chicago, IL: Haymarket Books.

Harper, V. (2014). Neoliberalism, democracy and the university as a public sphere: An interview with Henry A. Giroux. *Policy Futures in Education, 12*(8), 1078–1083. doi:10.2304/pfie.2014.12.8.1078

Jackson, S. (Ed.). (2011). *Lifelong learning and social justice: Communities, work and identities in a globalised world*. Leicester, England: National Institute of Adult Continuing Education.

Jacoby, D. (2006). Effects of part-time faculty employment on community college graduation rates. *The Journal of Higher Education, 77*, 1081–1103.

Janis, T. (2013). The community college: Bridge or roadblock to higher education for US adult immigrant English-language learners? *Research in Comparative and International Education, 8*(2), 149–165.

Kezar, A., & Maxey, D. (2012). *The changing faculty and student success: National trends for faculty composition over time.* Association of American Colleges and, U., & University of Southern California.

Kim, E., & Díaz, J. (2013). Immigrant students and higher education [Monograph]. *ASHE Higher Education Report, 38*(6), 1–163. doi:10.1002/aehe.20006

Lambert, M. T., & Callam, P. M. (2014). *Privatization and the public good: Public universities in the balance*. Cambridge, MA: Harvard Education Press.

Larrotta, C. (2010). English language learning for adults. In C. E. Kasworm, A. D. Rose, & J. M. Ross-Gordon (Eds.), *Handbook of adult and continuing education* (pp. 199–208). Thousand Oaks, CA: SAGE.

Levin, J. S. (2005). The business culture of the community college: Students as consumers; students as commodities. *New Directions for Higher Education, 129*, 11–26.

Levin, J. S., Kater, S., & Wagoner, R. L. (2006). *Community college faculty: At work in the new economy*. New York, NY: Palgrave Macmillan.

Lynch, K. (2006). Neo-liberalism and marketisation: The implications for higher education. *European Educational Research Journal, 5*(1), 1–17.

Ma, J., & Baum, S. (2016, April). *Trends in community colleges: Enrollment, prices, student debt, and completion* (College Board Research Brief). Retrieved from College Board website: https://trends.collegeboard.org/sites/default/files/trends-in-community-colleges-research-brief.pdf

Mackay, K. (2014). Neoliberalism and postsecondary education: A view from the colleges. *Academic Matters OCUFA's Journal of Higher Education*. Retrieved from http://www.academicmatters.ca

Marttila, T. (2013). *The culture of enterprise in neoliberalism: Specters of entrepreneurship*. Taylor and Francis. doi:10.4324/9780203094693

McGivney, V. (2004). Understanding persistence in adult learning. Open Learning, *19*(1), 33–46. http://dx.doi.org/10.1080/0268051042000177836

Mendoza, G. S. (2015). *Tuition benefits for immigrants*. Retrieved from National Conference of State Legislatures website: http://www.ncsl.org/research/immigration/tuition-benefits-for-immigrants.aspxMigration Policy Institute. (2014). *Largest U.S. immigrant groups over time, 1960-present*. Retrieved from http://www.migrationpolicy.org/programs/data-hub/charts/largest-immigrant-groups-over-time

Nakajima, M., Dembo, M., & Mossler, R. (2012). Student persistence in community colleges. *Community College Journal of Research and Practice, 36*(8), 591–613. doi:10.1080/10668920903054931

National Center for Education Statistics. (2017). *Undergraduate retention and graduation rates*. Retrieved from https://nces.ed.gov/programs/coe/indicator_ctr.asp

National Council of Teachers of English. (2008). *English language learners: A policy research brief.* Retrieved from http://www.ncte.org/library/NCTEFiles/Resources/PolicyResearch/ELLResearchBrief.pdf

Olssen, M. (2006). Understanding the mechanisms of neoliberal control: Lifelong learning, flexibility and knowledge capitalism. *International Journal of Lifelong Education, 25*(3), 213–230. doi:10.1080/02601370600697045

Passel, J. S., & Cohn, D. (2009). A portrait of unauthorized immigrants in the United States. *Pew Research Center.* Retrieved from http://www.pewhispanic.org/2009/04/14/a-portrait-of-unauthorized-immigrants-in-the-united-states/

Perkins, R., & Neumayer, E. (2014). Geographies of educational mobilities: Exploring the uneven flows of international students. *Geographical Journal, 180*(3), 246–259. doi:10.1111/geoj.12045

Peters, M. A. (2013). Managerialism and the neoliberal university: Prospects for new forms of 'open management' in higher education. *Contemporary Readings in Law and Social Justice, 5*(1), 11–26.

Pimentel, S. (2013). *College and career readiness standards for adult education.* Washington, DC: Department of Education, Office of Vocational and Adult Education.

Posecznick, A. (2014). On theorising and humanising academic complicity in the neoliberal university. *Learning & Teaching,* 7(1), 1–11. doi:10.3167/latiss.2014.070101

Razfar, A., & Simon, J. (2011). Course-taking patterns of Latino esl students: Mobility and mainstreaming in urban community colleges in the United States. *TESOL Quarterly, 45*(4), 595–627. doi:10.5054/tq.2011.268060

Rogers, G. S. (2015). Part-time faculty and community college student success. *Journal of Research and Practice, 39*(7), 673–684. doi:10.1080/10668926.2014.908426

Ryan, C. (2013). *Language use in the United States: 2011* (ACS Report No. 22). Washington, DC: U.S. Department of Commerce, Economics and Statistics Administration, U.S. Census Bureau.

Samee Ali, S. (2016, December 10). International college students leery of Trump could cost U.S. billions. *NBC News*. Retrieved from http://www.nbcnews.com

Saunders, D. (2007). The Impact of Neoliberalism on College Students. *Journal of College & Character, 8*(5), 1–9. doi:10.2202/1940-1639.1620

Saunders, D. B. (2014). Exploring a customer orientation: Free-market logic and college students. *The Review of Higher Education, 37*(2), 197–219. doi:10.1353/rhe.2014.0013

Schalge, S. L., & Soga, K. (2008). "Then I stop coming to school": Understanding absenteeism in an adult English as a second language program. *Adult Basic Education and Literacy Journal,* 2(3), 151–161.

Schram, S. F. (2014). The future of higher education and American democracy: Introduction. *New Political Science, 36*(4), 425–437. doi:10.1080/07393148.2014.954805

Shear, B., & Zontine, A. (2010). Reading neoliberalism at the university. *Learning and Teaching: The International Journal of Higher Education in the Social Sciences, 3*(3), 32–62. doi:10.3167/latiss.2010.030303

Shepherd, S. (2017). Managerialism: an ideal type. *Studies in Higher Education,* 1-11. Advance online publication. doi:10.1080/03075079.2017.1281239

Silva, A. (2016). Neoliberalism confronts Latinos: Paradigmatic shifts in immigration practices. *Latino Studies, 14*(1), 59–79. doi:10.1057/lst.2015.50

Sterne, J. (2006). A brief history of neoliberalism. *Tikkun, 21*(2), 75.

Stromquist, N. (2012). The educational experience of Hispanic immigrants in the United States: Integration through marginalization. *Race Ethnicity and Education, 15*(2), 195–221. doi:10.1080/13613324.2011.578125

Taylor, A. (2017). Perspectives on the university as a business: The corporate management structure, neoliberalism and higher education. *Journal for Critical Education Policy Studies, 15*(1), 108–135.

Teranishi, R. T. & Suárez-Orozco, C. & Suárez-Orozco, M. (2011). Immigrants in community colleges. *The Future of Children, 21*(1), 153-169.

Tirelli, V. (2014). Contingent academic labor against neoliberalism. *New Political Science, 36*(4), 523–537. doi:10.1080/07393148.2014.954791

Tucker, J. T. (2007). The ESL logjam: Waiting times for ESL classes and the impact on English learners. *National Civic Review, 96*(1), 30–37.

U.S. Department of Labor, Bureau of Labor Statistics. (2015). *Foreign-born workers: Labor force characteristics—2015* (USDL Publication No. 16-0989). Retrieved from http://www.bls.gov/news.release/pdf/forbrn.pdf

Warriner, D. S. (2016). 'Here, without English, you are dead': Ideologies of language and discourses of neoliberalism in adult English language learning. *Journal of Multilingual and Multicultural Development, 37*(5), 495–508, doi:10.1080/01434632.2015.1071827

Wu, H., Garza, E., & Guzman, N. (2015). International student's challenges and adjustment to college. *Education Research International,* Volume 2015 (2015), Article ID 202753, 9 pages. http://dx.doi.org/10.1155/2015/202753

CHAPTER 10

TEACHERS AS LEADERS

Accountability Era School Leadership and the Limits of Democratic Participation

Jessica Holloway, Jessica Kerr, and Jeffrey Zacharakis

ABSTRACT

The purpose of this chapter is to question the extent to which "democratic" ideals are made possible given new, neoliberal configurations of K–12 educational leadership. Set against the backdrop of a quasi-market schema that grounds leadership in managerial values and techniques, we use this chapter to question how neoliberalism is influencing the constraint and/or advancement of democratic possibilities for building/district leadership. Both in terms of function and structure, K–12 educational leadership has been refashioned to meet new policy demands that are grounded in market logics. In this market-based leadership schema, school principals function more like private sector managers who are forced to accomplish unprecedented levels of data collection and reporting. To accommodate the load, schools are breaking from the traditional, single-leader structure, to adopt more distributed forms of leadership where teachers are recruited to help absorb the additional tasks. The notion of teachers as leaders has been lauded by politicians as more democratically just and empowering of teachers. We use Reed's (1907) definition of the "democratic ideal" to argue that new policy initiatives

Convictions of Conscience: How Voices From the Margins Inform Public Actions, and Educational Leadership, pp. 181–197

(e.g., Teach to Lead) and related practices (e.g., teacher leadership) do not *necessarily* lead to more democratically-oriented forms of K–12 leadership.

INTRODUCTION

In the name of quality and efficiency, market-based logics have fundamentally reshaped public schools in the image of the market, whereby competition, choice, and product outcomes are highly valued and rewarded (Ball, 2003; Hursh, 2007; Rose, 1999). Consistent with any market entity, mechanisms are necessary to measure, evaluate, and compare the "products" of schools, or, in this case, student achievement. In the United States specifically, a series of federal policy initiatives, such as No Child Left Behind (NCLB), Race to the Top (RttT), and NCLB waivers, have introduced a set of accountability procedures and instruments that function to quantify, evaluate, compare, and rank various facets of education, including both students and teachers, as well as schools, districts, and states (Falabella, 2014; Koyama, 2011; Suspitsyna, 2010). These procedures and instruments allow for a systematic way for external stakeholders (e.g., government officials, taxpayers, parents, etc.) to make relative value judgments about the worth of a teacher, school, and so forth (Ball 2003; Hursh, 2007; Shore & Wright, 1999). As a result, school administrators have been inundated with unprecedented levels of accountancy tasks and responsibilities, especially in terms of increased data collection, analysis, and reporting on student achievement and teacher effectiveness.

The response to these needs has resulted in a (re)making of the school leader—one who acts as manager rather than educational leader. This new configuration has also reshaped school leadership structures, as more human capital is needed to respond to increased accountancy demands. In the United States, there is a proliferating trend to distribute leadership responsibilities among teachers, who serve in dual capacities as classroom teachers and school leaders. This practice has been incentivized at both state and national levels, touting greater "democratic" participation for teachers; but some scholars have questioned this proposition (Bolden, 2011).

The purpose of this chapter is to question the extent to which "democratic" ideals are made possible given new, neoliberal configurations of K–12 educational leadership. Set against the backdrop of a quasi-market schema that grounds leadership in managerial values and techniques, we use this chapter to question how neoliberalism is influencing the constraint and/or advancement of democratic possibilities for building/district leadership. Both in terms of function and structure, K–12 educational leadership has been refashioned to meet new policy demands that are grounded in market logics. In this market-based leadership schema, school principals function more like private sector managers who are forced to accomplish unprecedented levels of data collection and reporting. To accommodate the load, schools are breaking from the traditional, single-leader structure, to adopt more distributed forms of leadership where teachers are recruited to help absorb the additional tasks. Politicians have lauded the notion of teachers as leaders as more democratically just and empowering of teachers. We use Reed's (1907) definition of the "democratic ideal" to argue that new policy initiatives (e.g., Teach to Lead) and related practices (e.g., teacher leadership) do not *necessarily* lead to more democratically-oriented forms of K–12 leadership.

THE DEMOCRATIC IDEAL

The original intent of public education was to build civil society and be available and free to all citizens. John Locke argued that with consolidation of power, democracy is threatened by government autocracy and that there have to be other organizations to check this power (Dalton, 2014). Putnam (1993) described organizations, which spawn social capital, trust and shared values, as locations where civil society is built, and interconnected interests are developed creating opportunities for greater participation resulting in a more informed citizenry. In a civil society it is the role of mediating organizations such as unions, churches, schools, and other associations where citizens can participate and voice their collective interests to provide a counterbalance to government power.

We can trace the democratic spirit of education back to Aristotle who wrote that "education should be one and same for all, and that it should be public and not private" (Everson, 2000, p. 195). This theme was expanded by Rousseau (1923) who posited that public education is fundamental to government and society, and later used by Smith, Hume, and Condercet (Rothschild, 2001) who saw public education as a means to build a rational democratic society where all had equal opportunity. Early public education was seen as a bulwark against superstition, and the entrenched mindset of monarchies and its privileged class.

Public education is also embedded in the formation of the United States or the American ideal as advocated by Thomas Jefferson (1786) who supported the school law of Virginia to establish general education: "I think by far the most important bill in our whole code is that for the diffusion of knowledge among the people. No other sure foundation can be devised, for the preservation of freedom and happiness" (p. 1). Later Horace Mann (1840) would write: "Education must be universal! It is well, when the wise and learned discover new truths; but how much better to diffuse the truths already discovered to the multitudes!" (p. 58). And John Rawls (1993) accentuated the thought that public schools serve the common good by developing public reason. Public or general education and the diffusion of truths is the foundation on which the democratic ideal is built.

Milton Reed (1907) wrote that the democratic ideal is based on three principles: "liberty, equality of rights and opportunities, and justice" (p. 146). In his seminal article, he points out the romantic or naïve limitations of earlier philosophers such Plato, Aristotle, and Bacon's New Atlantis, as not addressing equality of opportunity when various classes or groups continue to oppress other groups either through economic structures or social structures. Liberty is not freedom to do what you want; it is something that must be regulated by the state to avoid anarchy and tyranny. Liberty is created by the state, and with these freedoms the state must also institute rules and order, all of which according to Reed are based on each citizen's obligation to all other citizens. This "obligation to others" is based on reciprocity and mutual help (p. 146). It is the state's responsibility to preserve freedom by preventing mob rule and the rise of despots, and "possession of enormous wealth, thereby generating sharp distinctions between classes, [which] is inimical to the Democratic Ideal" (p. 150). Reed continues that a democratic society "pre-supposes a tolerable measure of equality in possessions, and absence of class privilege" (p. 150). Hence freedom according to Reed in the democratic ideal is not unlimited and all citizens must share in a piece of their government to enact laws that limit greed and unlawfulness.

Lewis Lorwin (1935) argued that the democratic ideal has shifted over time being defined by each civilization reflecting their conditions. In his construct of the democratic ideal there is a common set of freedoms including the freedom to move, freedom of speech and thought, freedom to associate with others, and freedom to pursue their individual potentials (p. 114). He also noted that laissez-faire economics had resulted in violent strikes and the need for workers to organize unions—in essence these freedoms were threatened by unfettered economic policies.

These freedoms are preserved by allowing people to determine government policies; being able to replace peaceably any administration; forming public policy and opinion without fear of persecution; and inclusion of minority group opinions and their needs in the decisions of the majority. All these freedoms are preserved through the political process, voting, and, most importantly, an engaged citizenry. He pointed out that the liberal state that adheres to the democratic ideal has a balance and check to various economic orders, or what might be viewed as the liberal state regulating the economic capitalism. The purpose of the liberal state "is to put into political form the scattered economic powers of individuals and to make these powers serve a distinct collective purpose, namely, making the whole nation work together for a common good" (p. 116).

Dianne Ravitch and Joseph Viteritti (2001) argued that education is the cornerstone of a democratic society in that civil society is dependent upon public education where young people experience society's commonweal by participating in a setting that represents a cross section of that society to build a civil society. Whereas the historical purpose of general and public education was to assimilate diverse cultures and ethnic heritages toward an American commonweal of American community, when public schools embraced diversity in the 1980s and 1990s society became more fractured.

As the public schools shifted from being the central agency for promoting civic understanding to being an agency for sponsoring racial, ethnic, and cultural identity, faith in the public school ideal weakened. Because Americans have typically believed that their public schools played a key role in building the moral foundation for a robust democracy, there were inevitably questions about whether the schools' faltering commitment to civic assimilation was in some way connected to the decline of our civic spirit.

This notion of public schools assimilating diverse cultures into a common appreciation for a unified society is not static. Rather schools reflect society in as much as they direct society. This process is subjugated when schools become segregated by income and race or ethnicity, and is also threatened when competing ideas are stifled by strong cultural values and religious beliefs. But these forces are always in flux reflecting changing social and cultural dynamics (Putnam, 1993). Still schools are often the first arena where children are exposed to new ideas and other cultures apart from their family or tribe. It is in this setting where an individual's status quo is first challenged, at least subconsciously.

Though some might disagree with Ravitch and Viteritti's (2001) analyses considering the history of the United States is ripe with oppression and exploitation of disenfranchised groups such as African Americans, Latinos, and Indigenous persons, there is an element of truth in their argument if we combine Reed's (1907) thesis that in the democratic idea the role of government is to insure equal opportunity, Lorwin's (1935) thesis that the purpose of the liberal state is to focus on the common good, and Ravitch and Viteritti's thesis that schools are to help form a civil society where everyone has the knowledge to function as an informed and engaged citizen. By combining these three theses, the atrocities we committed as a country in the past, such as slavery and industrial exploitation of workers, can be rectified without negating or undermining the commonweal. The democratic ideal might best be captured by viewing Reed's (1907) three principles—liberty, rights, and opportunities, justice—through the metaphor of a three-legged stool. If one leg is missing, the stool tips over. If one group is denied equal rights and opportunity, then justice is not attainable. In the end the democratic ideal is dependent on the informed and engaged citizen who is not only allowed to express their ideas and opinions but who is also able to listen and understand the opinions of others.

Applying the three-legged stool metaphor to the call for expanded teacher leadership allows us to think about how contemporary, accountability-driven models of distributed leadership meet or challenge Reed's (1907) conceptualization of the democratic ideal. To bring his argument into the discussion of teacher leadership, we must contextualize this relatively new phenomenon within contemporary modes of K–12 educational leadership more broadly, begging the question: what does it mean to be a school leader in the contemporary, accountability era?

CONTEMPORARY EDUCATIONAL LEADERSHIP

The current accountability era is the product of a neoliberal discourse that has reoriented public services and goods in the image of the market which includes, but is not limited to, a reliance on numbers, standards, and modes of evaluation that have fundamentally reshaped contemporary education in the United States and abroad (Ball, 2003; Falabella, 2014; Koyama, 2011). This is defined as the period for which "accountability" is legitimized as a necessary mechanism to provide external stakeholders the information they need (e.g., quality indicators, comparative measures, etc.) to make market choices about public goods. In other words, public institutions, such as education, are rearticulated as market entities, and market values and techniques are used to define, discipline, and shape the institutions and the people who practice within them. Educational leadership, as a subject of public education, is constituted by the social, political and historical contexts within which it is currently produced. Thus we should think about the ways in which the neoliberal era provides particular conditions of possibilities for educational leadership to take shape in particular ways. One way in which educational leadership has been shaped by this era is through standards, standardization, and data-driven accountability.

Prior to the advent of national leadership standards and data driven modes of educational management, what constituted an "ideal" school leader, be they an administrator or teacher, came from the belief that an individual tasked with the responsibility of leading in an educational space would act rationally on behalf of the specifications and desires of the community they serve (Sackney & Mitchell, 2002). The day-to-day practice of leadership, albeit infused with hierarchical notions of knowledge and power, was left to a highly localized vision of what a given classroom/school/district should and could look like.

The emergence of a neoliberal, standards and data-driven model of governance has transformed educational leadership roles (Giles, 2013; Gleeson & Husbands, 2001). Education professional organizations that currently oversee what it *means to be* a person in an educational leadership role in the current regime of discourse maintain, "This era of higher standards and greater accountability requires a 'new breed' of school leaders" (Bottoms & O'Neil, 2001, p. 2). This demand for a new type of leader is coconstructed within an era of neoliberal rationality that simultaneously sees standards and assessment data as the tried and true assessment metric for what is best/maximized within a particular area of focus (Ross & Gibson, 2007).

The advent of standards, the use of data-driven assessment, and their underlying logics stand in stark contrast to the discourse, or "knowledge," of previous conceptualizations of education. In other words, the accountability regime, as an ontological framework (or "regime of truth," Foucault, 1980), has set the parameters for what can be said, thought, and done in education. A pre-standards understanding of assessment has now been cast as a highly subjective understanding of what was being observed, and therefore an inadequate view of determining the relative worth or value of the thing being assessed (Sackney & Mitchell, 2002). This change has cast into doubt previous answers to questions regarding how we know or can know an educated student within a particular content area, the overall effectiveness of a teacher, and for the purpose of this chapter, what constitutes effective leadership.

Within the contemporary standardized, data-driven model, the focus has transitioned to the observed subject. Knowledge is reconceptualized by the ability to generate data that provides information relative to the model. Followed out to its furthest end, by accessing these data, the assessor can have a more accurate understanding of the domain being studied when compared to both the model and to other examples of that "thing." Neoliberal, standards-driven discourse ultimately asserts that we can have a rational, unbiased version of the truth in data. It is with these data, truth, that we can order and discipline individuals, institutions, and behaviors with the overarching vision that best practice can be achieved through rewards and/or sanctions (Popkewitz & Kirchgasler, 2015).

Prior to assessment, however, what is optimal must be defined within an institutional governing framework, be it a student, a school, or practices within a content area. Standards driven logic subscribes to the notion that nothing can be left outside of the model; as the model stands for the most comprehensive vision of what is being measured. A standard, therefore is a vision and definition of the total nature of the subject, not excluding how they think and act, but extending to their "feelings, emotions, and sensitivities" (Popkewitz & Kirchgasler, 2015). All aspects of life, from who one is, to how one behaves are contained within the standard structure; nothing is outside. The effect of the standards-based mode has therefore been described as having the ability to "govern" the very souls of the individuals and spaces they produce (Popkewitz & Kirchgasler, 2015; see also Ball, 2003).

The standards are productive in that they discursively frame what it means to be a leader within an educational institution. As such, notions of political power are inscribed within the discourse of the standards, ranging from the text itself to the larger frame of educational leadership discourse; what is left in/left out of the standards to issues of enaction of the standards in practice. Simultaneously, contemporary standards address all aspects of the school environment, namely governing the day-to-day, inner-workings of building, teacher, and student life. In addition to elements that are more familiarly associated with educational leadership roles, standards models can include macro/micro levels of national, state, and school district educational change, along with the "dispositions, sensitivities, and awareness-es" (Popkewitz & Kirchgasler, 2015, p. 36) needed to be a successful educational leader in the 21st century (National Policy Board for Educational Administration, 2015)

Popkewitz and Kirchgasler (2015) say standards function to direct not just the tasks of educators or administrators but, "individual's feelings, emotions, and sensitivities" (p. 36). Standards as the pieces that are brought together, "not as a sum or the parts, or an evolution, [but] … a determinant category" (p. 36) of what constitutes the totalized vision of educational excellence. In this way, the standards and the data they generate as outputs can be seen as a governing framework for managing the life of the school, and therefore a technology for articulating the innermost qualities of the individual tasked with this professional/personal role.

These measures extend beyond quantifiable skills and attributes. They speak to a leader engaged in a reflexive process that includes self-thought, reflection, decision making, and who is capable through this process of manifesting oneself as inner leader (Peters, 2010). Ever present in the standards are technologies of power, audit and surveillance, self-discipline and improvement. The discourse of these mechanisms work on the soul of the educational leader to continually make oneself amenable to the vision of leadership "outputs" contained within the standards, as held to the gaze of data, no matter where they find themselves in the "chain of command" within their individual educational space (Peters, 2010). Within the data are elements that spell out actionable measures a school leader can take to oversee and improve school quality, equality, and effectiveness (National Policy Board for Educational Administration, 2015).

Simultaneously, school leaders are tasked to make ongoing quality checks, produce accountability reports, and make data-driven personnel decisions (e.g., teacher evaluation, professional development, termination and tenure decisions, etc.). As such, school leadership models have broken from traditional leadership structures to include more people to carry out the data collection, analysis, and reporting needs (Anderson & Herr, 2015; Eacott & Norris, 2014; Hartley, 2009). Disseminating leadership among teachers, by promoting classroom teachers to dual teacher-leader roles, has produced a more sustainable system for upholding the increased leadership responsibilities.

New forms of distributed leadership are touted as more democratically just for teachers because they putatively provide teachers the opportunity to serve in leadership capacities. However, we need to challenge whether this is the case and challenge the contemporary teacher leader as a subject of the neoliberal discourse that currently configures education and educators. In other words, we can begin to unpack the teacher leader subject as a product of a discursive framework grounded in market ideals and principles. We can also think about teacher leaders as products of a rapidly changing education landscape that is also shaped by market ideals and principles. To this end, we aim to demonstrate how prescribed teacher leadership is not necessarily a democratically just practice, but rather a response to increased accountability demands that require more human capital to uphold. We argue that new modes of prescribed teacher leadership, as are currently being incentivized on a national level, are producing a system of self-managed individuals who are strictly shaped by standards, data-intensive expectations, and accountability demands that do not help expand their capacities for democratic participation. We also argue that this is in direct contradiction to Reed's imaginary of the democratic ideal.

CONTEMPORARY TEACHER LEADERSHIP

Various forms of teacher leadership have been in place for some time; they have taken various forms and functions, and have been promoted on the grounds of various rationales (Bolden, 2011; Youngs, 2014). Teacher leadership as a field of study has analyzed and critiqued the practice from various perspectives, but, overall, it has taken kindly to teacher leadership (Crowther, Ferguson, & Hann, 2009; Graetz, 2000; Harris & Muijs, 2004; Murphy, 2005; see also Liljenberg, 2014). Some argued that instructional and curriculum coaches have had a positive impact on student achievement scores (as measured by standardized achievement tests) (Campbell & Malkus, 2011), and others claimed that such practices boost teacher morale and positive school culture (Griffin, 1995; Hulpia, Devos, & Rosseel, 2009).

Scholars also warned that teacher leadership must be carefully orchestrated in order to guarantee the necessary resources for sustainability and success (Liljenberg, 2014). Similarly, careful planning can help align teacher strengths with school needs, allowing for teachers to participate in leadership capacities in ways they find meaningful (Mascall, Leithwood, Straus, & Sacks, 2008). Teacher leaders must also be supported via leadership preparation and training, ongoing professional development, and the time necessary to conduct their classroom and leadership responsibilities (e.g., designated classroom release time to perform coaching duties) (Camburn, Rowan, & Taylor, 2003). Failure to meet these needs can lead to burn-out, dissatisfaction with the job, and high turnover. While teacher leadership received positive attention from some in the research community; it has also been heavily critiqued by others.

Critics of contemporary arrangements of teacher leadership ask us to consider the distribution of power as we make sense of distributed leadership (Hartley, 2009; Hatcher, 2005; Lumby 2013; Youngs, 2009). They warn that, while the distribution of leadership responsibilities may have some positive effects, it does not necessarily mean that power and authority are simultaneously distributed among the "leadership" participants. In other words, teacher leaders might help carry out leadership responsibilities (e.g., teacher observations, professional development workshops), but they may not be able to contribute in authentic ways to overall school-level decisions. They also caution that increased teacher leadership, and distributed leadership specifically, may be more a function of increased accountability demands rather than the democratic ideals that are often used to promote prescribed teacher leadership models (Holloway, Nielsen, & Saltmarsh, 2017).

Therefore, we question how, despite some of the original (and promising) intentions of teacher leadership, new policy demands require unprecedented levels of human capital to carry out the accountancy, resulting in a demand for teacher leaders. We argue that new policy demands create conditions whereby teacher leaders are needed to uphold the increased accountability demands (e.g., increased data collection, analysis, reporting). As such, we question the extent to which democratic ideals can be realized in this contemporary adoption of teacher leadership. We use The TAP System for teachers and student advancement as a case in point—an example of one popular teacher leadership model—to explore these lines of inquiry.

As mentioned previously, teacher leadership has manifested in many different ways, over the past several years. Recent federal- and state-level incentive awards have given rise to more systematic models of teacher leadership where "leadership" is treated as a reward for high performance. In these systems, teachers are promoted to leadership positions based on performance, and they often serve in dual capacities as classroom teachers and teacher leaders. For example, in 2014, then Secretary of Education,

Arne Duncan, announced the Teach to Lead: Advancing Teacher Leadership initiative that incentivized states and districts to implement programs where teachers could serve in leadership capacities (without leaving the classroom). Other models of systematic teacher leadership have manifested, in part, due to other tangentially related policy initiatives. The National Institute of Excellence in Teaching (NIET) developed The TAP System for Teacher and Student Advancement (referred to from here on as the TAP System), which is a comprehensive, performance-based pay, accountability system.

The TAP System is a career ladder model that incentivizes high-performing teachers to seek leadership roles. It includes three teacher ranks: career, mentor, and master. Career teachers are full-time teachers who spend 100% of their time in their respective classrooms. Mentor teachers are full-time teachers, but they also take on leadership responsibilities that include coaching and evaluating their peers. Master teachers have significantly reduced teaching loads so they can spend a majority of their time coaching and evaluating career and mentor teachers. Both mentor and master teachers participate on the school-level leadership team. The TAP System was developed as a response to various federal incentive awards, including Race to the Top and Teacher Incentive Fund (TIF) grants. The TAP System also met the requirements for the No Child Left Behind (NCLB) waivers for which states could apply to exempt them from the harsh penalties for not meeting NCLB stipulations. States and school districts around the United States have partnered with NIET to apply for these federal awards. This has provided the funds for said states and districts to implement the TAP System into their schools, creating a nationwide uptick in TAP use.

We use the TAP System as a case in point for a few reasons. First, it serves as an exemplar case because it is a comprehensive package designed specifically to meet the current accountability policy initiatives that are reforming U.S. schools nationwide. NIET has partnered with many TIF grant recipients, making the TAP System a popular teacher leadership model in the United States—another reason for which it should be considered emblematic of the greater teacher leadership movement across the country. That said, we do not intend to criticize the TAP System or the intentions behind the system (though the profitability of the company may warrant some critique). Rather, we aim to understand the contextual conditions that have made this type of prescribed teacher leadership model possible. This allows us to think about how teacher leadership has been made possible, in a particular way, at this particular sociohistoric moment. Then we can begin thinking about the democratic-orientation of this mode of teacher leadership that has manifested as a response to policy. As such, we see the TAP System as a product of these conditions, rather than an intentional actor in its development. We also see it as a vehicle for critiquing the putative democratic ideals often used to justify teacher leadership incentives (e.g., the Teach to Lead program).

TEACHER LEADERSHIP AND THE DEMOCRATIC IDEAL

In 2007, the National Comprehensive Center for Teacher Quality released a report about teacher leadership, including benefits of and strategies for promoting teacher leadership in K–12 schools. The authors of the report list seven benefits that schools reap from effective teacher leadership programs. Two of the stated benefits are directly related to the argument we are attempting to make in this chapter. The first:

> *Create a more democratic school environment.* When teacher leaders take on important schoolwide [sic] responsibilities and are centrally involved in school decision making, they are able to transform their school into a democracy. Students benefit from observing and experiencing democratic, participatory forms of government. They also benefit from higher teacher morale because their teachers are involved in democratic decision making and school leadership. (p. 4)

Calling on Reed's (1907) definition of the democratic ideal, one might be able to argue that including teachers in leadership discussions and decisions is more democratic for teachers. However, we must question the extent to which this is actually possible. When teachers are recruited to leadership positions to carry out more accountability tasks, such as peer evaluation, test data analysis and reporting, and other administrative tasks, are they actually participating in more democratic ways? Is their voice influencing change, or are they simply helping to sustain an otherwise unsustainable level of leadership tasks?

As if to highlight the point, the National Comprehensive Center for Teacher Quality report (2007) explicitly stated that another benefit to teacher leadership is:

> *Extend principal capacity.* Teacher leadership provides the additional person power needed to run the organizational operations of the school, which are too complex for principals to run alone. Indeed, teacher leaders are a source of reliable, useful, and professional help for the principal. "When teachers lead, principals extend their own capacity" (Barth, 2001). In addition, instructional teacher leadership can reduce the principal's workload. Teacher leaders are able to assume some of the principal's many responsibilities, including those of instructional leader. (p. 4)

The question to be raised here is whether teacher leadership is a manifestation of increased accountability need or an attempt to increase democratic participation? We do not assert that these are necessarily mutually exclusive. Teachers can expand the administration capacity while still contributing to school-level discussions and decisions. The problem, however, is that both are difficult to ensure, simultaneously, systematically, and consistently.

One of the major issues is that tangible, accountability tasks are easier to systematically assign and accomplish. For example, one of the key responsibilities of TAP teacher leaders is the evaluation of their peers. The teacher leaders are assigned a particular number of teachers to evaluate, which they complete throughout the year. These teachers also participate on the leadership team, where they take part in school-level discussions. However, this participation is relatively nebulous in that it is not something that can be checked off on a list. As such, what takes precedence: expanding leadership capacity to meet accountability demands, or ensuring that teacher leaders' voices are heard? According to one group of TAP teacher leaders, the former is privileged and the latter is ignored (Holloway, Nielsen, & Saltmarsh, 2017). Other scholars have found similar results, arguing that distributed leadership may be nothing more than the "emperor's new clothes" (Bolden, 2011; see also Crawford, 2012). They point out that assigning teachers to leadership roles often happens in name only, rather than offering teachers the authentic leadership voice that the title presumes.

Further, democratic leadership and distributed leadership are very different and should not be confused or used synonymously—*democratic* leadership is grounded in a set of philosophical values (Crawford, 2012; Woods, Bennett, Harvey, & Wise, 2004), while *distributed* leadership can serve various agendas and ideals. As such, leadership is not necessarily decentralized; rather, power is centralized and teacher "leaders" have their place in the hierarchy, accompanied by the relative level of influence. For example, if distributed leadership were grounded in democratic ideals, it would require leaders to be democratically elected, not appointed (Hartley, 2009), as is commonplace.

Further, as noted by Bolden (2011) and Hatcher (2005), distributed leadership does not necessarily equate with distributed power or authority. As argued here, prescribing teacher leadership roles might help schools respond to external policy demands, but it does not necessarily nurture opportunities for democratic participation. Rather than arguing that there is something inherently, or ethically, wrong with the TAP System or other models like it, we argue that leadership is remade into a commodity that can be used as an incentive and sanctioned for self-improvement, accountability, and regulation. We also argue that this form of distributed leadership is in response to a rise in policy demands, rather than a new form of increased democratic participation for teachers. Consistent with new managerialism, while TAP (and similar systems), as well as policies and practices associated with prescribed distributed leadership, might use the word "leadership," we must be aware of how the term "leadership" is co-opted and used, when "management" is the more appropriate descriptor.

To call again upon on Reed's (1907) three pillars of the democratic ideal—"liberty, equality of rights and opportunities, and justice" (p. 146)—we can see how the contemporary realization of teacher leadership does not quite live up to Reed's imaginary. With educational leadership structures and actors being constituted by market values, defined by strict standards, and consumed by accountability demands, teacher leaders become mechanisms for expanding the capacity for meeting such responsibilities. It would be remiss to assume that the title of "teacher leader" provides these teachers with the freedom to act, the platform to voice their opinions, or the protection to challenge the status quo. Therefore, we have a responsibility to challenge these policy- and accountability-driven models of teacher leadership. It is on teacher leadership scholars to critically investigate how teacher leadership is constraining or contributing to more democratic participation for teachers; and it is on school leaders to avoid systems of accountability checklists and instead build sustainable leadership structures that foster democratic participation.

REFERENCES

Anderson, G., & Herr, K. (2015). New Public Management and the new professionalism in education: Framing the issue. *Education Policy Analysis Archives, 23*(84), 1–9.

Ball, S. J. (2003). The teacher's soul and the terrors of performativity. *Journal of Education Policy, 18*(2), 215–228.

Bolden, R. (2011). Distributed leadership in organizations: A review of theory and research. *International Journal of Management Reviews, 13*(3), 251–269.

Bottoms, G., & O'Neil, K. (2001). Preparing a new breed of school principals: It's time for action. Retrieved from http://eric.ed.gov/?id=ED464388

Camburn, E., Rowan, B., & Taylor, J. E. (2003). Distributed leadership in schools: The case of elementary schools adopting comprehensive school reform models. *Educational Evaluation and Policy Analysis, 25*(4), 347–373.

Campbell, P. F., & Malkus, N. N. (2011). The impact of elementary mathematics coaches on student achievement. *The Elementary School Journal, 111*(3), 430–454.

Crawford, M. (2012). Solo and distributed leadership definitions and dilemmas. *Educational Management Administration & Leadership, 40*(5), 610–620.

Crowther, F., Ferguson, M., & Hann, L. (2009). *Developing teacher leaders: How teacher leadership enhances school success*. Thousand Oaks, CA: Corwin Press.

Dalton, B. (2014). Civil society: Overlapping frames. *Cosmopolitan Civil Societies: An Interdisciplinary Journal, 6*(2), 40–68.

Eacott, S., & Norris, J. (2014). Managerial rhetoric, accountability, and school leadership in contemporary Australia. *Leadership and Policy in Schools, 13*(2), 169–187.

Everson, S. (Ed.). (2000). *Aristotle: The politics and constitution of Athens.* Cambridge, England: Cambridge University Press.

Falabella, A. (2014). The performing school: The effects of market & accountability policies. *Education Policy Analysis Archives, 22*(70), 1–18.

Foucault, M. (1980). *Power/knowledge: Selected interviews & other writings 1972–1977.* New York, NY: Pantheon Books.

Giles, D. (2013). *Educational leadership and Michel Foucault.* London, England: Routledge.

Gleeson, D., & Husbands, C. T. (2001). *The performing school: Managing, teaching, and learning in a performance culture.* London, England: Routledge.

Graetz, F. (2000). Strategic change leadership. *Management Decision, 38*(8), 550–564.

Griffin, G. A. (1995). Influences of shared decision making on school and classroom activity: Conversations with five teachers. *The Elementary School Journal, 96*(1), 29–45.

Harris, A., & Muijs, D. (2004). *Improving schools through teacher leadership.* London, England: McGraw-Hill Education.

Hartley, D. (2009). Education policy, distributed leadership and sociocultural theory. *Educational Review, 61*(2), 139–150.

Hatcher, R. (2005). The distribution of leadership and power in schools. *British Journal of Sociology of Education, 26*(2), 253–267.

Holloway, J., Nielsen, A., & Saltmarsh, S. (2017). Prescribed distributed leadership in the era of accountability: The experiences of mentor teachers. *Educational Management Administration & Leadership*, 1–18. doi:1741143216688469.

Hulpia, H., Devos, G., & Rosseel, Y. (2009). The relationship between the perception of distributed leadership in secondary schools and teachers' and teacher leaders' job satisfaction and organizational commitment. *School Effectiveness and School Improvement, 20*(3), 291–317.

Hursh, D. (2007). Assessing No Child Left Behind and the rise of neoliberal education policies. *American Educational Research Journal, 44*(3), 493–518.

Jefferson, T. (1786). *Letter to George Wythe.* Retrieved from http://teachingamericanhistory.org/library/document/letter-to-george-wythe/

Koyama, J. P. (2011). Generating, comparing, manipulating, categorizing: Reporting, and sometimes fabricating data to comply with No Child Left Behind mandates. *Journal of Education Policy, 26*(5), 701–720.

Liljenberg, M. (2015). Distributing leadership to establish developing and learning school organisations in the Swedish context. *Educational Management Administration & Leadership, 43*(1), 152–170.

Lorwin, L. L. (1935). The plan state and the democratic ideal. *The Annals of the American Academy of Politial and Social Science, 180,* 114–118.

Lumby, J. (2013). Distributed leadership the uses and abuses of power. *Educational Management Administration & Leadership, 41*(5), 581–597.

Mann, H. (1840). *Lecture on education.* Boston, MA: Publisher.

Mascall, B., Leithwood, K., Straus, T., & Sacks, R. (2008). The relationship between distributed leadership and teachers' academic optimism. *Journal of Educational Administration, 46*(2), 214–228.

Murphy, J. (Ed.). (2005). *Connecting teacher leadership and school improvement.* Thousand Oaks, CA: Corwin Press.

National Comprehensive Center for Teacher Quality. (2007, October). *Enhancing teacher leadership.* Retrieved from http://www.gtlcenter.org/sites/default/files/docs/EnhancingTeacherLeadership.pdf

National Policy Board for Educational Administration. (2015). *Professional Standards for Educational Leaders 2015.* Retrieved from http://www.ccsso.org/Documents/2015/ProfessionalStandardsforEducationalLeaders2015forNPBEAFINAL.pdf

Peters, M. (2001). Education, enterprise culture and the entrepreneurial self: A Foucauldian perspective. *Journal of Educational Enquiry, 2*(2), 58–71.

Popkewitz, T. S., & Kirchgasler, C. (2015). Fabricating the teacher's soul in teacher education. In Fejes, A. & Nicoll, K. (Eds.), *Foucault and a Politics of Confession in Education* (pp. 35–47). London, England: Routledge.

Putnam, R. D. (1993). The prosperous community. *The American Prospect, 4*(13), 35–42.

Ravitch, D., & Viteritti, J. P. (2001). *Making good citizens: Education and civil society.* New Haven, CT: Yale University Press.

Rawls, J. (1993). *Political liberalism.* New York, NY: Columbia University Press.

Reed, M. (1907). *The democratic ideal.* Boston, MA: American Unitarian Association.

Rose, N. (1999). *Powers of freedom: Reframing political thought.* Cambridge, England: Cambridge University Press.

Ross, E. W., & Gibson, R. J. (Eds.). (2007). *Neoliberalism and education reform.* Cresskill, NJ: Hampton Press.

Rothschild, E. (2001). *Economic sentiments: Adam Smith, Condorcet, and the Enlightenment.* Cambridge, MA: Harvard University Press.

Rousseau, J. (1923). *The social contract and discourses by Jean-Jacques Rousseau* (G. D. H. Cole, Trans.) London, England and Toronto, Canada: J. M. Dent and Sons.

Sackney, L., & Mitchell, C. (2002). Postmodern expressions of educational leadership. In K. Leithwood & P. Hallinger (Eds.), *Second international handbook of educational leadership and administration* (pp. 881–913). Dordrecht, The Netherlands: Springer.

Shore, C., & Wright, S. (1999). Audit culture and anthropology: Neo-liberalism in British higher education. *Journal of the Royal Anthropological Institute, 5*(4), 557–575.

Suspitsyna, T. (2010). Accountability in American education as a rhetoric and a technology of governmentality. *Journal of Education Policy, 25*(5), 567–586.

Woods, P. A., Bennett, N., Harvey, J. A., & Wise, C. (2004). Variabilities and dualities in distributed leadership findings from a systematic literature review. *Educational Management Administration & Leadership, 32*(4), 439–457.

Youngs, H. (2009). (Un) Critical times? Situating distributed leadership in the field. *Journal of Educational Administration and History*, *41*(4), 377–389.

Youngs, H. (2014). Moving beyond distributed leadership to distributed forms: A contextual and socio-cultural analysis of two New Zealand secondary schools. *Leading and Managing*, *20*(2), 89.

ABOUT THE AUTHORS

EDITORS

Brenda J. McMahon is an Associate Professor of Educational Leadership at The University of North Carolina, Charlotte. She worked as a high school teacher and administrator in Canada. Her research focuses on the impacts of Whiteness on educational leadership, student engagement, resilience, and democracy in urban and rural high schools.

Lisa R. Merriweather is an Associate Professor of Adult Education at the University of North Carolina, Charlotte. Her research focuses on issues of equity and social justice within the historical discourse of adult education, informal education, and doctoral education. She explores the critical philosophy and sociology of race and antiblack racism and employs Africana Philosophy, Critical Race Theory, and qualitative and historical methodology to investigate topics found at the nexus of race and adult education.

AUTHORS

Thomas Archibald is an Associate Professor and Extension Specialist in Virginia Tech's Department of Agricultural, Leadership, and Community Education, where his research and practice focus primarily on evaluation capacity building and evaluative thinking in community development contexts. He is a 2017 recipient of the American Evaluation Association's

Marcia Guttentag Promising New Evaluator Award. He received his doctorate in Adult and Extension Education in 2013 from Cornell University.

Tracey Benson is an Assistant Professor of Educational Leadership at the University of North Carolina at Charlotte, where he offers courses in school law, education policy, and curriculum leadership. He received his doctorate in Education Leadership from the Harvard Graduate School of Education and Masters of School Administration from the University of North Carolina-Chapel Hill.

Ann K. Brooks is Professor in and former Director of the Adult, Professional, and Community Education PhD Program at Texas State University. She has published widely in the areas of workplace learning, organizational change, and identity, focusing on the learning and development necessary in an increasingly complex world.

Bettie Ray Butler is an Associate Professor of Urban Education in the Cato College of Education and the Director of Student Discipline Joint Task Force (SDJTF) at the University of North Carolina Charlotte. Her research looks closely at issues of equity, representation, and achievement by examining racial and gender disparities in school discipline.

Ami C. Camp, MA, is an Assistant Professor in the Department of Counselor Education and Supervision at Northeastern Illinois University. Her research interests include school counselors' training and support of students experiencing homelessness, multicultural and social justice counseling, and child-centered play therapy. As a former school counselor, Dr. Camp supported the academic, personal, socioemotional, and career development of high school students.

Raul Cantu has taught in Texas since 1997 and is currently an Associate Professor of English as a Second Language at Austin Community College. Raul received his BA from the University of Houston and his MEd from the University of Saint Thomas in Houston, Texas. Raul is currently pursuing a PhD in Adult, Professional, and Community Education at Texas State University in San Marcos, Texas.

Natalie Cook is a Program Evaluation Specialist for the Oklahoma Cooperative Extension Service and Agricultural Experiment Station of Oklahoma State University. In addition to her scholarship and practice of program evaluation and evaluation capacity building, Natalie is also interested in human development and family studies, contemporary pedagogy, transformative research and evaluation, and community engagement.

Amanda Cordova is a former social worker and K–12 teacher committed to educational leadership grounded in social justice and practices of equity. Her research centers relationships, pedagogies, curriculums, and policies that operate to reshape education as an emancipatory praxis where knowledge is no longer stultified along the appropriation of gender, race, ethnicity, or any other aspects of the intersections of identity.

Brian K. Corpening, PhD, is the Assistant Provost for Community Partnerships at the University of Oklahoma Health Sciences Center. His research interests are focused on African American educational history, the philosophy of miseducation and reeducation, and the history of resistance and rebellion throughout the African Diaspora. He has over 30 years of experience working in communities struggling for quality education and opportunities.

César A. Cruz, from marching 76-straight miles, to hunger striking for 26 days, Dr. Cruz is dedicated to justice. Raised in Guadalajara, Compton and Oakland, he is now a 23-year veteran educator, cofounder of HomiesEmpowerment.co which is evolving to become a school. He was the first Mexican immigrant male to receive his Doctorate in Education Leadership (EdLD) at Harvard University where he cotaught/cofounded the Ethnic Studies for Educators course.

Eric Feldman is the Associate Director for Student Success and Academic Programs at Florida International University in Washington, D.C. He leads the development of The Talent Lab, FIU's comprehensive support system for student with goals to make an impact in the nation's capital, through a cohort education model for students with DC internships, and funded, three day experiential learning "fly-ins." Previously, he developed and managed the university's international education cocurricular initiatives, and has served on the advisory board member for CWS Miami Immigrant and Refugee Program, and as a volunteer college coach for Peer Forward.

Sejal Parikh Foxx is an Associate Professor in the Department of Counseling. She serves as the Director of the School Counseling Program and Doctoral Program in Counselor Education and Supervision. She is coauthor of *School Counseling in the 21st Century,* 6th ed. In 2015, she received the Counselor Educator of the Year Award from the North Carolina School Counselors Association. She was appointed member of the NC School Counseling State Leadership Team and serves as Chair of the Higher Education Committee. Dr. Foxx is also a board member of CACREP. She teaches both doctoral and master's level courses and her special areas of interest are school counseling, multicultural and social justice, urban education, and college and career readiness. Her current research projects include college and career readiness in partnership with local schools.

William C. Frick, PhD, is the Rainbolt Family Endowed Presidential Professor of Educational Leadership and Policy Studies in the Jeannine Rainbolt College of Education at the University of Oklahoma. A graduate of The Pennsylvania State University, his research interests include the philosophy of administrative leadership, school system reform within urban municipality revitalization efforts, and broader cultural studies exploring the intersection of identity formation and schooling. He is a former Core Fulbright U.S. Scholar to the Republic of Georgia.

Encarnación Garza, Jr., PhD, is a Professor at the University of Texas at San Antonio in the department of Educational Leadership and Policy Studies. He received his PhD in Educational Administration from the University of Texas at Austin, where he was a fellow in the Cooperative Superintendency Program. As a scholar-practitioner whose scholarship employs a critical theory perspective, Dr. Garza's research focuses on four themes: (1) the study of minority student success, (2) the preparation of principals as leaders for social justice, (3) the exploration of school district/university partnerships with respect to preparing principals as social justice advocates, and (4) international perspectives of successful school leadership.

Jessica Holloway, PhD, is a postdoctoral research fellow within the Research for Educational Impact (REDI) Strategic Research Centre at Deakin University. She draws on post-structural theory to understand contemporary modes of accountability and its production of new teacher and leader subjectivities. Her recent publications include "Making Accountable Teachers: The Terrors and Pleasures of Performativity" (with Jory Brass) in the *Journal of Education Policy,* and "Datafying The Teaching Profession: Remaking the Professional Teacher in the Image of Data" (with Steven Lewis) in the *Cambridge Journal of Education.*

Rodney Hopson PhD, serves as Professor of Evaluation in the Department of Educational Psychology, College of Education, University of Illinois-Urbana Champaign. Relative to his research interests, Hopson raises questions that (1) analyze and address the differential impact of education and schooling on marginalized and underrepresented groups in diverse global nation states and (2) seek solutions to social and educational conditions in the form of alternative paradigms, epistemologies, and methods for the way the oppressed and marginalized succeed and thrive despite circumstances and opportunities that suggest otherwise.

Jessica Kerr, MA, is a doctoral student and instructor at Kansas State University. She is a community organizer around issues of equitable access to health care, housing, and education. This work deeply informs her graduate scholarship around social movements and rural subjectivities.

Juan Manuel Niño, PhD, is Assistant Professor at the University of Texas at San Antonio in the department of Educational Leadership and Policy Studies. He received his PhD in School Improvement from Texas State University. Juan Manuel's research, which takes a critical perspective on the practice of education and leadership in multiple contexts, addresses issues of social justice, equity and excellence in education for diverse communities, and the Latin@ experiences that influence identity and advocacy.

Tonette S. Rocco is a professor in adult education and human resource development at Florida International University in Miami, Florida. She is a Houle Scholar, a member of the 2016 class of the International Adult and Continuing Education Hall of Fame, and Editor-in-Chief of New Horizons in Adult Education and Human Resource Development.

Nicholas P. Triplett is an equity consultant in education in Raleigh, NC, and a lecturer in the College of Education at the University of North Carolina Charlotte. His research interests include equity and implicit bias in school discipline and the processes of social reproduction in K–12 school settings.

Kyung-Hwa Kay Yang, PhD, is an independent researcher and adult educator in the Chicago area. Her research focuses on agency, identity, and reflexivity in the context of adult education. She has explored participatory visual approaches to help marginalized adult learners advocate for themselves. She has worked with adult learners who are low-income, immigrants, and student veterans. She is affiliated with Nelson Mandela University in South Africa as a research associate.

Jeff Zacharakis, EdD, is a professor of adult learning and leadership. His research interests include history and philosophy of adult education, adult literacy, and community and organizational development.

Made in the USA
Las Vegas, NV
21 January 2021